Taxes, Loans, and Inflation

Studies of Government Finance: Second Series

TITLES PUBLISHED

Taxes, Loans, and Inflation
How the Nation's Wealth
Becomes Misallocated

C. EUGENE STEUERLE

Studies of Government Finance

THE BROOKINGS INSTITUTION

WASHINGTON, D.C.

Library of Congress Cataloging in Publication data:

Steuerle, C. Eugene, 1946–
    Taxes, loans, and inflation.

    Includes bibliographies and index.
    1. Capital levy—United States.   2. Income tax—
United States—Effect of inflation on.   3. Loans—
United States.   I. Title.
HJ4653.A3S75   1985   339.373   84-45980
ISBN 0-8157-8134-2
ISBN 0-8157-8133-4 (pbk.)

9 8 7 6 5 4 3 2 1

THE BROOKINGS INSTITUTION is an independent organization devoted to nonpartisan research, education, and publication in economics, government, foreign policy, and the social sciences generally. Its principal purposes are to aid in the development of sound public policies and to promote public understanding of issues of national importance.

The Institution was founded on December 8, 1927, to merge the activities of the Institute for Government Research, founded in 1916, the Institute of Economics, founded in 1922, and the Robert Brookings Graduate School of Economics and Government, founded in 1924.

The Board of Trustees is responsible for the general administration of the Institution, while the immediate direction of the policies, program, and staff is vested in the President, assisted by an advisory committee of the officers and staff. The by-laws of the Institution state: "It is the function of the Trustees to make possible the conduct of scientific research, and publication, under the most favorable conditions, and to safeguard the independence of the research staff in the pursuit of their studies and in the publication of the results of such studies. It is not a part of their function to determine, control, or influence the conduct of particular investigations or the conclusions reached."

The President bears final responsibility for the decision to publish a manuscript as a Brookings book. In reaching his judgment on the competence, accuracy, and objectivity of each study, the President is advised by the director of the appropriate research program and weighs the views of a panel of expert outside readers who report to him in confidence on the quality of the work. Publication of a work signifies that it is deemed a competent treatment worthy of public consideration but does not imply endorsement of conclusions or recommendations.

The Institution maintains its position of neutrality on issues of public policy in order to safeguard the intellectual freedom of the staff. Hence interpretations or conclusions in Brookings publications should be understood to be solely those of the authors and should not be attributed to the Institution, to its trustees, officers, or other staff members, or to the organizations that support its research.

Foreword

A MAJOR source of distortions in the modern U.S. economy is the uneven treatment of income from capital in both the tax system and the loan markets. This unevenness affects virtually every investment decision. Despite the pervasiveness of the problem, seldom are its threads woven into a single story either in the popular press or in the professional literature.

In this book, C. Eugene Steuerle provides a comprehensive analysis of the taxation of capital income at both the personal and the corporate levels. He closely examines tax arbitrage—essentially borrowing to buy tax-preferred assets. He shows that inflation plays an important part not only in creating disparities in the taxation of different types of income, but also in allocating loans among different households and businesses. New businesses and newly formed households are placed at severe competitive disadvantages in this type of environment.

The uneven treatment of capital income also explains some of the long-term limitations of monetary and fiscal policy; the failure of investment and saving incentives; organizational and financial arrangements involving mergers, leases, acquisitions, and divestitures among firms; and the nonprogressivity of the individual income tax with respect to capital income. This uneven treatment leads to prescriptions as seemingly diverse as comprehensive income taxes, expenditure taxes, flat-rate taxes, a return to the gold standard, and credit reallocation. After explaining the rationale behind each of these approaches, the author concludes that a broad-based, low-rate income tax represents the best of the alternatives.

Steuerle wrote this book while he was a federal executive fellow at Brookings. He currently serves as deputy director (domestic taxation), Office of Tax Analysis, Department of the Treasury, and economic staff coordinator of the Treasury Department's Project for Fundamental Tax Reform. Parts of the discussions in chapters 2, 4, and 9 were first published in the *Public Finance Quarterly*, the *Wayne Law Review*, the *National Tax Journal*, and *The Brookings Review*.

For helpful comments the author is grateful to Martin David, Charles R. Hulten, Harvey Galper, Jane G. Gravelle, Joseph A. Pechman, Emil Sunley, and Vito Tanzi. Barry P. Bosworth, Joseph J. Cordes, Larry L. Dildine, Don Fullerton, Richard Goode, John J. Hoven, Richard A. Musgrave, and Graham M. Patterson read the manuscript in its entirety and offered many useful suggestions. The author wishes especially to acknowledge Richard Goode, who made the phrase "gentleman and scholar" come to life. Karen J. Wirt edited the manuscript, Carolyn A. Rutsch verified its factual content and provided valuable research assistance, Susan F. Woollen typed the original manuscript, Chisolm B. Hamilton prepared it for typesetting, and Florence Robinson compiled the index. This book is the twenty-first in the second series of Brookings Studies of Government Finance.

The views expressed here are those of the author and should not be ascribed to the Treasury Department, to the persons whose assistance is acknowledged above, or to the trustees, officers, or staff members of the Brookings Institution.

BRUCE K. MACLAURY
President

April 1985
Washington, D.C.

Contents

Taxes, Loans, and Inflation

CHAPTER ONE

Introduction

INCOME from capital receives uneven treatment in the United States both in the tax system and in the loan markets. This nonuniform treatment, as it has developed over time, affects almost every investment decision made by individuals, businesses, and government and causes major distortions in the economy. In many ways the story is unique to the modern economy and is related closely to the interactions among three relatively new, but important, factors: a tax system that imposes high statutory rates on income from capital but excludes much of that income from taxation in a variety of ways; record flows of interest payments and receipts and the major participation of the household sector as a borrower in the financial markets; and an inflation rate that has an expected presence in the economy, often at high rates.

The tax system creates distortions whenever, for each household or firm, it taxes economic income differently according to such factors as the source of income, the institutional arrangement by which the income is received, and the amount of borrowing by the taxpayer. Distortions thus exist when a taxpayer pays significantly different taxes depending upon, for example, whether a net dollar of economic income comes from rental housing or a machine tool, flows through a corporate share or a life insurance policy, is financed through equity or debt. Some tax-induced distortions were created in the attempt to meet other goals for the economy, such as an increase in saving and investment. Many disparities result from the difficulty of taxing accruals, rather than realizations, of income. The net result of this disparate treatment is an income tax base for capital income that is only loosely related to economic income from capital.

Changes in the loan markets also have affected investment and interacted with the tax system in a number of ways. Many interest payments are deducted on one side of the ledger at the same time that interest receipts are excluded from taxable income on the other side.

1

Higher interest rates and greater amounts of interest payments have magnified this problem.

tax arbitrage

Tax and loan considerations come together in part through tax arbitrage—basically a process whereby taxpayers borrow for the purpose of purchasing preferred assets. The difference in the tax treatment of receipts of preferred income, on the one hand, and deductions of interest payments received, on the other, has an enormous effect on almost all investment decisions. Tax arbitrage is an important determinant of which investments are made, of who will own which particular types of assets, and how large the aggregate demand will be for loans. Many loans and tax reductions are provided to persons who play tax arbitrage "games" in which no additional saving or investment is generated in the economy. As will be seen, an important consequence of widespread tax arbitrage opportunities is instability in the financial markets.

All these problems are exacerbated by inflation. A higher inflation rate raises interest rates and usually makes tax arbitrage more profitable per dollar of borrowing and investment. Some investment uses capital unproductively because the value of the output made possible by the investment is actually less than the cost of the investment itself. In addition, a high inflation rate creates severe problems of cash flow for many persons. Potential real economic returns from *new* activities become less important in channeling loanable funds among borrowers; instead, cash flow from *other* activities has become necessary to secure loans for each new venture.

Accounting for Economic Income

Many of the problems of nonuniform treatment of capital income arise because the methods of accounting for taxable income, financial income, and cash flow are becoming increasingly separated from a true measure of economic income. For a given economic unit, economic income over a finite accounting period equals its accretions to real wealth, which in turn equals its consumption plus its change in real net worth. In this book I use the terms *taxable income* to refer to the income tax base of the unit;[1] *financial income,* the measure of income typically

1. If taxes were based on consumption, the tax base could be measured theoretically by subtracting accretions to real wealth from economic income. In a world of consumption

reported on financial statements;[2] and *cash flow,* a measure of the cash receipts less cash payments of the economic unit.

Cash flow is closely related to income because cash receipts less cash payments is the base from which all practical measures of financial income or taxable income are made. Although some adjustments are made to this base, they are insufficient to bring the measures of taxable income or financial income close to a true measure of economic income.[3] In the case of capital income, implicit flows of services from housing and durables do not fall in the taxable income base nor in accounting for income on most financial statements. Also seldom counted as income are accruals of rights to future benefits provided through insurance and pension plans. Accruals of gains and losses on assets generally are not realized at either the household or firm level unless there is a cash recognition of that income. For a typical physical asset, cost recovery of the initial purchase price is allowed to business, but on schedules (one for financial purposes, one for tax purposes) that do not reflect economic loss or income.

With no inflation and an income tax assessed on real income, many of these differences among the measures of economic income, taxable income, financial income, and cash flow would be of far less importance than at present. Inflation increases enormously the disparity between these various methods of accounting.[4] With inflation, nominal cash flows from financial assets are recognized as income for financial and tax purposes regardless of the effect of inflation on the underlying value of the assets. Interest rates rise; the nominal value of real, physical assets

---

taxes, one might be equally concerned if the taxable consumption base differed from a true measure of economic consumption.

2. For a household the term *financial income* is used loosely to mean any income measure typically used by the household or by a financial institution or financial adviser in dealing with the household. Financial accounting for income of households is seldom precise or subject to as many rules as are applied to firms.

3. For instance, acquisitions of liabilities and purchases of assets affect cash flow, but these acquisitions are not allowed to change the measure of income; accrual accounting is often used for such items as inventories and accounts receivable; and investment in plant, equipment, and buildings is treated differently from other expenses.

4. For a more detailed description of the effects of inflation on tax accounting see Henry J. Aaron, ed., *Inflation and the Income Tax* (Brookings, 1976). Inflation also increases disparities in effective rates on different investments, as demonstrated in Don Fullerton and Yolanda Kodrzycki Henderson, "Incentive Effects of Taxes on Income from Capital: Alternative Policies in the 1980s," in Charles R. Hulten and Isabel V. Sawhill, eds., *The Legacy of Reaganomics: Prospects for Long-term Growth* (Washington, D.C.: Urban Institute, 1984), pp. 45–89.

increases; and the real cost of an asset purchased in the past is under-stated in today's dollars. Although some accounting adjustments have been made—for instance, in tax accounting, accelerated methods of cost recovery compensate in crude ways for the understatement in today's dollars of the cost of depreciable assets—the disparities among the different methods increase when the inflation rate rises.

The Treatment of Saving and Investment

Much of the nonuniformity in the treatment of capital income also comes from the mistaken identification of both saving and investment with acts of purchase, deposit, or retention.[5] This identification results because the latter acts often occur at the same time that investment and saving take place.

An individual act of deposit cannot be equated with net saving by the individual or with aggregate saving by society. A new deposit may come simply from the sale of assets, in which case the deposit merely reflects asset shifting. Individuals may hold both debt and interest-bearing assets simultaneously. Thus a deposit of financial investment can be made possible by increased borrowing. In addition, net saving by one individual may also go to finance net dissaving or additional consumption by another individual, or government may increase its own borrowing without any increase in investment. Although aggregate saving will equal aggregate investment in a closed economy, there is no reason to believe that an increase in an individual's gross deposits necessarily implies an increase in the savings of either the individual or the economy.

The problem of identifying nonfinancial investment is slightly differ-ent from that of identifying saving. Investment is often associated narrowly with purchases of buildings or equipment that can be readily measured or checked. In fact, any purchase or expenditure that provides some future worth—not merely current consumption—involves some amount of investment. Expenditures on plant, equipment, and buildings do not necessarily produce a higher rate of return than harder-to-measure investments in such intangible items as training of new employees or the acquisition of know-how. If one were to add expenditures on education, training, research and development, and similar variables to national

5. These disparities are also exacerbated by inflation.

income measures of business investment, total investment in the economy would multiply severalfold.[6] Similarly, returns to capital owners include not only returns to investment in plant, equipment, and buildings, but returns to ideas and inventions, to goodwill and for the provision of insurance, to investment in inventories and land, to training of employees, and to the taking of risks. Each of these sources of return to capital owners does not stand alone but is complementary to other sources in the production of each good or service provided by a firm.

The Treatment of New and Old Wealth

Many disparities in the treatment of capital income are also a result of policies that favor "old" wealth over "new" wealth. More precisely, tax and loan policies have combined in such a way to create broad discrimination between new and old businesses and between newly formed and established households. Thus for a given marginal investment, new participants must face higher tax rates and reduced access to the loan markets than established firms and households. Although the equity effects of this discrimination are fairly apparent, the focus in this book is primarily on the efficiency implications. In effect, tax and loan policies have often prevented the channeling of investments and loans to those persons and businesses that can make best use of them and who often have the ideas necessary to build a new and more productive society.

Ideas, innovation, and technological change have long been recognized as important factors influencing economic growth. As John Hicks has stated, "The mainspring of economic progress is . . . invention, invention that works through the rate of profit."[7] Empirical work consistently has failed to explain much, if not most, improvement in aggregate output simply by growth in the availability of capital and labor.

6. See Robert Eisner, Emily R. Simons, Paul J. Pieper, and Steven Bender, "Total Incomes in the United States, 1946–1976: A Summary Report," *Review of Income and Wealth,* vol. 28 (June 1982), pp. 133–74. In this study nonresidential business investment in structures and equipment was estimated at $157 billion in 1976, while gross domestic capital accumulation equaled $1,293 billion, including $37 billion in research and development and $436 billion in education and training.

7. See the speech delivered by John Hicks in Stockholm, Sweden, in April 1973 upon receiving the Nobel Prize in Economic Science. John Hicks, "The Mainspring of Economic Growth," *American Economic Review,* vol. 71 (December 1981), pp. 23–29.

Indeed, recent bouts of stagnation in the United States have been accompanied by rates of gross investment and growth in the supply of labor that were higher, not lower, than in previous periods.[8]

In this book, tax and loan policies are shown to have acquired certain institutional and design features that often inhibit the efficient operation of markets by favoring certain participants—primarily those with old wealth—over other participants with ideas and prospects of equal or greater merit. These problems become severely aggravated in an inflationary economy and thus contribute to the poor economic performance often observed during long periods of high inflation. new vs. old

The Plan of the Book   unequal treatment, and wealth,

Part one of this book offers an explanation of the major sources of the nonuniform treatment of capital income and their development over time. Chapters 2 and 3 analyze the ways in which returns to capital are taxed through both the individual and corporate income taxes. Chapter 4 looks at the loan markets and traces flows of interest from borrowers to lenders. Special attention is given to the distortions caused by tax arbitrage in chapters 5 and 6. The effects of inflation are examined in chapter 7.

Part two applies the analysis developed in these early chapters to some related issues: long-term limitations of macro policy initiatives in chapter 8; the failure of saving and investment incentives in chapter 9; organizational and financial arrangements involving mergers, leases, acquisitions, and divestitures among firms in chapter 10; and the nonprogressivity of the income tax with respect to capital income in chapter 11.

Part three examines a broad range of tax and other prescriptions for more uniform treatment of income from capital. Chapters 12 and 13 describe proposals seemingly as diverse as consumption taxes, comprehensive income taxes, flat-rate taxes, a return to the gold standard, and attempts at credit reallocation. The last chapter presents an agenda for reform.

8. See, for instance, Edward F. Denison, *Accounting for Slower Economic Growth: The United States in the 1970s* (Brookings, 1979); Barry P. Bosworth, *Tax Incentives and Economic Growth* (Brookings, 1984); Edward F. Denison, "The Interruption of Productivity Growth in the United States," *Economic Journal,* vol. 93 (March 1983), pp. 56–77; and Barry P. Bosworth, "Capital Formation and Economic Policy," *Brookings Papers on Economic Activity, 2:1982,* pp. 273–317.

PART ONE

The Allocation of Capital

CHAPTER TWO

Taxation of the Capital Income of Individuals

No ANALYSIS of the treatment of capital in a society can proceed without first examining the tax system. The focus of this part of the analysis is on the myriad ways in which capital income is taxed—in particular, the various preferences and penalties applying to capital income according to sources of income and financial arrangements of taxpayers. This chapter looks at taxes on capital income that are paid by individual taxpayers.

Income Subject to Tax

If an income tax system taxed all income equally, capital income, regardless of source, would be treated in the same way as wage income. The individual income tax in the United States, however, is designed so that tax treatment of capital income varies widely according to source and differs greatly from the tax treatment of wage income.

National income data for 1982 were used to provide rough estimates of the amount of net income from capital in the U.S. economy. These estimates are presented in table 2-1. Total net income from capital for that year is estimated at $446.1 billion. Sources of income include corporate profits, proprietors' income, rental income, income from consumer durables, and net interest income.

Capital income is estimated here net of inflationary returns (such as inflationary increases in the value of inventories), corporate income taxes and property taxes, interest payments from individuals to business, and the value of financial services (such as on checking accounts) furnished by financial intermediaries.[1] To ensure that only real income

1. A conventional measure of returns to capital owners is used for these purposes. Some returns to investment, especially investment in education or human capital, show up as returns to labor rather than to capital.

Table 2-1. *Estimated Income from Capital, 1982*
Billions of dollars

Source of income	Amount
Real corporate profits[a]	**98.4**
Dividends	69.2
Retained earnings (adjusted)[b]	29.2
Proprietors' income from capital	**37.0**
Total income	117.9
Less: inventory valuation adjustment	0.5
Less: capital consumption adjustment	6.3
Less: imputed return to labor[c]	74.1
Real rental income of persons[d]	**51.5**
Rental income	88.4
Less: capital consumption adjustment	36.9
Income from consumer durables[e]	**42.2**
Net interest income	**217.0**
Net interest income, including services in kind	260.9
Less: certain services furnished[f]	43.9
Total net income from capital	**446.1**

Source: Data derived from U.S. Department of Commerce, Bureau of Economic Analysis, "Revised Estimates of the National Income and Product Accounts," a supplement to *Survey of Current Business*, vol. 64 (July 1984), tables 1.11 and 8.7. Figures are rounded.
  a. After indirect business taxes, transfer payments, and subsidies.
  b. Adjusted as follows: profits before tax, 165.5; less profits tax liability, 60.7; less dividends, 69.2; less inventory valuation adjustment, 9.5; after capital consumption adjustment, 3.1.
  c. Equals two-thirds of proprietors' total income after inventory valuation and capital consumption adjustments.
  d. Includes imputed rent to owner-occupied housing. Real estate taxes and interest expenses are effectively subtracted from gross rental income in the rental income figure shown here.
  e. Net income from durables after personal property tax payments. The estimate assumes a 4 percent real rate of return to the stock of durables as reported in Board of Governors of the Federal Reserve System, *Balance Sheet for the U.S. Economy, 1945–83* (The Board, November 1984), p. 75.
  f. Without payment by financial intermediary. The value of these financial intermediary services may under alternative assumptions be counted as income to capital.

is measured, corporate profits are reported net of inventory valuation and capital consumption adjustments, thus excluding profits resulting from the inflationary increase in value of inventories and equipment and eliminating the corresponding overstatement of inventory profits and understatement of depreciation.

The estimate of interest income is effectively adjusted for inflation because the overstatement of interest income by individuals as creditors (and owners of debt instruments) is offset by the understatement of their income as debtors (and owners of institutions with outstanding debt). For instance, in the case of businesses that are owned by individuals, the decline in real value of the firms' indebtedness matches the overstatement of income by the interest recipients. Since national income accounts exclude government interest from national income, also excluded is net interest paid by government to persons and business. The measure of aggregate interest income here therefore represents real income and, if anything, is understated by the exclusion of government interest and the value of financial services.[2]

Although the estimated total net income from capital shown in table 2-1, $446.1 billion, represents real income from capital, the tax system is actually based upon nominal rather than real income. If various inflationary accruals of wealth were included, nominal income from capital would have been significantly larger than real income. Nominal capital gains on land, residential housing, and other physical assets would add several hundred billion dollars annually to the nominal amount of income from capital. For instance, capital gains on land held by households, farm business, and unincorporated business alone averaged $235 billion per year between 1979 and 1983.[3]

From a sample of filed tax returns it is estimated that only $143.5 billion in net income from capital was reported on individual income tax returns in 1982. A summary of the amount of capital income reported on individual income tax returns is presented in table 2-2.

Because the estimates of income from capital in the economy are net of interest payments, real estate taxes, and personal property taxes, consistency requires that the estimate of income from capital subject to individual income taxation also be reported net of deductions for such expenses. The largest deduction is for interest payments; in most years, interest deductions reported by taxpayers who itemize are almost equal in size to interest receipts reported on all returns.

The $143.5 billion of net income from capital reported on individual income tax returns represents only 32 percent of the $446.1 billion of net (real) capital income in the economy. If income from capital in the economy had been measured on a nominal basis similar to that used to report income on tax returns—for instance, if capital gains were included in the estimate of income from capital in the economy—then the

2. In general, the method of estimation used here was conservative and may have led to a slight overstatement of the amount of capital income reported on individual tax returns. Even major changes in method of estimation, however, would not significantly change the overall results. For details see Eugene Steuerle, "Is Income from Capital Subject to Individual Income Taxation?" *Public Finance Quarterly*, vol. 10 (July 1982), pp. 283–303. Portions reprinted by permission of Sage Publications, Inc.

3. See Board of Governors of the Federal Reserve System, *Balance Sheets for the U.S. Economy, 1945–83* (The Board, November 1984), p. 75.

Table 2-2. *Declared Income from Capital Subject to Individual Income Tax, 1982*
Billions of dollars

Income declared	Amount
Income from dividends and capital gains	**78.5**
Dividends[a]	47.1
Net realized capital gains in adjusted gross income	31.4
Proprietors' income from capital	**21.9**
Proprietors' total income[b]	65.7
Less: imputed return to labor	43.8
Rental and royalty income	**22.7**
Rental income	1.8
Nine-tenths of royalty income	2.7
Less: real estate tax deduction	27.2
Net interest	**33.5**
Interest income	142.0
Less: interest deductions[c]	108.5
Net income from consumer durables	**2.2**
Income from consumer durables	0.0
Less: personal property tax deductions	2.2
Other income received by or through financial intermediaries	**34.5**
Small business corporation income	0.9
Estate and trust income	4.8
One-half of pension and annuity income	28.8
Total income from capital subject to tax	**143.5**

Source: Data derived from the individual income tax model of the U.S. Department of the Treasury. Figures are rounded.

a. Gross dividends before exclusion, 52.0, less dividend exclusion, 1.8.

b. Equals two-thirds of proprietors' total income.

c. Interest deductions for mortgages on owner-occupied housing are subtracted from net interest in this table and from rental income in table 2-1.

percentage of capital income reported on individual tax returns would have been even smaller.

Some of the revenue effects of the individual taxation of income from capital are shown in table 2-3. The various components are shown for income from capital gross of certain personal itemized deductions and for income from capital net of these deductions. Ignoring the deductions for the moment, $281.6 billion of capital income was reported in 1982, of which $245.4 billion was subject to tax at a rate greater than zero. Deductions for interest and property taxes, however, reduced the net income from capital figures to $143.5 billion reported, and $141.9 billion subject to tax at a positive rate.

The change in tax reported for each of these income measures is the average marginal rate on all capital income calculated at the margin above labor income. That is, the tax estimate is the difference between the tax that is currently collected and the tax that would be collected if the income from capital were excluded from taxation. Measuring at the margin is a useful means of examining the economic impact of capital income taxation. However, that measurement does not allow a comparison of the taxes on capital with the taxes on wages. If capital income had been treated as the base, with wage income as marginal income, the estimate of the amount of tax paid by capital would be significantly lower.

Dividing tax revenues of $33.3 billion on net income from capital by the amount of net capital income in the economy yields an effective rate of federal individual income tax of 7.5 percent on all capital income. This number should not be interpreted as the marginal rate that would apply to an extra dollar of income received and recognized for tax purposes. Compared to the typical dollar of capital income, the last reported dollar of an individual, if it was *fully reported,* would have a higher tax rate because it would be added to all other income and thus be subject to the highest marginal rate. The rate of 7.5 percent should also not be interpreted as the effective rate of tax for all taxes on income from capital. For 1982 the federal corporate tax liability of $46.5 billion (see the next chapter) on corporate income alone was well in excess of the $33.3 billion estimate of individual tax liability on all capital income.[4] Adding this corporate tax liability to both the estimate of income from capital and to the individual tax liability yields an effective federal tax rate for both corporate and individual income taxes of 16.2 percent. State and local income taxes, as well as property and indirect business taxes (to the extent that they are considered a tax on capital income), would raise the number even higher.[5]

Assets and Liabilities of Individuals

An easy means to see why so much income from capital, whether real or nominal, is not subject to individual income taxation is to examine

4. *Survey of Current Business,* vol. 64 (July 1984), table 3.2.

5. Unlike capital income, most labor income is reported on individual income tax returns. At the same time, there is no additional corporate tax on such income. Depending upon the margin at which the calculation is made, wage income is taxed at a much higher rate than some capital income and at a much lower rate than other capital income. Some implications will be discussed in chapter 11.

Table 2-3. *Income from Capital Reported and Taxed on Individual Income Tax Returns, 1982*
Billions of dollars

Income class (dollars)	Total tax on all income	Income from capital gross of interest and tax deductions				Net income from capital			
		Total claimed	Income taxable at a positive rate[a]	Tax on capital[b]		Total claimed	Income taxable at a positive rate[a]	Tax on capital[c]	
				Amount	Percent of total tax			Amount	Percent of total tax
0–5,000	0.0	3.3	1.9	−0.1	...	−0.3	1.4	−0.1	...
5,000–10,000	5.7	19.6	15.0	1.0	17.5	14.1	13.6	0.9	15.8
10,000–15,000	15.1	24.5	21.0	2.4	15.9	17.0	17.6	1.9	12.6
15,000–20,000	20.6	21.9	19.6	2.8	13.6	12.1	13.4	1.7	8.3
20,000–30,000	53.5	38.6	36.1	6.5	12.1	9.6	14.3	1.4	2.6
30,000–50,000	85.6	57.2	53.0	13.3	15.5	9.4	11.5	0.3	0.4
50,000–100,000	52.2	49.5	46.0	15.9	30.5	28.0	26.2	7.9	15.1
100,000–200,000	25.1	28.1	24.7	10.4	41.4	21.0	18.8	7.7	30.7
200,000 or more	23.4	38.7	28.0	13.0	55.5	32.7	25.1	11.7	50.0
Total	281.2	281.6	245.4	65.2	23.2	143.5	141.9	33.3	11.8

Source: Data derived from the individual income tax model of the U.S. Department of the Treasury. Figures are rounded.
a. Change in taxable income less zero bracket amount (taxable income less zero bracket amount constrained to be zero or greater) if all reported capital income is excluded from taxation.
b. Difference in total tax actually collected, and tax that would be collected if the income, gross of interest, real estate tax, and personal property tax were not subject to tax.
c. Difference in total tax actually collected and tax that would be collected if the income were not subject to tax.

the portfolio of assets and liabilities held by individuals in the United States. Although 1984 data are examined, most of the existing exclusions, exemptions, and deductions of capital income have actually been allowable for years and are not a new phenomenon. In large part these preferences indicate that the tax system generally taxes *realized* flows of cash and excludes or defers from taxation both unrealized accruals of income and receipts of in-kind service flows, such as those from housing and durables.

As shown in table 2-4, there were approximately $13.8 trillion in assets held by individuals at the beginning of 1984. Tangible assets—such as housing, consumer durables, and land—accounted for roughly $7.7 trillion of this; financial assets, $6.1 trillion. Very little of the income from tangible assets held by individuals is taxed. Income from investment real estate is not taxed fully, in part because the owners of these assets are allowed generous investment credits and depreciation or cost-recovery allowances.

Much of the total return from both household and business investment in land and real estate consists of appreciation in value. Little tax is collected on this appreciation because of the capital gains exclusion and, more important, because of provisions in the tax code that defer increases in value from taxation until they are realized or exclude them completely from taxation in the event of death.[6]

Taxpayers who are age fifty-five and older receive a generous exclusion for gains from the sale of owner-occupied housing, while younger taxpayers are allowed to defer such gains by purchasing houses of equal or greater value. Compliance data also indicate a substantial amount of underreporting of rental income and income from farms and noncorporate businesses.[7]

Of the $6.1 trillion held in financial assets, about 25.6 percent, or $1,563 billion, was in the form of life insurance and pension reserves. Earnings on savings in life insurance and annuities are usually deferred, often permanently, from taxation.[8] Deferral of tax on compensation

---

6. For some administrative reasons for deferring tax on appreciation in value see Richard Goode, *The Individual Income Tax* (Brookings, 1976), pp. 27–32.

7. See U.S. Department of the Treasury, Internal Revenue Service, *Income Tax Compliance Research: Estimates for 1973–1981* (IRS, 1983), p. 22. Reported rental income in 1981 equaled 37 percent of the amount that should be reported; for nonfarm proprietor income the figure was 50.3 percent. Farm proprietor income of $11 billion should have been reported rather than the −$2 billion that was actually reported.

8. Thomas Neubig and C. Eugene Steuerle, "The Taxation of Income Flowing

Table 2-4. *Assets and Liabilities of Individuals in the United States, Outstanding at the Beginning of 1984*[a]
Billions of dollars

Item	Amount
Tangible assets	**7,721**
Reproducible assets	4,971
Owner-occupied housing	2,220
Other residential structures	545
Consumer durables	1,164
Inventories and nonresidential plant and equipment	1,041
Land	2,750
Owner-occupied	1,166
Farm business and nonfarm noncorporate business	1,515
Other	70
Financial assets	**6,104**
Currency, savings accounts, and money market funds	2,198
Demand deposits and currency	376
Time and savings accounts	1,659
Money market fund shares	163
Securities	1,967
U.S. savings bonds	71
Other U.S. government securities	257
State and local obligations	174
Corporate and foreign bonds	45
Open-market paper	8
Corporate equities[b]	1,412
Pension and life insurance reserves	1,563
Life insurance reserves	241
Pension fund reserves	1,322
Miscellaneous assets	376
Total assets	**13,825**
Less: total liabilities	2,664
Home mortgage	1,207
Consumer credit	437
Other mortgage debt	533
Other debt	487
Equals: net worth	**11,161**

Source: Board of Governors of the Federal Reserve System, *Balance Sheets for the U.S. Economy, 1945–83*. Figures are rounded.

a. The Federal Reserve Board defines individuals as the sum of households, farm business, and nonfarm, noncorporate business. Beginning of year 1984 is equivalent to end of year 1983.

b. Excludes corporate farms.

deposited in pension funds and on the earnings within the funds is often treated as equivalent to complete exemption of capital income within the pension plans. This theoretical equivalence requires that taxpayers be in the same bracket when they receive their pensions as when wages are paid by the employer—or, in the case of an individual retirement account (IRA) or a Keogh plan, the individual—into the pension plan.[9] In fact, the taxpayer is usually in a lower bracket by the time of withdrawal or retirement. The tax preference given to income from pension savings, therefore, could be argued to provide a net subsidy to such income.[10]

Another approximately $1.4 trillion of the financial assets of individuals was held directly in corporate stock. For the individual taxpayer, holdings of corporate stock are given favorable tax treatment through the exclusion of 60 percent of long-term capital gains from taxation; a dividend exclusion of $100 per taxpayer ($200 per joint return); a deferral from taxation and eventual conversion to capital gains for a limited amount of dividends reinvested in public utility stock; and, most important, the combination of tax deferral of any gains until they are realized and the exclusion from taxation of all gains unrealized at the time of a taxpayer's death. One can compare the several hundred billion dollars of nominal capital gains earned in most years since the early 1970s[11] with the $31.4 billion that, when treated as net, was subject to taxation in 1982. It quickly becomes apparent that most capital-gains income is excluded from taxation, not because of a 60 percent exclusion of gains actually realized, but because of the deferral of realization of most gains and the permanent exclusion of many gains at death.

Individuals also held $174 billion worth of state and local obligations, the income from which is generally nontaxable, and $71 billion worth of U.S. savings bonds, the income from which can be deferred from taxation until the bonds are redeemed.[12] Other interest income is excluded by

---

through Financial Institutions: General Framework and Summary of Tax Issues,'' Office of Tax Analysis Paper 52 (Treasury Department, September 1983).

9. Emil M. Sunley, Jr., ''Employee Benefits and Transfer Payments,'' in Joseph A. Pechman, ed., *Comprehensive Income Taxation* (Brookings, 1977), pp. 75–106.

10. If W is taxed at rate t_1, and interest i is not taxed, the individual will have $P_1 = [W(1 - t_1)] (1 + i)^N$ after N years. Equivalently, if the income W and the interest is not taxed until withdrawal, and the tax rate is t_2, the individual will have $P_2 = [W(1 + i)^N] (1 - t_2)$. Then $P_1 = P_2$ if $t_1 = t_2$, and $P_2 > P_1$ if $t_2 < t_1$.

11. Board of Governors of the Federal Reserve System, *Balance Sheets for the U.S. Economy, 1945–83*, pp. 72–75.

12. Income from government bonds does not actually represent returns from real

being paid in the form of in-kind financial services or simply by not being reported.

⟨In aggregate, then, about 80 percent of the $13.8 trillion in individual assets is in forms for which some or all related income can be excluded or deferred from taxation.⟩

On the liability side of the ledger, much of the interest paid on individual liabilities is deductible immediately. It is quite common for individuals to borrow and take deductions at the same time that they invest in assets (pensions, land, housing, corporate stock) for which income is deferred or excluded from taxation. The tax laws do place some limits on investment deductions in excess of investment receipts, but even these limitations can be avoided easily because much borrowing, such as borrowing against equity in housing or against assets used in business, is not subject to these limits. Borrowing to purchase preferred assets is a crucial issue in the taxation of capital income and will be treated in more depth in subsequent chapters.

Some Implications

This peculiar system of taxing capital income at the individual level has important implications, four of which are discussed below.

A Discretionary Tax

The first implication is that, insofar as capital income is concerned, the individual income tax is primarily a discretionary tax. Most capital income does not flow through to individuals for reporting on tax returns. Of the amount that does flow through, much is avoidable. An obvious example is capital-gains income. A tax on capital gains is the most discretionary of all taxes. One should not be surprised, therefore, if a reduction in the actual tax rate or inclusion rate for realizations brings about an increase in such realizations.[13] The correct interpretation of

---

capital. Such income was excluded from the measure of real capital in the economy in table 2-1.

13. See, for instance, Martin Feldstein, Joel Slemrod, and Shlomo Yitzhaki, "The Effects of Taxation on the Selling of Corporate Stock and the Realization of Capital Gains," *Quarterly Journal of Economics,* vol. 94 (June 1980), pp. 777–91; Joseph J. Minarik, "The Effects of Taxation on the Selling of Corporate Stock and the Realization

this occurrence is that persons will be willing to recognize more income if the discretionary tax rate is reduced.

Not a Tax on Income

Second, the discretionary individual tax on capital income is a tax on liquidity, risk reduction, and diversification rather than a tax on income. A corollary is that taxpayers pay unnecessary taxes because of the simplicity of their filing response or their lack of knowledge of the tax laws. About half of all interest and dividend receipts reported on individual returns is reported by taxpayers aged sixty-five and over. These persons are often in need of current receipts or liquid assets to cover consumption needs in the near future. For persons anticipating that savings may need to be spent soon, risk can also be reduced substantially by increasing the percentage of interest-bearing assets in the portfolio. Those who realize capital gains or interest income also have greater opportunity for diversification relative to those who hold on to unrealized gains. Diversification is useful both for reducing risk and converting to assets with higher expected rates of return.

Many taxpayers do not make elaborate portfolio calculations to achieve the maximum expected after-tax rate of return. For these taxpayers, and to some extent for all taxpayers, there is a "tax" on simplicity—or the failure to engage in complex transactions—and on lack of knowledge of the tax laws.

It is not hard to find examples. Many employees still make nondeductible employee contributions to pension plans rather than avoid taxation by having employers act on their behalf. Many retirees recognize income on distributions of stock from employers that could easily be rolled over into IRAs and taxed at lower rates in later years of life. Other taxpayers own shares of mutual funds that regularly recognize gains. If these taxpayers were willing to own diversified portfolios similar to those offered by the mutual funds, they could easily realize less taxable income. Still other taxpayers can convert ordinary interest income into

of Capital Gains: Comment," *Quarterly Journal of Economics*, vol. 99 (February 1984), pp. 93–110; Gerald E. Auten and Charles T. Clotfelter, "Permanent versus Transitory Tax Effects and the Realization of Capital Gains," *Quarterly Journal of Economics*, vol. 97 (November 1982), pp. 613–32; and Gerald E. Auten, "Capital Gains: An Evaluation of the 1978 and 1981 Tax Cuts," in Charls E. Walker and Mark A. Bloomfield, eds., *New Directions in Federal Tax Policy for the 1980s* (Ballinger, 1983), pp. 121–59.

interest income of deferred annuities from which withdrawals, just like withdrawals from savings accounts, are allowed. Taxes owed would then be reduced by deferral of tax on part or all of the interest income.

All these means of tax reduction could be achieved with little or no loss in return or increase in risk. Three related groups of taxpayers fail to take advantage of this available tax reduction. First, there are taxpayers who know the tax laws but simply do not consider it worth their time (or other expense) to avoid taxes through alternative investment. This behavior is entirely rational, but it again implies that the "income" tax is not a tax on income. Second, there are those who are knowledgeable and would benefit on the basis of time or expense by altering their portfolios, but at some point they find it distasteful to devote further efforts to activities that may be personally profitable but socially unproductive.[14] Finally, there are those who are ignorant of many aspects of the tax laws. In many ways, ignorance of tax laws is not much different from ignorance of other products. Billions of dollars are lost each year to savers who simply are ignorant of alternative opportunities and keep their savings in low-yielding forms such as passbook savings. Billions of dollars are also lost by consumers who purchase name-brand products when identical products are available at lower costs. It should not be surprising, therefore, that a large amount of tax is paid owing to ignorance. Actually, I conjecture that most taxpayers pay some amount of tax because of all three reasons listed here.

A Declining Tax with Deferred Consumption

The third implication of the tax system is that to the extent there is an explicit individual tax on capital income, or an implicit tax through lower yields on preferred assets, the rate of tax will decline significantly the longer the taxpayer is willing to defer consumption. In effect, the income tax bestows many of the benefits of an expenditure or consumption tax— nontaxation of income from capital—to those willing to defer or forgo consumption for long periods.

Tax preferences are generally granted for assets with some amount of short-term risk relative to interest-bearing assets. This risk, however,

14. For empirical evidence that persons do not always take maximum advantage of situations in which costs can be passed on to others see Gerald Marwell and Ruth E. Ames, "Economists Free Ride, Does Anyone Else?" *Journal of Public Economics*, vol. 15 (June 1981), pp. 295–310.

declines substantially as time passes; more technically, the variance in end-period wealth declines over time. For the purpose of this discussion, therefore, I define risk not as the variance in rate of return over some period of time, but rather as the probability of not being able to finance a fixed amount of consumption at some point in the future. Over a short period of time, interest-bearing assets can be shown to have relatively lower risk and lower expected returns relative to a diversified portfolio of stocks. As time passes, however, a stock portfolio may show not only more expected returns, but also reduced risk. Because of inflation, interest-bearing assets carry a significant risk of loss in real value. What this implies is that the tax on risk reduction borne by those who expect to hold assets for relatively short periods of time will not be borne by those who hold assets for longer periods. Equivalently, any tax preference given to those who bear greater short-term risk than others is also given to those who bear no more, and often less, long-term risk.

This third implication is supported empirically by some common examples of investor behavior. The interest income from pensions and IRAs, taxed at the equivalent of a negative rate, is generally no different from other interest income; that is, there is no implicit tax paid through a lower rate of return, and there is no difference in risk. The only implicit tax that the taxpayer may face is some loss of liquidity or opportunity for current consumption (actually this can sometimes be avoided too, as is discussed below). Yet despite liberalization of the allowance in 1981, more than 80 percent of eligible taxpayers did not take advantage of the provision.[15] Many nonparticipants still receive taxable interest income from other accounts.

A second example is provided by almost any asset for which the tax on capital income is deferred until the asset is sold—stocks, annuities (purchased with after-tax income), and U.S. savings bonds. As the deferral period increases, the effective tax rate declines.

Tax-exempt state and local bonds also show some interesting variations in returns. Here there is no explicit tax, but rather an implicit tax rate or loss of interest relative to taxable bonds. This implicit tax declines at a steady rate over time until the bond matures. The implicit rate declines from about 43 percent for periods of one year to 19 percent for thirty-year periods (see figure 2-1). This result is difficult to interpret since the annual yield is received currently rather than unrealized and

15. Preliminary data provided by the Statistics Division of the Internal Revenue Service.

Figure 2-1. *Implicit Tax Rates of Tax-Exempt Bonds for Different Maturities, 1954–82*[a]

Percent

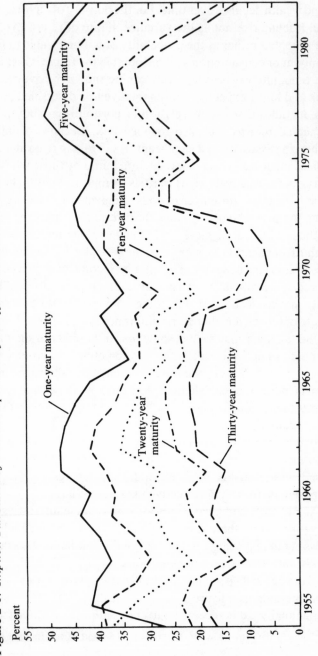

Source: Data prepared by Thomas Neubig of the Department of the Treasury from data provided by Salomon Brothers in "An Analytical Record of Yields and Yield Spreads, 1984."
a. The implicit tax rate is the sum of taxable yield minus tax-exempt yield divided by taxable yield. Taxable yields are for new prime issues (Aaa) released on approximately the first day of the month. Both yields are annual averages. The average implicit tax rates for 1954–82 for the various maturities are as follows: one year, 43 percent; five years, 37 percent; ten years, 31 percent; twenty years, 23 percent; and thirty years, 19 percent.

held within the asset or account.[16] The implicit tax rate on tax-exempt bonds is also strongly affected by the activities of banks and property and casualty insurance companies. Most wealthy persons actually hold only a small percentage of their assets in tax-exempt bonds, a fact that implies they achieve higher after-tax returns elsewhere.[17] In effect, there may be no bidding up of the price of tax-exempt bonds with substantial periods to maturity because the explicit tax rate on equally risky assets is also low.

Distortions

The fourth implication of this system of timing individual income is that the myriad tax penalties and preferences for income from capital distorts the allocation of investment in the economy and the distribution of assets and liabilities among individuals. In an inflationary economy, income from a number of assets may be overstated for tax purposes because of the overstatement of real capital gains, the understatement of the real value of depreciation, and the overstatement of interest income.[18] Yet while tax penalties are placed on income from some assets or on particular uses of capital, other capital income receives tax preference. Taxing the returns from different types of investments in these myriad ways creates the various tax wedges that contribute to an inefficient economy.

This system of penalties and subsidies also affects the distribution of assets and liabilities among individuals. This last problem is more than just one of nonoptimal portfolio diversification or risk reduction: capital

16. The term structure of the tax rates on tax-exempt bonds is consistent with the notion that the tax rate declines with an increase in the short-term riskiness of the asset. Because income is received currently in this case, however, one needs the additional evidence from other portfolio behavior to make the connection between deferral of consumption and tax rates. One such piece of evidence is the relative tendency of tax-exempt bonds to be held in wealthy estates—that is, in estates of persons who obviously deferred consumption of large amounts of income—even though these estates hold only a small percentage of assets in this form.

17. See U.S. Internal Revenue Service, *Statistics of Income: Personal Wealth Estimated from Estate Tax Returns,* various years.

18. For more detail on capital gains see Martin Feldstein and Joel Slemrod, "Inflation and the Excess Taxation of Capital Gains on Corporate Stock," *National Tax Journal,* vol. 31 (June 1978), pp. 107–18; on interest income see Martin Feldstein and Lawrence Summers, "Inflation and the Taxation of Capital Income in the Corporate Sector," *National Tax Journal,* vol. 32 (December 1979), pp. 445–70.

and labor in an economy should be managed by persons who can use them most productively.

Persons with substantial current taxable income have much more incentive to purchase and own those items of capital that are tax-preferred, regardless of whether they are the persons most capable of using that capital most efficiently. A piece of farmland, for instance, may produce much of its return from nonrealized appreciation in value. When compared with alternative investments such as interest-bearing assets, a person with a high tax rate will find the farmland much more attractive than will a person with a lower tax rate, all other things being equal. The former will then outbid the latter for the land even when the latter may be capable of obtaining a higher crop yield on the land. The opposite side of the coin is that the former taxpayer will be less likely to supply the savings that could in turn be borrowed and used by other taxpayers even when, from a social standpoint, the income of both could be increased by such an arrangement. That is, the high-income taxpayer has a strong disincentive to place dollars with financial intermediaries who would make those dollars available to other investors in real capital. The tax system thus prevents financial institutions from performing their important role as intermediaries between savers and the investors who are capable of making best use of savings.

tax system - prevents financial inst from performing efficiently.

CHAPTER THREE

Taxation of Corporate Income

WHETHER a tax is assessed directly on individuals or businesses, of course, persons actually bear the tax burden. The previous chapter examined the taxation of capital income as it is reported on individual tax returns. In this chapter the taxation of business income is investigated in depth, with emphasis on the chief means by which such income is taxed: the corporate income tax.[1]

Corporate Tax Collections

Corporate tax liability on corporate income alone is much greater than individual tax liability on all income from capital, including distributed corporate income. In 1982, for example, corporate tax liability of $46.5 billion was well in excess of the $33.3 billion estimate for individual tax liability on all capital income.[2]

Corporate taxes are the basic source of revenue from the taxation of income from capital. One of the major reasons that corporations pay tax is often ignored. Managers of publicly traded corporations have a strong incentive to report high and growing levels of profits. The value of the corporate stock, as well as the manager's salary and value of stock options, are dependent in large part upon reported earnings. Perhaps nothing gives more evidence of this bias than the slowness with which many corporate managers accept optional tax reductions when these

1. Many of the features of corporate tax design are discussed in Joseph A. Pechman, *Federal Tax Policy* (Brookings, 1983); Alan J. Auerbach, "Corporate Taxation in the United States," *Brookings Papers on Economic Activity, 2:1983*, pp. 451–505; J. Gregory Ballentine, *Equity, Efficiency, and the U.S. Corporation Income Tax* (Washington, D.C.: American Enterprise Institute for Public Policy Research, 1980); and Richard Goode, *The Corporation Income Tax* (Wiley, 1951).
2. *Survey of Current Business*, vol. 63 (July 1983), table 3.2.

reductions effectively require that the measure of corporate financial income also be lowered. The adoption of LIFO (last in, first out), an accounting method that adjusts for inflationary increases in the value of inventories, for instance, is still resisted by many companies. Businesses were also slow in making optional adjustments to new, more beneficial, methods of depreciation.[3]

This incentive for full reporting of income for financial purposes is offset by an opposite tendency to understate taxable income. In many ways the former incentive is a powerful means of attaining compliance with the tax laws at minimum cost of enforcement. Thus estimates of underreporting of business income on individual returns generally are much higher than estimates of underreporting for corporate income.[4]

Although corporate tax payments are large relative to individual tax payments on income from capital, they have been declining relative to the size of the economy since the early 1950s (see figure 3-1). In the early postwar era corporate tax payments were often 5 percent or more of net national product, but they have decreased steadily since then to about 2 percent in 1983. This decline is the result of three separate factors: a reduction in the earnings of capital in the corporate sector; an increase in the share of earnings of corporate capital that is treated as income of the holders of corporate debt and, therefore, is not subject to corporate tax; and statutory tax changes in the treatment of new investments— changes that were often offset by increases in effective tax rates on returns from old investments as higher inflation rates lowered the real value of depreciation allowances.

Figure 3-1 demonstrates some of these effects. Domestic income paid out of the product of nonfinancial business corporations actually increased as a percentage of net national product during the postwar period; by the late 1970s it had reached a fairly stable level of 52 percent of net national product. Compensation of employees took an increasing share of this product, while payments to capital declined.

Corporate profits with inflation adjustments for changes in inventories (IVA) and allowances for real depreciation (CCA) alone declined from 10.7 percent of net national product in 1948 to 5.8 percent in 1983; as a

3. Thomas Vasquez, "The Effects of the Asset Depreciation Range System on Depreciation Practices," Office of Tax Analysis Paper 1 (U.S. Treasury Department, May 1974).
4. See U.S. Department of the Treasury, Internal Revenue Service, *Income Tax Compliance Research: Estimates for 1973–1981*, pp. 22, 243.

Figure 3-1. *Income and Taxation of Nonfinancial Corporations as a Percentage of Net National Product, 1948–83*

Percent

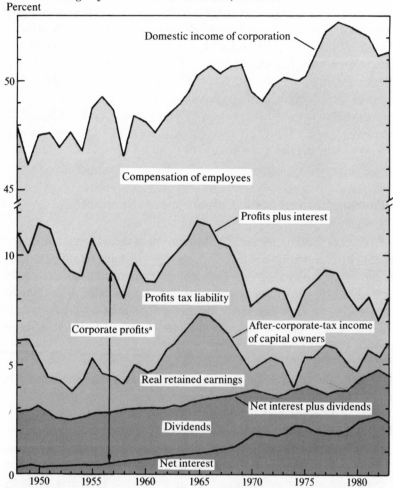

Source: U.S. Department of Commerce, Bureau of Economic Analysis, *The National Income and Product Accounts of the United States, 1929–76 Statistical Tables,* a supplement to the *Survey of Current Business,* vol. 64 (July 1984), tables 1.13 and 1.7.

a. With real depreciation and inflation adjustments for inventories.

share of domestic income of nonfinancial corporations, this decline is from 22.4 percent to 11.4 percent.[5]

5. U.S. Department of Commerce, Bureau of Economic Analysis, *The National Income and Product Accounts of the United States, 1929–76 Statistical Tables,* a supplement to the *Survey of Current Business* (U.S. Government Printing Office, 1981), table 1.13; and *Survey of Current Business,* vol. 62 (GPO, July 1984), table 1.13.

These statistics are dramatic but somewhat misleading. The real income of corporations paid to owners of capital includes both corporate profits and interest payments. Profits plus interest payments decreased from about 11 percent of net national product in 1948 to around 8 or 9 percent by the late 1970s. About half the decline in corporate profits during the postwar era was therefore offset by an increase in the amount of income paid as net interest. The remaining decline is more difficult to interpret, partly because of the volatility of corporate profits and corporate taxes over the business cycle.[6] Considering the poor status of the economy during 1979–82, it may be surprising that total profits plus interest did not decline even more.

Postwar Changes in the Corporate Tax Structure

Profits tax liability, essentially the amount of federal, state, and local tax paid by corporations on their income, also declined steadily throughout the postwar period. Profits tax liability as a percentage of real profits remained fairly steady during this same period (see figure 3-2). Changes in the corporate tax structure—principally legislated tax decreases and inflation-caused tax increases—combined to bring about this rather constant ratio of tax liability to profit.

Congress actually enacted several changes in the tax laws that reduced tax rates, especially for firms purchasing new plant and equipment. The principal modifications were an allowance for investment credit for new purchases of plant and equipment and various accelerations of the deductions allowed for recovery of the cost of these purchases.

Investment credits of up to 7 percent were provided for investments in plant and equipment through the Revenue Act of 1962. After two suspensions between 1966 and 1967 and between 1969 and 1971, the investment credit was reinstated in 1971 and liberalized. In 1975 the maximum credit allowance was increased to 10 percent. Higher credit amounts for shorter-lived assets were allowed in 1981.

Depreciation or cost-recovery allowances have been accelerated four different times since World War II: (1) the adoption of the Internal Revenue Code of 1954 allowed accelerated methods such as "double declining balance" or "sum-of-the-years'-digits"; (2) the 1962 "Guidelines for Depreciation" reduced write-off periods by about 30 to 40

6. Pechman, *Federal Tax Policy*, p. 147.

Figure 3-2. *Profits Tax Liability of Nonfinancial Corporations as a Percentage of Real Profits Earned, 1948–83*[a]

Ratio of tax liability to profits (thousandths)

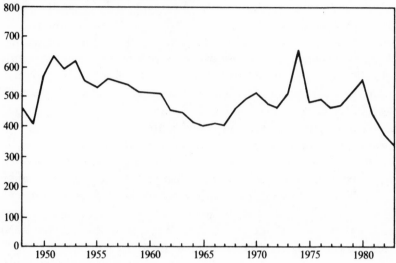

Source: Same as figure 3-1.
a. Real profits earned excludes effect of inflation on net interest payments. See text discussion.

percent;[7] (3) the introduction of the asset depreciation range (ADR) system in 1971 allowed taxpayers to base calculations on tax lives that were 20 percent shorter than the guidelines defined; and (4) the 1981 accelerated cost-recovery system (ACRS) generally shortened these lives, classified assets into five categories (but only four lives), and effectively accelerated the portion of deductions that could be realized in years immediately following an investment. Congress offset some of the 1981 changes in 1982 by limiting the extent to which firms could write off a portion of the costs that they did not incur. Before that time, firms were allowed to write off the gross cost of most investments even though net cost was equal to gross cost less the investment credit. After 1982 the basis for recovery was reduced by one-half of the value of the investment credit.[8] In 1984, depreciation allowances for real estate were made slightly less generous.

Other postwar changes in corporate taxation were less significant but

7. U.S. Internal Revenue Service, *Internal Revenue Bulletin,* Cumulative Bulletin 1962-2 (July–September 1962), pp. 418–86.
8. The 1981 tax act called for further acceleration of cost-recovery deductions to be phased in between 1985 and 1986, but this prospective acceleration was eliminated in 1982.

applied to more than just plant, equipment, and buildings. The statutory corporate tax rate was reduced from 52 percent for years before 1964 to 48 percent by 1965, then was temporarily raised by a surtax from 1968 to 1970, and finally was lowered to 46 percent for 1979 and thereafter (see figure 3-3). Gains from sales of inventories were often reported by firms on a first-in, first-out (FIFO) basis, a method of accounting that effectively included gains from inflation in the measure of income. Firms were allowed to use the dollar-value LIFO method after 1948, although various less-used forms of LIFO have been allowed on and off since the origin of the income tax. The LIFO method defers indefinitely the tax on inventory gains for a growing or stable firm.[9]

An estimate of the effective marginal corporate tax rate applying to new investment in the past three decades is also presented in figure 3-3. This estimate actually measures the effective tax rate that would apply if the tax laws and the rate of inflation over the life of investment remain the same as they were when the investment was made. Although there are different ways of making this type of marginal estimate, the trend toward lower tax rates at the margin is a common element.[10]

Given this history of legislated tax reduction, why do corporate tax collections remain a fairly constant percentage of corporate income? An important factor throughout the 1960s and 1970s was an inflation rate that crept upward from one economic cycle to the next. As the inflation rate increased, it reduced substantially the value of depreciation allowances based upon original cost. The inflation rate also overstated the gains from selling inventory for firms not adopting a LIFO method of accounting and for firms that reduced their stock of inventory. To the extent this increase was unexpected, it operated as a lump-sum tax on existing assets.

It is important to note that Hulten and Robertson's calculations of the marginal corporate tax rate in figure 3-3 are ex ante in nature. That is, they figure the effective tax rate on new investment as if inflation

9. For a firm with steady or growing inventory, the last piece of purchased inventory likely has a higher price than older inventory; if the time between the latest purchase and the most recent sale is small, there are few inflation gains on a sale accounted for through LIFO. Another way to view this process is to think of the firm as selling the older inventory, but then being allowed to roll over the inflation gains by subtracting them from the basis value of the new inventory.

10. Different assumptions can be made about the real before- or after-tax rate of return required from assets, as well as the appropriate way to calculate or weight the proportions of investment directed toward different types of assets.

Figure 3-3. *Statutory Corporate Tax Rate and Marginal Effective Corporate Tax Rates on Plant and Equipment, 1952–83*[a]

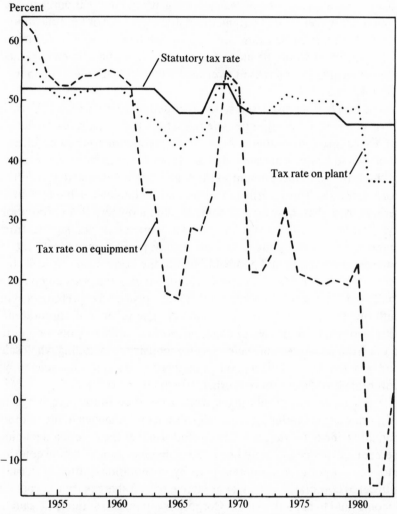

Source: Data derived from Charles R. Hulten and James W. Robertson, "The Taxation of High Technology Industries," *National Tax Journal,* vol. 37 (September 1984), p. 337.

a. Estimates assume an after-tax rate of return of 4 percent. Rates for 1981–83 assume a 6 percent rate of return. The 1981 and 1982 rates are calculated as averages of the two years.

remained at the level it was when the investment was undertaken. This is certainly an appropriate method of trying to assess the effect of tax changes on expectations of managers regarding marginal purchases of capital. However, to understand the historical record of tax collections, tax payments must be examined ex post. On this basis, the tax rate on any investment would be much higher than would have been expected whenever inflation increased over levels that existed when the investment was made.

The two factors discussed so far operated in large part to offset each other in terms of average effective tax rates—the rising rate of inflation increased taxes on existing assets, while tax reductions on new purchases of plant and equipment reduced taxes. It is a common fallacy, however, to think that only investment in plant and equipment is subject to the corporate tax. The return that ideas and technological improvement receive may also show up as income of capital owners.[11] A corporation may profit from the ideas of its own workers or managers, from investment in their education, and it may profit from investment in patents, inventions, and goodwill outside the corporation. Recall that the economic definition of capital investment encompasses much more than that physical investment receiving special tax preferences or suffering from an additional inflation tax. The income of corporations may also reflect monopoly or oligopoly profit or unique opportunities to profit from economies of scale. Service industries, including wholesale and retail trade, provide a good example of broad activities generating corporate profit from sources other than plant and equipment.

Since corporate profits taxes were a fairly constant percentage of corporate profits (after inflation adjustments for changes in inventories and allowances for depreciation), it follows that they were a declining percentage of income, including interest income, paid to capital contributors to corporations. Interest paid by corporations, after all, is not subject to corporate tax, yet it has increased as a share of total corporate income paid to capital owners. Corporate capital can actually be said to be the source of three types of nonlabor income: dividends, real retained earnings, and interest payments. When added together, the real income (after corporate taxes) of holders of corporate stocks and bonds has

11. Stiglitz has even suggested a model in which ideas are capitalized into the equity of the firm, and financing of capital to implement ideas is accomplished entirely by debt. See Joseph E. Stiglitz, "Taxation, Corporate Financial Policy and the Cost of Capital," *Journal of Public Economics*, vol. 2 (February 1973), pp. 1–34.

fluctuated slightly around 5.5 percent of net national product throughout the postwar era. Again, making an inflation adjustment for interest payments will not affect this result. Whatever the negative adjustment for bondholders might be, a positive adjustment of equal size will be made for stockholders.

More Recent Trends

The 1981 change to ACRS substantially lowered the effective rate of tax on new investment in plant and equipment. When policymakers enacted this and previous changes affecting business income, they acted in the belief that they could receive a "free ride" for a few years with such a change. By applying the incentives only to new investment, the revenue losses were expected to be minor in the first year or two, while the full-scale incentive effect supposedly was to occur immediately.

After the first few years, however, the revenue losses become much more substantial. A larger percentage of the capital stock makes use of the new allowance. Five-year Treasury Department estimates show that the combined effect of the 1981 and 1982 tax acts will be a reduction in the corporate tax revenues by about 22 percent to 25 percent between 1984 and 1988.[12]

There are at least two other predictable shifts in the future measure of the activity and taxes of corporations.

One likely future shift will be in the sectoral measure of capital income from bondholders to equity owners. If inflation is lower than it has been in past periods, there will be a corresponding decline in the overstatement of real interest paid by equity owners and in the overstatement of real interest received by bondholders. If interest rates decline with a lowering of the inflation rate, the nominal income of bondholders will decline and that of equity owners will rise even if there is no change in their real income. On the other hand, if real interest rates stay high, the shift in the measure of sectoral income will also occur if the higher rates cause an increase in the amount of new equity financing relative to debt financing.

Another possible shift, portended perhaps in the 1982 and 1984 tax acts, may be to stabilize or increase the amount of taxes paid by corporations. Such a shift would occur under many recent proposals to reform the income tax.

12. Estimates from the Office of Tax Analysis, Treasury Department.

Permanence of Corporate Tax Reductions

In noting the effect of changing inflation rates on taxes, it is important to distinguish between individual income taxes and corporate income taxes. The corporate tax is essentially a flat-rate tax; thus there is no bracket creep. Although an increase in the rate of inflation lowers the value of a depreciation allowance, the continuation of a rate of inflation simply maintains that allowance at the same (lower) value. Thus corporate taxes are raised, all other things being equal, not by a continuation of an inflation rate, but only by an increase in that rate. Individual income taxes, on the other hand, are progressive in nature. Without indexing of individual income tax brackets for inflation, any constant rate of inflation causes bracket creep or an increase in the tax rate. Under that condition, inflation does not need to increase for individual income tax rates to rise; it simply needs to be greater than zero.

This simple difference explains a great deal of past and future trends in the relative tax revenues provided by the individual income tax and the corporate income tax. In the 1960s and 1970s Congress often argued that one-fourth or so of tax reductions should apply to businesses and three-quarters to individuals. At a given rate of inflation, the above discussion makes it apparent that the business reductions were actually permanent in nature, whereas the individual reductions merely offset some of the tax increases due to bracket creep. Even if the permanent business tax reductions were initially offset by business tax increases due to higher rates of inflation, a lowering of the rate of inflation will eliminate those tax increases, while leaving intact the permanent tax cuts. Lower inflation rates will not, however, eliminate any of the past tax increases due to bracket creep. This phenomenon, as much as any other, explains how past tax cuts could be thought of as going primarily to individuals, while at the same time tax rates for businesses were declining and those for individuals were rising both as a percentage of national income and as a percentage of all tax collections.

Even with indexing of individual brackets, individual income tax rates will not go down as inflation declines. Indeed, real growth in the economy will continue to raise these tax rates. Increases in average real incomes cause bracket creep, although at a slower rate than in a system indexed for neither inflation nor real growth. For business income, however, a decrease in the rate of inflation will mean a real decrease in the rate of tax applying to equity investment in depreciable assets.

Variations in Tax Rates

At one time the income tax was at least theoretically supposed to be based upon income. Two individuals or two firms would be required to pay the same amount of tax if their incomes were equal. While there were many deviations from this rule of uniformity of treatment, such deviations were often judged to be violations of the standard that had been set.

In the case of business income, inflation did have a severe impact upon the measure of real income. Because depreciation allowances were allowed to vary with the rate of inflation, there was a substantial break with the notion that all income should be treated equally. Yet the failure to make the necessary adjustment seems not to have been the result of any conscious decision to violate the uniformity standard. Instead, the failure to index depreciation seems to have resulted from (1) a political fear of all issues of indexing, both those related to income measurement and those related to bracket creep; (2) technical problems in designing schemes for indexing, especially indexing for capital gains and interest income; and (3) a belief that the political or administrative costs of indexing were not worthwhile in periods of low inflation and a related hope that high rates of inflation were temporary.

With the adoption of investment credits and various forms of accelerated depreciation, no such claim of accidental cause and effect can be made. It seems clear in both these cases that Congress and the executive branch were quite willing to abandon the notion that the income tax should tax income. Investment credits technically did not change the measure of income, and thus, on a pure measurement basis, one might be less critical of the these credits. Nevertheless, Congress lowered, relative to other income, the effective tax rate on income generated by investment eligible for the credits. Accelerated depreciation changes further led to abandonment of the notion that the tax system would require accurate accounting for economic income. One could argue that the 1954 change in depreciation law, and to a lesser extent the legal changes in the 1960s and 1970s, were designed to offset the mismeasurement caused by inflation. In these cases, the measurement of marginal income from new investment initially yielded a total that was too low, but the understatement of income from new assets was to offset overstatement of income from old assets. At least in principle, moreover, the economic lives of assets were still to be measured even if those lives were shortened substantially in reporting income for tax purposes.

In 1981 the term *accelerated cost-recovery system* was adopted to convey the notion that the tax system would not be based upon the measure of the real economic depreciation or economic loss from holding assets. Thus the economic term *depreciation* is no longer used even to describe the tax calculations related to cost recovery and the Treasury Department completely eliminated the office whose task was to estimate the economic lives of assets. As an important aside, there is still a need for sources of data on economic depreciation rates of assets. As the economy changes and new forms of capital are developed, such sources become more necessary to estimate the net national product and national income. More recent proposals, including the 1984 Treasury Department report on tax reform, suggest that some office is necessary to compare economic depreciation rates across assets.

Table 3-1 shows the types of problems that develop when the tax laws are developed without any clear relation to the measure of economic income. This table shows the effective tax rates on equity investments in assets of various types under various tax laws allowing investment credits and accelerated cost recovery. These rates vary enormously. For example, after 1982 the effective rate for commercial structures equaled 35.6 percent, while ships and boats were taxed at 5.1 percent.

Generally economists believe that efficiency losses increase as the differential between tax rates on assets increases. If a system of investment credits and depreciation allowances were developed with a focus on measures of real income and real depreciation, it would be possible to eliminate many of the differences shown in table 3-1 without necessarily changing the overall level of average taxation. For instance, the effective tax rate on engines could be brought more into line with the tax rate on furniture, thus decreasing the difference between the two and increasing the efficiency of investment in the economy.

Although these types of changes would clearly be of substantial benefit, I believe that far too much emphasis has been placed on this particular source of inefficiency. It would be a mistake to believe that the discrepancies between ACRS types of deductions and measures of actual economic depreciation are the only major source of inefficiency caused by the taxation of income from corporate capital or other income from capital. Many more serious disparities in tax rates—and therefore much greater inefficiency—are caused by other factors.

Table 3-1. *Effective Tax Rates, by Asset Type*
Percent

Asset type[a]	Law in effect before 1981	Law enacted in 1981[b]	Law enacted in 1982
Equipment			
Automobiles	17.0	−32.8	9.6
Office, computing and accounting equipment	2.3	−49.4	11.9
Trucks, buses, and trailers	10.1	−45.2	11.3
Aircraft	17.7	−31.4	8.9
Construction machinery	7.6	−29.7	8.6
Mining and oil field machinery	16.7	−28.5	8.3
Service industry machinery	20.3	−28.5	8.3
Tractors	8.9	−28.2	8.3
Instruments	20.7	−17.5	13.1
Other equipment	13.4	−25.6	7.7
General industrial equipment	20.6	−14.0	11.7
Metal working machinery	13.2	−20.2	6.7
Electric transmission and distribution equipment	29.2	3.2	24.2
Communications equipment	22.6	−21.1	6.7
Other electrical equipment	12.6	−21.1	6.7
Furniture and fixtures	7.1	−20.0	6.4
Special industrial equipment	12.6	−19.0	6.1
Agricultural equipment	6.6	−18.1	5.9
Fabricated metal products	26.8	−1.4	18.2
Engines and turbines	31.8	16.3	30.2
Ships and boats	27.9	−15.1	5.1
Railroad equipment	24.8	11.1	25.3
Plant			
Mining exploration, shafts, and wells	8.5	8.5	8.5
Other mining[c]	51.7	41.6	41.6
Industrial structures[c]	49.6	38.4	38.4
Public utility structures	27.3	15.5	25.7
Commercial structures[c]	46.8	35.6	35.6
Farm structures[c]	41.1	35.8	35.8

Source: Jane G. Gravelle, "Capital Income Taxation and Efficiency in the Allocation of Investment," *National Tax Journal*, vol. 36 (September 1983), p. 299.

a. Assets are approximately ordered from fastest to slowest economic depreciation rates.

b. These rates would have been effective in 1986 had not they not been overidden by 1982 tax law changes.

c. Under 1984 tax law, the following effective tax rates are changed: other mining, 44.6 percent; industrial structures, 41.3 percent; commercial structures, 38.4 percent; and farm structures, 38.7 percent (communicated to the author by Jane Gravelle).

First, while equity investment in most equipment may be taxed at close to a zero rate and investment in structures at a higher rate, much variation exists between these and other investments. Equity investment in land and inventories continues to be taxed at a higher rate still. With the use of LIFO, for instance, corporate income from inventory sales is taxed at a corporate rate of 46 percent, plus any amount of expected future tax on the gains that are deferred from tax. Research and development expenditures are usually written off as wage payments—a favorable treatment—but the high returns to such investment are often fully taxable.

Second, corporate income is likely to flow through to individuals in different ways. Individuals may hold their investments in tax-deferred or partially tax-exempt form through the use of pensions, life insurance, and other retirement accounts. Thus the tax rate on this corporate source income will vary widely according to the institutional means through which individuals hold property.

A third source of disparity arises from the different rules applying to the three sources of corporate capital income: interest, retained earnings, and dividends. Interest income is not subject to corporate tax; retained earnings often generate additional capital gains taxes; and dividend income is subject both to corporate taxation and individual taxation unless the individual holds corporate assets through pensions or life insurance. In addition, the interest costs are deductible to the owners of equity capital, although taxable to the owners of the debt. For a given asset with a fixed rate of return, the negative rate of tax on the interest payments may exceed both the positive rate of tax on the return from the asset and the positive rate of tax on the interest receipts.

When one combines all possible ways in which income can be taxed—by type of plant or equipment, by investment in inventory, plant, or ideas, by the institutional means through which individuals hold assets, and by source of corporate capital payment—the effective tax rate on different types of income attributed to capital owners can be seen to vary tremendously. For instance, if inventories are purchased and sold under a FIFO method, which taxes inflationary gains, while income is paid out as dividends to taxable individuals, the tax rate may easily be in excess of 100 percent. If new equipment is purchased in a corporation through retained earnings, on the other hand, the effective tax rate may be close to zero. If that equipment is purchased with borrowed dollars—

effective tax rate varies a lot

with the interest being deducted by the corporation and excluded from tax by a nontaxable recipient such as a pension plan—the tax rate may be close to minus 100 percent.

This variation in marginal tax rates is so great that one can argue that capital income is overtaxed or undertaxed simply by choosing the appropriate type of margin on which to make a calculation. Since so many of these arrangements for taxation are discretionary, the researcher can make almost any case he wants. Indeed, the debate about whether marginal returns to investment are overtaxed or undertaxed has divided the economics, finance, and accounting professions.[13] By often focusing on the issue of what the marginal (or average marginal) tax rate on capital should be, people fail to note that one rate does not apply to all capital. One essentially has to average certain numbers to come up with an estimate. Some adopt average tax collections, arguing that only this takes into account all the multiple tax provisions. Others assume some average ratio of debt to equity and some average dividend rate, ignore a variety of provisions, and then try to calculate the present value of taxes on investments that face some average (often top corporate) statutory rate on receipts and certain deductions. Both approaches are revealing—and both have been mentioned or quoted herein—but both are limited by looking only at certain tax provisions and by the very discretionary nature of many taxes.

One estimate of the variation in specific types of investment in machinery, buildings, and inventories, according to different industries, sources of finance, and types of owners is provided by King and Fullerton.[14] Results for the United States are summarized in figure 3-4. Although this type of study requires a number of assumptions about which reasonable people may disagree, those disagreements relate to the extent to which current investment falls into certain categories and, to a lesser extent, to the simplifying assumption that, given the previous discussion, had to be made in each category. The qualitative results emphasized here, however, would not change. The effective tax rate on

13. See the discussions in chapters 5 and 6 on how tax arbitrage can be used to change tax rates and on why no ratio of debt to equity can be assumed to provide a stable equilibrium in the financial markets.

14. Mervyn A. King and Don Fullerton, eds., *The Taxation of Income from Capital: A Comparative Study of the United States, the United Kingdom, Sweden, and West Germany* (University of Chicago Press, 1984).

Figure 3-4. *Proportion of Investment Taxed at Selected
Rates of Taxation, 1980*

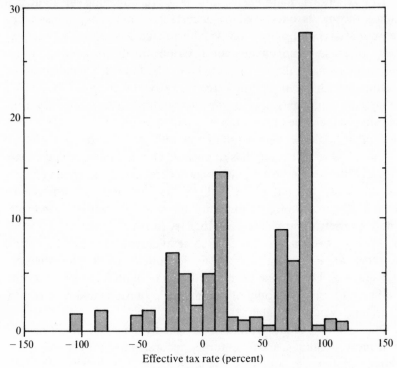

Percent of corporate capital

Effective tax rate (percent)

Source: Mervyn A. King and Don Fullerton, eds., *The Taxation of Income from Capital: A Comparative Study of
the United States, the United Kingdom, Sweden, and West Germany* (University of Chicago Press, 1984), p. 299.

different types of investment would still vary enormously. This variation,
by the way, is not confined to the United States; similar results can be
seen in most countries around the world.

It is difficult to measure precisely how much these variations have
quantitatively affected aggregate investment or welfare. Some traditional
economic analyses have attempted to measure the welfare losses associated with the change in investment that would take place if there were
essentially one investor in the economy and all investments were equity
investments in which no loans were involved. Such analyses usually
determine a loss of a few percent in aggregate output or welfare in the

economy.[15] These analyses, however, ignore many of the crucial problems that are highlighted in this book. They ignore discrimination among individual investors, including crucial entry barriers that new businesses experience. They completely ignore financial questions by assuming essentially that they are unimportant—in much the same way that many microeconomic studies have trouble incorporating macro variables such as the amount of loanable funds made available by monetary authorities.

Some Implications

Some implications that relate to the analysis of corporation income tax are outlined below.

First, the gradual separation of economic, financial, and tax accounting is a major threat to the establishment of an efficient and uniform method of taxing capital income, as well as to the collection of taxes on capital income generally. As noted in chapter 2, financial income and taxable income have always differed from economic income because of differences in accounting for such items as accrued gains. Because neither financial nor tax accounts are indexed for inflation, however, the expected presence of inflation in the modern economy has caused even greater disparities between these accounts and one that would be designed to measure economic income. Now, in addition, the tax laws accommodate a cost-recovery schedule that differs from the schedule of depreciation claimed in financial accounts. As all these measures become further separated from one another, it will become more difficult to measure and interpret the economic activity of business as a whole and to design tax and expenditure programs that maintain or restore neutrality across investments of various types. Finally, the incentive for corporate managers to report profits for financial purposes will also become a less powerful counterforce to the tendency to understate income for tax purposes.

Second, fundamental differences exist in the types of capital employed in the nonfinancial corporate and nonfinancial, noncorporate sectors.

15. See, for instance, Jane G. Gravelle, "Capital Income Taxation and Efficiency in the Allocation of Investment," *National Tax Journal,* vol. 36 (September 1983), pp. 297–306.

Businesses that make their profit from the sales of goods or services to many parts of the economy tend to be relatively more concentrated in the corporate sector, while the noncorporate sector is composed primarily of smaller service enterprises and businesses with large proportions of investment assets in real estate.

There is a logical reason for such separation. The production and selling of goods often tend to be much riskier than the selling of individual services. The former often involves large enterprises in which economies of scale are important. Noncorporate businessmen and farmers too face many risks, but they generally are not those associated with being the first to develop a new or better product for a national marketplace. Their investments are likely to be more localized and involve smaller economies of scale, as in the case of most investment in real estate.

Incorporation gives two important and related benefits to owners. One way is that the risk of sizable losses is transferred from the owners to the government. A corporation may declare bankruptcy, yet its owners may maintain sizable wealth in assets other than the bankrupt corporation. Even if the corporate tax rate is higher than the individual tax rate, the government will bear more of the burden of losses that occur.[16] The tax benefits of these losses may even be transferred through merger and consolidation. Some unprofitable corporations, for instance, may sell their losses to other corporations, which in turn will compensate the losing corporations for the tax benefits of deducting those losses; or, alternatively, the corporation with substantial cumulated losses may find ways to purchase other corporations with taxable gains.

Incorporation is also beneficial because it makes much easier the selling of shares in a business. The market for noncorporate shares is much less developed (although a recent expansion of the market for limited partnerships is due to tax incentives). The more developed and liquid stock market enhances the ability of the original owners of firms to generate new funds for a business or simply to sell some of their own shares in order to consume, diversify their asset holdings, or move on to other ventures. The major reason that the corporate stock market is more developed may be related again to the risk reduction possible there. Many purchasers of shares do not exercise much control over the

16. See also Richard A. Musgrave, *The Theory of Public Finance: A Study in Public Economy* (McGraw-Hill, 1959), p. 320.

companies they own, and they would enter the market only if the liability for losses were kept to some minimum.

For many products with large potential markets, economies of scale often mean that only a limited number of sellers or makers of different types of goods will survive. Once a new product or method of production is developed—whether it entails a new technological innovation or simply a new, more efficient method of distribution—the firm that can capitalize on that idea soonest may be one of the few survivors, or at least a survivor with a low ratio of cost to price of product. It is therefore crucial to be able to generate capital for investment and expansion early in the life of many businesses, especially those offering goods and services on a wide scale.

Incorporation generally takes place long before a business becomes quite large. Once incorporated, the present value of the expected cost of future taxes may actually be reflected in the price of the stock. It is highly likely that this expected value is lower than the value of the risk reduction and increased share price that came about because of early incorporation.

Third, tax shelters and shelter industries tend to be unincorporated. The existing concentration of shelters outside the corporate sector is in part a consequence of the previous two implications. Since corporations tend to want to report income for financial purposes, they are less likely to engage in substantial transactions involving assets in which most income is accrued as capital gains. Those gains could not be reported unless realized, but if realized, would put a corporation at a competitive disadvantage relative to individuals or firms that held those assets and realized less of the economic income for tax purposes.

Some authors have argued that there exists a group of "natural deferral" industries including real estate, livestock feeding and breeding; fruit, tree, nut, and vegetable farming and forestry; and other agricultural activity.[17] In these industries much of the income (such as sales of timber or livestock) is treated as capital gains rather than ordinary income. The argument made is that the advantage of corporate earnings retention for

17. Harvey Galper and Dennis Zimmerman, "Preferential Taxation and Portfolio Choice: Some Empirical Evidence," *National Tax Journal*, vol. 30 (December 1977), pp. 387–97; and Joseph J. Cordes and Steven M. Sheffrin, "Taxation and the Sectoral Allocation of Capital in the U.S.," *National Tax Journal*, vol. 34 (December 1981), pp. 419–32.

individuals in high-income brackets is much less when only a portion of the income is subject to taxation because of the capital gains exclusion. All other things being equal, therefore, industries benefiting from the capital gains exclusion would be more likely to be unincorporated.

I agree with these authors on both their logic and on their identification of many "natural deferral" industries. In my view, however, more emphasis should be placed on the benefits arising from capital gains deferral (and exclusion at death) than upon the partial exclusion for realizations. In light of previous arguments, publicly traded corporations simply are more reluctant to reduce stated earnings by deferring gains for long periods of time.[18]

Shelter industries are held directly by individual taxpayers and unincorporated partnerships for another reason also. Even when economic income is positive, income reported for tax purposes and cash flow is much more likely to be negative when the income from investment comes as accrued capital gains. Negative taxable income from one activity is of primary benefit to firms or individuals with other taxable income. Since for tax purposes individuals may offset both labor income and other capital income whereas corporations may offset only capital income, individuals are more likely to be able to take advantage of the favorable tax treatment. Lending institutions may also require cash flow adequate to service a loan; again, the individual is more likely to have positive cash flow from noncapital sources. Thus for investments that are unlikely to yield sufficient cash flow to pay off a loan, the lending institution usually has recourse against the labor income and capital income of the individual, but only against the capital income of the corporation.

For businesses that buy and sell goods, inventory accumulation is kept to a minimum, and income is reflected fairly immediately in receipts and cash flow and taxable income. Buying, producing, selling, and distributing goods are normally not shelter activities and are therefore relatively more concentrated in the corporate sector where the opportunity for risk reduction and diversification by owners is not outweighed by the potential for tax sheltering, essentially of accrued capital gains.

Fourth, the system of tax penalties and subsidies for income from various types of assets distorts the allocation of investment in the economy and the distribution of assets and liabilities among individuals.

18. These authors also include oil and gas extraction in this category because preferential deductions allow ordinary income to be converted into capital gains.

This conclusion is exactly the same as one reached when examining the individual income tax in chapter 2. The cost is much greater than one would estimate by comparing only average tax rates for income of individuals and of corporations or between two types of investments such as investments in inventories or in plant. Marginal tax rates vary enormously and set up false and confusing signals for each person and business as to the types of investments that would be optimal for society as a whole. This confusion is reinforced by the complicated signals emitted by a system with different accounting rules for financial income, taxable income, and real economic income.

CHAPTER FOUR

Flows of Interest and Loan Markets

THE NEXT STEP in examining the allocation of capital in the economy is to take a close look at the loan markets, where much of the surplus saving of households or firms is made available to others for investment or consumption. This chapter examines this market for loans primarily by tracing interest flows between borrowers and lenders.

The market for loanable funds is especially important to the new business or the business with inadequate resources of its own to expand beyond its current capability. Without efficient capital markets, this business would either have to pay unnecessarily high costs for borrowed dollars or have to delay expansion until it could generate enough saving internally.

The separation of the functions of saving and investment, as well as the development of a market that will channel saving efficiently to the investment with the highest rate of return, is therefore essential to the growth of the modern economy. This financial market potentially "unties" millions of decisions so that persons wanting to save need not be burdened with personally finding the optimal use of their saving, and persons wanting to invest need not undertake the saving. Competition then allows savers to find the highest rate of return on their saving, while investors can appeal to a variety of sources in searching for loans at the lowest possible cost. No government, firm, or individual can possibly make these millions of decisions in any reasonable fashion. The market for loanable funds, when properly functioning, can be said to actually free individuals to make just the decisions that they themselves are best capable of making.

Interest as a Measure of Income

Although interest receipts are viewed as income of the recipients, an increase in aggregate interest receipts does not necessarily imply an

46

increase in income in the economy. Interest is a means of payment that may or may not be related to the production of real income. Unlike real assets and labor, there is no output generated by interest-bearing assets. While the owner of an interest-bearing asset is entitled to some payment by the person with the corresponding debt, that payment may come from the debtor's current income or wealth without any increased investment or output on the debtor's part. It is not uncommon for a debtor to use debt to buy equipment or inputs necessary for a business, in which case people tend to associate the debt with an increase in investment and output. On the other hand, the debt may be used for consumption purposes. In that case, the saving of the lender may be offset by the dissaving of the borrower, and neither additional investment nor income may have been generated.

One reason that lending is associated with investment is that collateral is often put up to obtain a loan. The collateral commonly is an asset purchased at the same time that the loan is negotiated. Even here, it is misleading to associate the lending with an increase in investment. Much more information is needed to ascertain the effect of the loan, such as whether the loan allowed the borrower to undertake investment that would not have taken place otherwise and whether there was a net increase in both the borrower's assets and the total real assets in the economy. A firm that borrows more, invests more, and pays more dividends cannot necessarily be said to have borrowed for investment purposes. Similarly, a person who sells a $75,000 house with an associated mortgage of $30,000 and buys an $80,000 house with a mortgage of $65,000 undertakes only $5,000 of investment at the same time that borrowing increases by $35,000. The other $30,000 of debt may be spent on clothes, durables, education, or any other purpose, and even the $5,000 of investment may have taken place in the absence of the loan.

If one looks at stocks rather than at flows of funds, a similar conclusion is reached. Interest-bearing assets and liabilities are simply two sides of a ledger. The net worth of society does not increase if these assets and liabilities increase by the same amount, just as an increase in interest receipts does not imply an increase in income in the economy if those receipts are matched by an equivalent amount of interest payments. Thus if person A loans $1,000 to person B and pays $100 in interest, while person B in turn loans $1,000 to person A and pays $100 in interest, there is no change in net worth or income in the economy because of these transactions. Total assets and liabilities nonetheless increase by $2,000, while aggregate interest payments and receipts each rise by $200.

Tracing Interest Payments and Receipts

The next task in this examination of loan markets is to trace interest payments from their sources to their ultimate recipients.[1] In 1981 the total payments by nonfinancial corporations, sole proprietorships and partnerships, and persons with real estate and consumer debt were equal to $385.4 billion (see table 4-1). Except for about $55 billion of payments by individuals, this income is deducted by business and persons on their tax returns.[2] When the net payments by the federal government and foreigners and the payments of state and local interest are added, the total reaches $491.1 billion.[3] If all this interest were received directly by taxable businesses and individuals, it would be reported as income subject to taxation on tax returns.

Most interest is not paid directly to ultimate recipients, but instead flows through financial intermediaries. Intermediaries have monetary interest receipts ($449.1 billion) close to the amount of interest payments from original sources.[4] Their monetary payments, however, are $130.3

1. The issue is made complex by several factors. First, when financial intermediaries are involved, each dollar of interest paid by a borrower is likely to generate not only a dollar (approximately) of receipt by a lender, but also another dollar of both payment and receipt by a financial intermediary. Second, some interest receipts are received in the form of wages or other payments to factors employed by financial institutions. These factors in turn often provide nontaxable financial services to consumers in lieu of interest payments. Third, payments by governments add to personal income, but not to national income or product. For further analysis of these issues see Eugene Steuerle, "Tax Arbitrage, Inflation, and the Taxation of Interest Payments and Receipts," *Wayne Law Review*, vol. 30 (Spring 1984), pp. 991–1013 (reprinted by permission of Wayne State University).

2. This number represents the difference between individual taxpayer payments, as estimated by the Department of Commerce, Bureau of Economic Analysis, and the amount actually deducted on individual income tax returns.

3. Here an attempt was made to measure the net amount of interest payments that would be included on returns of domestic taxpayers in the absence of intermediation and tax preferences. A more extensive analysis might treat the foreign sector and the state and local sector in more detail. One might, for instance, examine gross payments by foreigners to determine the extent to which these payments are deducted abroad while not being included on domestic tax returns. For state and local interest, one might want to include in total interest the value of interest forgone in return for tax savings; this forgone interest, or implicit tax, however, would still not be collected by the federal government, but rather by state and local authorities. Such extensions of the analysis would not change the general results and conclusions reached here.

4. The difference between interest payments by original sources and interest receipts of financial intermediaries should not be interpreted as the measure of payments not made through intermediaries. Intermediaries also make payments among themselves.

billion less than their receipts. This difference is composed of payments to pensions and life insurance companies ($55.1 billion), and a remainder that represents almost entirely interest paid as in-kind services to businesses, individuals, and governments.

After accounting for intermediation, another $108.1 billion flows out in one nontaxed form or another: state and local governments receive $37.6 billion for their pension funds and other trusts, while taxpayers and businesses receive $6.5 billion in nontaxable state and local interest. Other amounts are exempted because they pass through nonprofit institutions, IRA and Keogh plans, and other accounts with special exclusions. Legitimate nonfilers receive about $9.2 billion, while non-taxable filers receive about $10.6 billion. Finally, about $31.1 billion more remains nontaxed, primarily due to underreporting of income on tax returns, but this last number is a residual and may be due to other factors such as errors of measurement.

In summary, of the $491.1 billion of interest payments made directly or indirectly to domestic recipients in 1981, about $220.1 billion was received in one nontaxed form or another. The remaining $271.0 billion showed up as income of taxable individuals or businesses, or as income of those providing financial services to business.

These numbers give some idea of the extent to which interest income is deducted and used to reduce tax liabilities on one side of the ledger, but flows through in a nontaxed form on the other. This issue is so important to the efficient operation of the economy that it is treated in more depth in chapter 6.

Historical Comparisons

When interest payments and receipts are compared during the 1948–81 period, perhaps the most remarkable trend observed is the increase in interest flows as a percent of gross national income. Total interest paid out, including government payments, rose from between 4 and 5 percent of GNP in the early postwar years to between 15 and 17 percent by 1980–81, as shown in table 4-2. Net interest paid rose from less than 1 percent of GNP to between 7 and 8 percent by 1980–81. The principal reason for this increase was the rise in nominal interest rates.

Despite persistent deficits during this postwar period, net federal government payments relative to GNP actually fell in the early postwar period, then rose slowly to the 1948 level by the late 1970s. The reason

Table 4-1. *The Flow of Interest Payments and Receipts, 1981*
Billions of dollars

Item	Amount
Total payments potentially deductible	**385.4**
Nonfinancial corporations	161.1
Sole proprietors and partnerships	60.4
Personal payments	
Real estate and co-ops	108.8
Consumer payments	55.1
Total nondeductible payments	**105.7**
Net federal government payments	72.3
State and local government payments	23.7
Net foreigners' payments	9.7
Total receipts potentially taxable without exemptions or financial intermediation	**491.1**
Financial intermediation	
Monetary receipts	449.1
Less: monetary financial intermediation payments	318.8
Difference	**130.3**
Services to business[a]	30.0
Services to individuals[a]	37.0
Services to government[a]	3.4
Retained receipts of pensions and life insurance companies	55.1
Retained financial interest	4.8
Total taxable after intermediation	390.8
Services to business[b]	30.0
Interest only	**360.8**
Taxable as business interest[b]	**86.3**
Nonfinancial corporations	79.0
Other private business	0.4
Financial noncorporate business	6.9
Exemptions	**108.1**
Receipts of state and local governments in their own pensions, trusts, and other accounts	37.6
Receipts by individuals and businesses of nontaxable state and local interest	6.5
Nonprofit institutions	10.4
Individual retirement accounts and Keogh plans	4.6
Interest exclusions	8.7
Legitimate nonfilers	9.2
Individual underreporting plus discrepancy	31.1

Table 4-1 (*continued*)
Billions of dollars

Item	Amount
Interest income of individuals	**165.3**
Reported as interest in adjusted gross income	139.9
Other	25.4
Mutual fund dividends	12.6
Proprietors' income	3.5
Other income	3.3
Trust income	6.0
Less: other nontaxed receipts	10.6
Reported as interest of nontaxable filers	9.0
Reported as other income of nontaxable filers	1.6
Total reported interest on taxable returns of individuals[b]	154.7
Addenda	
Total taxed interest receipts	271.0
Total nontaxed interest receipts	220.1

Source: Eugene Steuerle, "Tax Arbitrage, Inflation, and the Taxation of Interest Payments and Receipts," *Wayne Law Review*, vol. 30 (Spring 1984), p. 997. Figures are rounded.

a. Services to business are treated as intermediate, while those to persons and government are treated as final and paid out of before-tax income. Since a large portion of these services represents profits of banks and other institutions (rather than taxable wages of their employees) which pay little tax, the procedure may overstate the extent of taxable interest payments.

b. Components of total taxable income.

for this relatively small increase in interest payments relative to GNP, of course, was that inflation was driving up nominal GNP (the denominator), while old debt had been sold at interest rates that were quite low relative to new debt. Ex post most of these rates were negative in real terms. More recent trends are in the opposite direction. Between 1978 and 1981 alone, net federal government payments rose from 1.7 percent to 2.5 percent of GNP and continued to rise in 1982 and 1983. Large deficits, if maintained, will combine to raise that percentage significantly unless interest rates fall at the same time.[5]

Although the tax code may have increased the number of exclusions, deductions, and special preferences for interest income, a greater percentage of total interest payments was nontaxed in 1948 (71 percent) than in 1981 (45 percent).[6] The relative importance of the sources of nontaxability, however, has changed significantly. With low interest

5. See Henry J. Aaron, "The Choices Ahead," in Joseph A. Pechman, ed., *Setting National Priorities: The 1984 Budget* (Brookings, 1983), pp. 201–24.

6. The percentage of interest payments nontaxed in 1981 was especially low compared with 1980 and appears to be the result of the dramatic increase in short-term relative to long-term rates in effect during 1981.

Table 4-2. *Interest Flows as a Percentage of Gross National Product, Selected Years, 1948–81*

Type of payment or receipt	1948	1955	1961	1967	1973	1976	1977	1978	1979	1980	1981
Payments											
Total receipts potentially taxable[a]	**4.5**	**5.4**	**7.3**	**8.5**	**10.7**	**11.4**	**11.7**	**12.3**	**13.6**	**15.1**	**16.7**
Total payments potentially deductible	2.6	3.9	5.5	6.6	8.8	9.0	9.2	9.9	11.1	12.1	13.1
Federal government, net	1.6	1.2	1.2	1.3	1.4	1.6	1.6	1.7	1.8	2.0	2.5
State and local government	0.2	0.3	0.4	0.5	0.6	0.7	0.7	0.7	0.7	0.8	0.8
Foreign net	0.1	0.1	0.1	0.1	0.1	0.1	0.2	0.1	0.0	0.1	0.3
Receipts											
Total taxed	**1.3**	**1.6**	**2.2**	**3.1**	**4.5**	**4.9**	**4.9**	**5.3**	**6.2**	**7.6**	**9.2**
Interest on taxable returns of individuals	0.5	0.6	1.0	1.7	2.5	2.8	2.8	2.8	3.2	4.2	5.3
Taxable business interest	0.3	0.3	0.5	0.7	1.2	1.3	1.4	1.6	2.1	2.5	2.9
Services to business	0.5	0.6	0.7	0.7	0.8	0.8	0.7	0.8	0.9	0.9	1.0
Total nontaxed	**3.2**	**3.9**	**5.1**	**5.4**	**6.2**	**6.5**	**6.7**	**7.0**	**7.4**	**7.5**	**7.5**
Pension and life insurance	0.5	0.7	1.1	1.2	1.2	1.3	1.4	1.5	1.5	1.7	1.9
IRAs and Keoghs	0.0	0.0	0.0	0.0	0.0	0.0	0.0	0.1	0.1	0.1	0.2
Receipts by state and local governments	0.1	0.2	0.3	0.5	0.7	0.8	0.8	0.8	1.1	1.2	1.3
Financial services	0.6	0.8	1.0	1.1	1.3	1.4	1.5	1.6	1.7	1.6	1.4
Nonprofit, nonfilers, and nontaxable	0.3	0.3	0.5	0.6	0.7	0.8	0.9	0.9	0.9	0.9	1.0
Underreporting and discrepancy	1.0	1.2	1.4	1.3	1.4	1.2	1.2	1.3	1.6	1.5	1.1
Other exclusions[b]	0.1	0.1	0.1	0.1	0.2	0.2	0.2	0.2	0.2	0.2	0.5
Other differences	0.6	0.6	0.7	0.5	0.8	0.8	0.7	0.7	0.4	0.3	0.2
Addendum											
Net interest[c]	0.9	1.5	2.5	3.5	4.5	5.1	5.3	5.6	6.4	7.1	8.0

Source: Steuerle, "Tax Arbitrage, Inflation, and the Taxation of Interest Payments and Receipts," p. 999. Figures are rounded.
a. No exemptions or intermediation.
b. Includes state and local bonds.
c. Data are from the U.S. Department of Commerce, Bureau of Economic Analysis.

rates in the early postwar era, including zero rates on deposits in checking accounts, much of total interest simply went to financial institutions to cover the costs of their services.[7] The underreporting or discrepancy term was also quite large in the early postwar era. This should not be a surprise. Many individuals were pulled into the income tax system either in World War II or during the postwar era because of the steady decline in tax-exempt levels relative to average household income.[8] While withholding on wages was adopted during the war, it was not until the early 1960s that banks and other savings institutions began to make reports to the government on the interest they paid to individuals.

Relation between the Interest Rate and the Tax Base

The problem created by the differential treatment of interest receipts and payments has nonetheless become much more serious. The gap between interest payments and deductions is a *real* gap that increases with a rise in the interest rate (or the amount of private debt). Suppose, for instance, that the rate of interest increased from 5 percent to 10 percent, that payers of interest who formerly paid $5 billion in interest now pay $10 billion, and that one-half of all interest payments was nontaxed. While real income (interest receipts less interest payments) equals zero in both cases, net real interest deductions in excess of taxed receipts rise from $2.5 billion to $5 billion.

If the increase in interest rates is due to inflation, the loss in the tax base is attributable directly to the mismeasurement of income. Because interest payments are both deducted from the payer's income and counted in the recipient's income, any overstatement of the recipient's income would be matched by an understatement of the payer's income. Suppose that the increase in the interest rate was due to an increase in the inflation rate by 5 percentage points, from a 0 percent rate to a 5 percent rate over the two periods. One could certainly argue that the real receipts of lenders had not increased. The real payments of borrow-

7. One can reasonably debate the extent to which these financial services should be counted as final rather than intermediate. While an interpretation different from that of the national income accountants would change the numbers in the text somewhat, it would have little effect on the overall trends of the postwar era.

8. Eugene Steuerle and Michael Hartzmark, "Individual Income Taxation, 1947–79," *National Tax Journal*, vol. 34 (June 1981), pp. 145–66.

ers also did not change, yet they would be allowed to deduct the increase in nominal payments as if they were declines in real income![9]

One aspect of this relationship warrants examination. Payments on government debt are not deducted by any taxpayer even though some of those payments are included in taxable income by recipients. Thus if taxable government debt forms a large portion of total outstanding debt, the increase in interest payments on government debt partially offsets the decline in the tax base due to the increase in deductible private payments relative to includable private payments. It should also be noted that some amount of private payments, principally consumer payments, are not deducted because they are made by nontaxable businesses or individuals, or by individuals who do not itemize.

In simple algebraic terms, if the tax base equaled national income except for interest receipts and deductions, then

$$Tax\ base = i\,[a(D_p + D_g) - bD_p] + Y,$$

where i = interest rate

$\quad D_p$ = private debt

$\quad D_g$ = taxable government debt

$\quad Y$ = national income

$\quad a$ = percentage of total payments flowing through in taxable form

$\quad b$ = percentage of private interest payments deducted.

If both sides are divided by Y and a value of 0.5 is assigned to a and 0.85 for b—parameters roughly approximating the postwar experience—the equation becomes

$$Tax\ base/Y = -i[0.35(D_p/Y) - (D_g/Y)] + 1.$$

This equation ignores general equilibrium effects on a and b themselves, the effect on government debt of a change in r, and the different tax rates that may apply to interest receipts and deductions that do fall within the tax base. Nonetheless, the equation provides a simplified explanation of why the increases in the interest rate, i, and in the relative amount of private debt, D_p/Y, and the decreases in the relative amount of taxable public debt, D_g/Y, contributed to a decline in the tax base over the postwar era.

9. This, by the way, also has a number of implications for measurements of sectoral saving and income flows; one example is the poor measurement of real corporate income discussed in chapter 3.

Table 4-3. *Estimated Taxes Paid on Interest Income in 1981*
Billions of dollars

Type of payer or recipient	Taxes paid
Interest paid	
Nonfinancial corporations	−48
Sole proprietors and partnerships	−18
Other individuals who pay interest	−31
Interest received	
Nonfinancial corporations[a]	19
Individuals[b]	38
Businesses[c]	7
Financial intermediaries	4
Total	−29

Source: Steuerle, "Tax Arbitrage, Inflation, and the Taxation of Interest Payments and Receipts," p. 1007.
a. Includes a small amount from financial noncorporate business.
b. Includes receipts of estates and trusts.
c. Services to businesses. See discussion in text and table 4-1, note b.

Taxes Paid on Interest Income

Table 4-3 goes a step beyond the previous analysis and attempts to measure the net revenues actually collected on interest payments and receipts. Taxes on interest paid and received were estimated with personal and corporate tax models by successively subtracting interest payments and receipts from the measure of income in the various sectors.[10] This table should not be interpreted as showing the general equilibrium effect of lowering to zero the inclusion rate for both interest receipts and payments. Such a step would obviously cause substantial shifting of assets, payment of debts, and other activities that would affect both the interest rate itself and overall tax liability.

Because government and foreign interest payments were not deducted on tax returns, total interest payments in 1981 were $106 billion in excess of the amount potentially deductible (see table 4-1). If interest receipts were included in income at the same tax rate at which they were deducted, the taxation of interest income would result in large positive net tax collections. If the average marginal rate on both were 0.30, for instance, the taxation of interest income would have yielded a net revenue of $32 billion in 1981. In fact, net collections of tax on interest were negative

10. Because of the interaction between the two estimates, it was actually necessary to stack the estimate of taxes paid on interest income on top of taxes remitted because of interest deductions.

and equal to about − $29 billion. This implies that taxpayers paid about − $61 billion in taxes on private interest transfers in 1981. This number represents about one-seventh of all federal individual plus corporate income taxes collected and one-half of total income taxes collected on income from capital.

Inflation often plays a major role in this loss. Since the inflation rate was 9.4 percent in 1981 and interest rates around 14 to 15 percent,[11] much of this loss was attributable to the mismeasurement of real interest receipts and payments. In effect, about two-thirds of this loss might be viewed as the value of the inflation-induced subsidy of borrowing in excess of an inflation-induced penalty for lending.

11. Inflation here is measured by the GNP implicit price deflator and interest rates by three-month Treasury bill rates, yields on corporate Aaa bonds, and new home mortgage yields. See U.S. Council of Economic Advisers, *Economic Indicators* (Government Printing Office, November 1983), pp. 3, 30.

CHAPTER FIVE

Tax Arbitrage

ARBITRAGE is a process whereby profit is generated from price discrepancies through the simultaneous, or nearly simultaneous, purchase and sale of assets or goods. The focus here is on arbitrage in the capital and financial markets, a process encouraged by differences in rates of return or payment on different assets. *Financial arbitrage* is defined here as arbitrage that would be profitable regardless of tax considerations. For the purposes of this discussion I include buying and selling assets of different risks. Thus borrowing (or selling a promise to deliver cash) at a 10 percent interest rate and simultaneously purchasing an asset that produces a rate of return of 12 percent is a typical example of financial arbitrage.[1]

By *tax arbitrage* I refer to arbitrage activity that is influenced by the different tax treatment of the returns (or rates of payment) on various assets (or debts). The most common form of this tax arbitrage is simply borrowing and making deductible interest payments while purchasing assets whose returns are tax-preferred—that is, taxed at a comparatively lower rate than interest-bearing assets. Because returns from housing, pension accounts, equipment purchases, and other assets are almost all preferred to interest income, borrowing to purchase most assets will turn out to involve tax arbitrage, even when unintended. In this chapter, therefore, attention is directed to the effects of tax arbitrage opportunities on most investment decisions. The next chapter shows how the discretionary nature of capital income taxation, as well as the presence of international markets, prevents prices or rates of return on assets from reaching a stable equilibrium in financial markets.

---

1. Financial arbitrage serves a useful function in the economy by helping to equate rates of return for assets of equal risk. This activity helps send correct signals to investors as to the social return made possible by an investment. For less sophisticated investors, near-to-market rates of return are obtained even when investments are made randomly or with little knowledge of the market itself.

The Special Case of Interest

[handwritten annotation: Greatly — no taxes on accrued income]

When the taxation of capital income was examined at both the individual and the business level, it was found that most assets yield income that is not subject to tax to the full extent of both cash yield plus change in value over time. Almost 80 percent of the assets of individuals benefit from some preference or another. These preferences arise in large part because, for most individuals the tax system essentially taxes realized flows of cash and generally excludes or defers from taxation both accruals of income and receipts of service flows, as from housing and durables. For businesses many equipment purchases are given a treatment close to expensing or a zero rate of tax, while initial deductions for new purchases of plant and buildings have reduced the effective tax rate below its statutory level—even though later deductions for depreciation may be understated, especially in periods of inflation.

Because of these many preferences the rule applying to the return from most assets is that not all nominal income—cash flow plus change in value—must be reported for tax purposes. The return from one asset stands out as a conspicuous exception. When reported on tax returns either as a deduction or as a source of income, interest is fully included. Even though the nominal interest rate equals the real interest rate plus the rate of inflation, both the real interest and the inflationary interest component are treated as income for tax purposes. This inclusion of the entire inflationary component is true for almost no other asset.[2] Capital gains are excluded or deferred for most real assets, and many types of special exclusions, deductions, deferrals, and accelerated allowances are permitted for other real and financial assets.

Although interest income is generally fully includable *when reported* as a deduction or as a receipt of a nonfinancial business or individual, as a receipt it is often not reported because it is excluded from taxable income by flowing through certain entities.[3]

The combination of high (negative) tax rate on interest deductions, a high tax rate on reported interest receipts, a lower tax rate on income

2. The main exception is an asset that is sold in the short term so that all returns, both yield and gain, are recognized currently.

3. In chapter 4 it was shown that almost half of potentially taxable interest receipts was excluded from taxation by flowing through financial intermediaries, pension plans, state and local governments, and other entities.

from almost all other assets, plus a zero tax rate on excluded or nonreported interest receipts creates enormously complex financial markets and has a significant effect on flows of interest and loans. Among the consequences are substantial reallocations of assets and liabilities among individuals and significant incentives to increase the aggregate amount of borrowing in society and the leverage (or debt-to-equity ratio) of many individuals and businesses.

Types of Tax Arbitrage

Businesses and individuals have obvious incentives to deduct all payments, including interest payments and short-term losses, on their tax returns. When these payments or deductions are includable at a higher rate than the receipts from almost all assets, there is powerful inducement for tax arbitrage. Because of the relatively high tax rate on interest payments, the most common form of tax arbitrage involves borrowing to purchase tax-preferred assets. Except where otherwise noted below, therefore, I analyze tax arbitrage in its most common form.[4]

Two types of tax arbitrage can be distinguished. Under the first type, a taxpayer borrows and then purchases a tax-preferred asset such as a house or equipment that receives generous cost-recovery allowances.[5] Technically the income from the asset need not be preferred in an absolute sense, but only have an inclusion rate or tax rate on total nominal income lower than that applying to the nominal interest payment. I define this as *normal tax arbitrage* because it occurs in most investment processes in which borrowing is used to purchase assets.

4. See the discussion of issues related to tax arbitrage in statement of Donald C. Lubick in *Tax Incentives for Savings,* Hearings before the House Committee on Ways and Means, 96 Cong. 2 sess. (Government Printing Office, 1980), pp. 3–26; statement of John E. Chapoton in *Savings and Retirement Proposals,* Hearings before the Subcommittee on Savings, Pensions, and Investment Policy of the Senate Committee on Finance, 97 Cong. 1 sess. (GPO, 1982), pp. 48–68; and David F. Bradford, "Issues in the Design of Savings and Investment Incentives," in Charles R. Hulten, ed., *Depreciation, Inflation, and the Taxation of Income from Capital* (Washington, D.C.: Urban Institute, 1981). The testimonies were drafted by me. The coining of the term *tax arbitrage* is, I believe, due to Bradford.

5. In the case of tax arbitrage, it is assumed that the taxpayer is comparing after-tax rates of return on the asset with the after-tax interest rate. It is still possible that the borrowing associated with an asset purchase goes to finance consumption.

Because the interest is entirely deductible, while the total nominal income from the preferred asset is not included in income subject to tax, the taxpayer will often find that total tax payments are less than zero on an investment purchased entirely with borrowed funds. While there may be before-tax gain or loss from borrowing and purchasing the preferred asset, the negative taxes will increase any gain and may more than offset any loss. As long as the after-tax rate of return on the preferred asset is greater than the after-tax rate of payment on the borrowing, the taxpayer will find this arbitrage profitable.

The second type of tax arbitrage is similar to the first, only in this case the taxpayer essentially buys and sells the same asset; for example, he borrows (sells an interest-bearing asset) and buys an interest-bearing asset.[6] Acquiring a second mortgage while depositing funds in an individual retirement account (IRA) would be a typical example. This type of activity is termed *pure tax arbitrage* because all the gains from these transactions are induced by pure manipulation of the tax system. Without tax preference for the income receipts, little or no nontax gains are possible when the taxpayer is buying and selling the same, or essentially the same, asset. In the case of interest-bearing assets and liabilities, for instance, interest receipts directly received are generally taxable to the recipient. Therefore pure tax arbitrage usually takes place by floating assets or receipts of interest through a tax-favored entity such as a pension fund or an insurance company. While a tax-favored entity may use the deposits to purchase interest-bearing assets, it will relabel the payments to the ultimate beneficiary as pension income, annuity income, or other preferred income that is excluded or deferred from taxation. The taxpayer has thus managed to deduct interest on one side of the ledger, while excluding interest income on the other side.

Many types of purchases, especially of financial assets that are noninterest bearing, involve arbitrage of both types. Purchases of corporate stock, for instance, may be characterized as normal tax arbitrage with respect to the real assets of the corporation. If the interest earned by the corporation is somehow deferred or excluded from taxation, or if the corporate tax rate on interest earnings is less than the individual tax rate on interest deductions, pure tax arbitrage also takes place. A person may also borrow to invest in a pension fund. If the

6. Because individuals cannot both buy and sell tax-exempt bonds, borrowing to purchase these bonds is defined as normal tax arbitrage. Supply limitations also distinguish borrowing to purchase these particular types of interest-bearing assets.

pension fund purchases real estate with its increased deposits, it facilitates normal tax arbitrage, while if it purchases interest-bearing assets, it is a case of pure tax arbitrage.

Some Implications of Normal Tax Arbitrage

To clarify the process of tax arbitrage, I begin with an example of normal tax arbitrage. There are two assumptions: an interest rate of 10 percent and an asset with a nontaxable nominal return of 7 percent. A simple progressive tax system imposes a 30 percent tax rate on taxable income of $20,000 or less, and a 50 percent tax rate on taxable income between $20,000 and $50,000. A taxpayer is assumed to have an income of $50,000 before tax arbitrage and portfolio reallocation. This $50,000 may be composed entirely of wage income, or perhaps the individual found some limited opportunity to invest in an asset with an extremely high rate of return or had a special opportunity or invention with limited applicability, which also contributed to total income. At this point, however, the taxpayer wants to maximize after-tax income and reduce the taxes owed. The taxpayer therefore borrows $300,000 and invests the money in the tax-preferred asset.

Excluding tax savings, the taxpayer deducts $30,000 in interest payments and is compensated only by an increase of $21,000 in income from the preferred asset. This $9,000 loss in before-tax income, however, is more than offset by a decrease in taxes of $15,000 (see the example, which I labeled case 1, in table 5-1).

Suppose this taxpayer obtained an additional $2,000 in cash income, perhaps from a increase in wages or from the realization of capital gains. In case 2 of this example, the taxpayer compensates for this increase in income by borrowing an additional $20,000, paying deductible interest of $2,000, and receiving an additional $1,400 in income from the preferred asset.

In both cases 1 and 2, the taxpayer does not pay the government any tax on income in excess of $20,000 but does pay an implicit tax rate of 30 percent on that income. This implicit rate is equal to the before-tax difference between the rate of return on the interest-bearing asset and the rate of return on the preferred asset, divided by the rate of return available on the interest-bearing asset.

Table 5-1. *An Example of Normal Tax Arbitrage*
Dollars unless otherwise indicated

Item	Case 1	Case 2
Before arbitrage		
Taxable income	50,000	52,000
Taxes	21,000	22,000
After-tax income	29,000	30,000
After arbitrage		
Interest deductions	30,000	32,000
Taxable income	20,000	20,000
Taxes	6,000	6,000
Other nontaxable income	21,000	22,400
After-tax income	35,000	36,400
Case 2 versus case 1		
Addition to income	...	2,000
Addition to after-tax income	...	1,400
Implicit tax rate on additional income (percent)	...	30

Source: Author's calculations.

Tax Arbitrage and Portfolio Theory

The model of normal tax arbitrage is in many ways an extension of models of portfolio theory that require an investor to maximize the after-tax rate of return from various investments.[7] The simplest statement of this theory that is the investor, after adjusting for risk, always invests in the asset that produces the highest after-tax rate of return. A common example compares returns from tax-exempt and taxable bonds. If the taxable interest rate is 10 percent and the tax-exempt rate is 7 percent, investors with marginal tax rates above 30 percent will prefer tax-exempt bonds, while those with rates below 30 percent will invest in taxable bonds. Assets will thus be reallocated among individual portfolios according to the marginal tax rates of the taxpayers.[8]

7. Limits on tax arbitrage investment, which are not apparent in these simple models, are discussed in the last section of this chapter.
8. The effect of tax preferences on before-tax rates of return on assets is examined in Martin J. Bailey, "Progressivity and Investment Yields under U.S. Income Taxation," *Journal of Political Economy*, vol. 82 (November–December 1974), pp. 1157–75. Allocation effects of differential tax rates are detailed in a variety of general equilibrium models, including some that examine household portfolio choices. See, for example, Joel Slemrod, "A General Equilibrium Model of Taxation with Endogenous Financial Behavior," in Martin Feldstein, ed., *Behavioral Simulation Methods in Tax Policy*

Normal tax arbitrage extends simple portfolio theory by allowing for a variety of borrowing opportunities. Portfolio theory at a minimum argues that the taxpayer will, in an ex ante sense, always invest in one asset or another to maximize after-tax yield. The model of tax arbitrage additionally asserts that the implicit plus explicit tax rate, in an ex post sense, can be minimized through combinations of borrowing and purchases of preferred assets.[9] Thus tax arbitrage can be used to offset wage income as well as income from capital, and the taxpayer need not have any stock of net savings. In addition, taxpayers can actually find themselves with ex post income from almost any source, including unexpected returns from risky investment, and still benefit from tax arbitrage. In case 2 above, for instance, the taxpayer received an additional $2,000 of income subject to tax and still was able to reduce the tax on that income.

Graphical Representation of Normal Tax Arbitrage

Figure 5-1 extends the simple example to encompass taxpayers with different levels of income who face a progressive tax system with multiple (actually a continuous series of) tax rates. Again I assume that the alternative investment A yields a nontaxable rate of return, r, which is lower than the rate of interest, i, on the loans and borrowings. The breakeven level of taxable income (Y^T in the figure) is defined as the level of taxable income at which after-tax rates of return on the two assets are equal. As long as potential nominal income from all sources is above the breakeven level, the taxpayer can engage in tax arbitrage and thereby

---

Analysis (University of Chicago Press, 1983), pp. 427–58; and Patric H. Hendershott and James D. Shilling, "Capital Allocation and the Economic Recovery Tax Act of 1981," *Public Finance Quarterly*, vol. 10 (April 1982), pp. 242–73. In many cases, portfolio theory subsumes the problem of tax arbitrage by assuming fixed ratios of debt to equity for various types of purchases.

9. One application of both clientele effects and of tax arbitrage is captured in the finance literature on dividend payments by corporations. Taxpayers in lower tax brackets may tend to hold shares with higher payout rates, as, for instance, in Merton H. Miller and Franco Modigliani, "Dividend Policy, Growth, and the Valuation of Shares," *Journal of Business*, vol. 34 (1961), pp. 411–33. Any increase in receipts, however, can be offset by an increase in borrowing and a simultaneous increase in assets held through insurance companies or other intermediaries, as discussed in Merton H. Miller and Myron S. Scholes, "Dividends and Taxes," *Journal of Financial Economics*, vol. 6 (December 1978), pp. 333–64. The former point is a special case of what is referred to here as portfolio theory, while the latter point is a special case of tax arbitrage.

Figure 5-1. *Normal Tax Arbitrage in a Progressive Income Tax System*

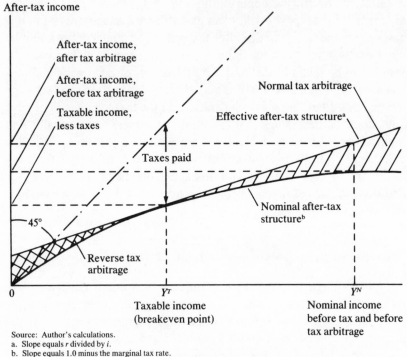

After-tax income

After-tax income,
after tax arbitrage

After-tax income,
before tax arbitrage

Taxable income,
less taxes

Normal tax arbitrage

Effective after-tax structure[a]

Taxes paid

Nominal after-tax
structure[b]

45°

Reverse tax
arbitrage

0   Y^T Y^N

Taxable income
(breakeven point)

Nominal income
before tax and before
tax arbitrage

Source: Author's calculations.
a. Slope equals *r* divided by *i*.
b. Slope equals 1.0 minus the marginal tax rate.

increase after-tax income. For instance, suppose the taxpayer can
generate a nominal before-tax income of Y^N. In the absence of a tax
system, this would equal the actual income of the individual. Recognizing
the potential for tax arbitrage, the taxpayer instead borrows enough
funds to lower taxable income to Y^T and reduce taxes paid. Although
there is a loss in income resulting from paying a higher interest rate on
the borrowings than is received on the investment in the preferred asset,
the tax reduction more than offsets this loss. The net loss in income, or
implicit tax, for income above Y^T is effectively $1 - r/i$.

Effect on Progressivity

Note in theory what has happened to the so-called progressive tax
structure. While it is still nominally progressive on all taxable income,
actual tax payments are now zero for income above the breakeven point.
Because in this example the preferred asset has a lower rate of return

than the interest rate, the taxpayer pays a net implicit tax, but the effective rate structure of this implicit tax is simply proportional for income above the breakeven point. The illustration thus generalizes the proportional result obtained when going from case 1 to case 2 in the examples in table 5-1.

If this model were to hold perfectly in the real world, no persons would pay tax above some given marginal tax rate as implied by the breakeven point. Taxpayers above that rate would outbid other taxpayers for available loanable funds, then invest those funds in the preferred asset. Their return for holding the preferred asset would necessarily be greater than the return to taxpayers in lower marginal tax brackets.

The Relation between Rates of Return

Tax arbitrage is demanded to offset income that would potentially fall in marginal tax brackets above $1 - r/i$. The closer the two measures of before-tax returns, r and i, therefore, the lower the marginal tax rate above which tax arbitrage is profitable. As the breakeven point becomes lower, the number of taxpayers who seek tax arbitrage is greater, as is the amount of gain they can obtain, or the amount of taxable income they can offset, per dollar of loanable funds used for tax arbitrage purposes.

In the extreme case, as i approaches r, the flat line defined as the effective after-tax structure approaches the 45-degree curved line at which before-tax income equals after-tax income. At that point, taxpayers in all positive tax brackets want to borrow to purchase preferred assets. When i is less than or equal to r in a riskless world without limits on the supply of loanable funds, the demand for tax arbitrage is limited only by the amount of income taxes paid. I return to this relation between rates of return in the next chapter.

Some General Equilibrium Effects

The simple theory of normal tax arbitrage holds that taxpayers potentially in higher brackets bid up the price of the preferred assets relative to the nonpreferred assets. If i is thereby raised above r in the process, portfolio reallocation is required not only for taxpayers with tax rates in excess of the rate applying at the breakeven point, but for taxpayers with rates below that level as well. For taxpayers with tax

Table 5-2. *An Example of the General Equilibrium Effect*
Value in dollars

Item	Taxpayer 1	Taxpayer 2
No tax system (rate = interest = 7 percent)		
Asset A	200,000	400,000
Interest-bearing assets	0	0
Liabilities	0	0
Income from net worth		
(same as after-tax income)	14,000	28,000
Tax system (rate = 7 percent,		
interest = 10 percent)[a]		
Asset A	0	600,000
Interest-bearing assets	200,000	0
Liabilities	0	200,000
Income from net worth	20,000	22,000
Taxes collected	4,000	−8,000
After-tax income	16,000	30,000

Source: Author's calculations.
a. With a marginal tax rate of 20 percent for taxpayer 1 and 40 percent for taxpayer 2.

rates below $1 - r/i$, investment in the preferred asset is never profitable. All their savings should be devoted to interest-bearing assets. In this case, the bidding up of the price of the preferred asset relative to interest-bearing assets could result in an increase in the interest rate for these taxpayers over what they might receive otherwise. In a sense, then, some of the implicit tax paid by taxpayers in high tax brackets would be transferred to taxpayers in lower brackets who made loanable funds available to those engaging in tax arbitrage.

This more general equilibrium effect can again be demonstrated through an example. In a riskless world, the rate of return on all assets should be the same, or else taxpayers would purchase only the asset with the highest rate of return. Suppose that, in absence of a tax system, taxpayer 1 holds $200,000 in asset A, earns $14,000 at a rate of return of 7 percent on that asset, and holds nothing in interest-bearing assets. Taxpayer 2 in turn holds $400,000 in asset A and earns $28,000 on that asset (see table 5-2).

Where a tax system is imposed on these taxpayers, the marginal tax rate for taxpayer 1 is 20 percent, while the rate for taxpayer 2 is 40 percent. Because both taxpayers have taxable wages and other sources of income (besides returns from asset A, interest payments, and interest receipts), the return from asset A is exempted from taxation, while interest income is fully taxable both as a payment and as a receipt. Suppose both taxpayers independently turn to the financial markets.

Taxpayer 2 realizes that an interest rate up to 11.67 percent is affordable, yet a profit could still be made by borrowing to invest in the preferred asset if it continues to pay a rate of return of 7 percent. Taxpayer 1, in turn, recognizes that if the taxable interest rate rose above 8.75 percent, it would be profitable to change from the nontaxable asset to interest-bearing assets. Now suppose that the perceptions of these prototype taxpayers, along with those of persons like themselves, resulted in the interest rate rising to 10 percent. The savings of taxpayer 1 would then be made available to taxpayer 2; taxpayer 2 would borrow these funds and invest in asset A; and both would profit from the exchange.[10]

This example brings out several general equilibrium aspects of normal tax arbitrage. First, both taxpayers who engage in tax arbitrage and those who make their savings available for such arbitrage may share in the tax reduction generated. In this example, the taxation of income from capital is actually negative in the aggregate. One can observe that the taxation of the preferred asset results in collections of zero, while the aggregate tax collections on interest income, counting both sides of the ledger, is negative. Second, tax arbitrage substantially increases the demand for loanable funds in society.[11] Third, there are large portfolio shifts caused by this arbitrage.

These portfolio shifts entail more than just accounting differences. Taxpayers in low tax brackets often fail to invest in preferred assets such as farmland or real estate even if their knowledge and skills would allow them to generate a higher rate of return by such investment than could taxpayers in high brackets. By the same token, a high-bracket taxpayer would not loan other taxpayers the funds necessary for investment even if, in the absence of taxes, such transfers would result in the most efficient use of the money.

Some Implications of Pure Tax Arbitrage

Let us now turn to the case of pure tax arbitrage. While both normal and pure tax arbitrage increase the aggregate amount of tax savings

10. Even without borrowing associated with tax arbitrage, substantial portfolio shifts are induced when taxpayers in different tax brackets face rates of tax or inclusion rates that vary among assets. See Harvey Galper and Eric Toder, "Transfer Elements in the Taxation of Income from Capital," in Marilyn Moon, ed., *Economic Transfers in the United States* (University of Chicago Press, 1984).

11. The supply of loanable funds, however, is influenced by a variety of factors unrelated to tax arbitrage.

achieved through borrowing, there are important distinctions between the two. With normal tax arbitrage, there generally must be an exchange of assets and liabilities between two different tax entities with different marginal tax rates. The arbitrage involves borrowing at a tax rate (of the first entity) higher than the tax rate (of the second entity) on interest received. Without this difference in tax rates, no additional tax reduction is achieved in the aggregate through borrowing. That is, in the absence of a difference in tax rates, the tax reduction on additional interest paid would equal the tax increase on additional interest received. The tendency to favor the preferred asset would be sufficient by itself to yield all available tax savings.

With pure tax arbitrage, there is no need for a second taxpayer to hold onto the interest-bearing asset. For instance, a person may simply borrow from a bank and deposit the money in an IRA at the same bank. Because the preferred income is from the same type of asset as the income that is deducted, the taxpayer in a sense engages in transactions with himself. In the case of pure tax arbitrage with interest-bearing assets and liabilities, for instance, the taxpayer furnishes the necessary deposits to achieve his own borrowing. That does not mean that he actually has to trace his deposited dollars and borrow them back. In an aggregate sense, however, other members of society borrow no more or no less. The only immediate real effect of pure arbitrage is that the arbitrager achieves a tax reduction effectively by deducting the payment on his liability, while excluding or deferring from taxation his interest receipts. In a riskless world with no transactions costs, pure arbitrage would have little or no effect on most real variables. Such arbitrage would simply involve an equal increase in the economy's total assets and total liabilities and in its total interest payments and total interest receipts.[12]

Normal tax arbitrage may become unprofitable for some or all taxpayers if the price of preferred assets rises or, correspondingly, if interest rates rise too high relative to the returns on preferred assets. Pure tax arbitrage, on the other hand, is profitable at all positive interest rates and all positive tax rates regardless of the returns on other assets. If the deductible interest rate paid on debt rises, so does the nontaxable interest rate received. Except for certain transaction costs, therefore,

_____

12. There may actually be an "income" effect because the tax savings increases the after-tax income of the taxpayer. Repercussions could also occur from the decline in government revenues.

the interest rate paid on the liability and received on the preferred asset will be the same.

In a related manner, pure tax arbitrage has a different effect on incentives for aggregate investment and saving. Normal tax arbitrage lowers the taxes on returns to capital, as the net tax paid on the net interest income is negative. If the investment and saving take place regardless, the tax savings from normal tax arbitrage may merely have financed consumption. Nonetheless, at least initially, normal tax arbitrage lowers the taxes that would be paid on a leveraged investment. These lower taxes may create an inducement for a higher relative interest rate and a net increase in savings by some households. Investment may therefore increase if this surplus is not used to finance increased consumption of other households. This is an extraordinarily complicated, inefficient, and inequitable way of accomplishing these goals, but it still differs from the case of pure arbitrage.

With pure arbitrage, there is no incentive for more saving, but simply for a society to hold greater amounts of debt. This can be seen by contrasting the tax reductions achieved by an arbitrager and by a true saver investing in an interest-bearing asset. The before-tax rate of interest is 10 percent for both interest received and interest paid in the example below. Suppose the interest income received is favored through a partial

	Taxpayer 1 (arbitrager)	Taxpayer 2 (saver)
Earnings on the asset	$1,000	$1,000
Interest paid	1,000	0
Change in taxable income before exclusion	0	1,000
Exclusion or other tax preference	500	500
Tax subsidy	250	250

exclusion so that the taxpayer need include only half of the 10 percent rate of return in income subject to tax. Since the interest paid on the borrowing can be deducted fully and immediately, the taxpayer has an incentive to purchase the asset—but does not necessarily have an incentive to undertake any net saving. In this example, a taxpayer in the 50 percent tax bracket who *borrows* $10,000 and invests it in the tax-favored asset realizes a tax subsidy equal to $250 while engaging in no net saving. If that taxpayer invests $10,000 of *new savings* in the asset, the tax subsidy received still equals $250. Thus the tax preference provides no additional return for increasing net saving.

Although the arbitrager has made no additional savings available to the economy, he has increased financial assets and liabilities. In a simple theoretical model, this joint increase should have no effect on other real variables. In a world of risk with a monetary authority exercising control on the supplies of loanable funds, however, this type of behavior may have harmful effects. In either case, little saving incentive—even through general equilibrium effects on the behavior of others—is possible in the case of pure tax arbitrage.[13]

Specific Cases of Tax Arbitrage

Tax arbitrage is not a theoretical problem that has limited application to the real world. Tax arbitrage is pervasive throughout the economy, and it affects almost every investment decision made by individuals, businesses, and governments. Hundreds of billions of dollars of tax base are lost annually because of tax arbitrage, and the threat always exists that the loss will increase from year to year as new mechanisms and means are found to take advantage of differential tax rates on interest and income from various assets.[14] Literally hundreds of pages of tax laws and regulations attempt, often unsuccessfully, to cope with tax arbitrage of all types.

Before proceeding with some common examples of tax arbitrage, it is important to clarify that taxpayers do not have to plan to engage in tax arbitrage for it to occur. The collateral for borrowing may have no association with the purpose for which that borrowing was spent. A taxpayer may purchase tax-exempt bonds, for instance, and, later, when he is short of cash to finance consumption, he may borrow a similar amount of money through a second mortgage. Moreover, taxpayers need not know how borrowed dollars are actually spent, as these dollars commingle with other sources of funds and all the money becomes fungible with regard to its actual uses. A corollary to this proposition is that taxpayers need not know that they are engaging in tax arbitrage.

Borrowing to Purchase Housing and Consumer Durables

The first example of tax arbitrage is one of the most pervasive. Tax arbitrage is performed routinely by taxpayers when they borrow to

13. In the strictest sense, almost any tax reduction might be a saving incentive to the extent that it directly or indirectly lowers marginal tax rates on other income.

14. These new mechanisms are required in part because of limits discussed in the next section.

Typical tax arbitrage — both — deduction of income flows,) deduction of interest

) borrowing for home purchase.

purchase housing and consumer durables for themselves. The nontaxation of the income flows from housing and durables, combined with the deduction of the interest payment, results in a substantially negative rate of tax on these investments. This negative tax is used to offset taxes due on other income, including wages. The reader should note, however, that local property taxes often offset this negative tax rate for many low- and moderate-income taxpayers.

Borrowing to Purchase Pension Assets and IRAs

Pure tax arbitrage, as well as normal tax arbitrage, is commonly obtained when taxpayers borrow at the same time that they invest in pension assets. An example is an itemizing taxpayer in the 30 percent tax bracket who borrows $2,000 and, at the same time, invests $2,000 in an IRA. Actually it makes little difference whether he borrows in order to put $2,000 in an IRA or uses the money to buy an automobile and then puts his own $2,000 in an IRA. He would immediately receive a $600 tax reduction for his deposit. At a 10 percent interest rate, the taxpayer would pay $200 in interest each year while receiving another $60 in tax reduction on those payments. Meanwhile, his IRA account would be accumulating and compounding interest, with $200 received in the first year. While the taxpayer might later owe taxes on withdrawals, the value of his tax reductions are far in excess of future taxes owed. The earlier deductions have a greater present value, and the taxpayer may later be in a lower tax bracket. Indeed, the taxpayer may owe little or no taxes if he later becomes nontaxable, as are about half of elderly persons today. No saving at all has taken place, yet the taxpayer has generated a tax reduction. Chapter 2 showed that the tax treatment of equity contributions to IRAs and pension plans is generally even better than nontaxation of the interest income itself. In this case, therefore, increased leverage or borrowing makes the rate of tax on these investments even more negative.

Borrowing from Pension and Life Insurance Accounts

A related type of arbitrage is accomplished by those who directly borrow from pension plan assets or the savings component of their life insurance policies. The income on those assets will still be deferred or excluded from taxation, but the payments on the borrowing will be deductible immediately. Of course, taxpayers need not borrow from these sources. As long as taxpayers have other access to the loan market, they need merely have the knowledge that those pension or life insurance assets are available for future consumption. Taxpayers can borrow from any source while buying whole life insurance and annuities or encouraging an employer to contribute toward a pension plan.

Purchases of State and Local Bonds

One of the more widely known examples of tax arbitrage is borrowing at taxable rates to purchase tax-exempt securities of state and local governments. Technically speaking, it is not legal to borrow directly in order to purchase tax-exempt securities. If one borrows with other assets as collateral, however, the exact association or pairing of each use and source of funds would be both theoretically and practically difficult to establish. Banks and property and casualty insurance companies are allowed to borrow money from depositors at taxable rates, and then can invest the financial institution's excess funds (the income from which effectively accrues to the owners of the institutions) in nontaxable state and local bonds.

Tax Shelters

Tax shelters are explicitly designed to generate negative taxable income for taxpayers in the early years of the investment. One of the primary sources of the negative income is the interest payment. Real estate investments partially financed with debt, for instance, obtain early interest deductions and defer realization of capital gains. Investment credits, depletion allowances, and accelerated cost-recovery allowances are also used.

Tax arbitrage is an essential ingredient in almost all tax shelters. Because debt is heavily used, sellers of shelters will often try to find devices to limit the risk of buyers. In recent years many assets have actually been removed from the corporate sector where taxpayers cannot as easily take advantage of the negative taxable income generated within the shelters.

Borrowing to Purchase Equipment and Other Investment Assets

Many firms borrow to purchase equipment and other assets. This combination results in a negative rate of tax for investments financed with sufficient debt.[15] In some cases, as is discussed in chapter 7, firms may even obtain a positive rate of after-tax income when the before-tax return from the investment asset is negative—that is, it may cost society more to build the asset than the asset returns in value to society.

Financial Transfers within Businesses or Corporations

Companies often transfer assets internally to generate interest income in nontaxable form while still obtaining full deductions of interest payments. Investment professionals and academics such as Fischer Black,[16] for instance, have urged companies with pension portfolios to sell their own stock and buy their own bonds; at the same time, outside the pension accounts, the same companies are encouraged to sell bonds of their corporation and buy back their own stock. In these transactions the combined debt and equity of the pension fund and the corporation together is not changed, nor is its overall level of saving and investment. The fundamental change is in the amount of taxes collected: the increased amount of interest payments of the corporation become deductible at the same time that the increased amount of interest receipts in the pension fund escapes taxation.

Financial Institutions

Financial institutions have a variety of other means of achieving tax arbitrage both for their customers and themselves. In addition to special treatment of pension and life insurance reserves, customers may borrow to purchase financial assets, the income flow from which is used to provide services directly (such as term insurance or checking services). The effective interest and income used to pay for those services is seldom

15. See Calvin H. Johnson, "Tax Shelter Gain: The Mismatch of Debt and Supply Side Depreciation," *Texas Law Review*, vol. 61 (March 1983), pp. 1013–55. Johnson documents a number of ways in which the tax benefits of the investment credit and accelerated cost-recovery system, when combined with the tax treatment of debt, create a negative tax for debt-financed investments in depreciable property. King and Fullerton show how debt-financed investments in machinery, buildings, and inventories, weighted together, have a negative total tax rate (even after personal tax on interest income). See Mervyn A. King and Don Fullerton, eds., *The Taxation of Income from Capital: A Comparative Study of the United States, the United Kingdom, Sweden, and West Germany* (University of Chicago Press, 1984), pp. 242–50.

16. See A. F. Ehrbar, "How to Slash Your Company's Tax Bill," *Fortune* (February 23, 1981), pp. 122–24.

subject to tax at the individual level. Many special deductions and exclusions also allow financial institutions to deduct interest paid on their own liabilities, while deferring or excluding their receipts from taxation.[17]

Payments to and from Foreigners

Interest payments to and from foreigners have each grown from less than 0.1 percent of GNP in 1948 to between 1.4 and 1.6 percent of GNP by 1983.[18] In many cases the payments made may be deducted by the payers in the respective country, while the payments received are excluded from tax in the other country. These international payments may thus create serious problems for the tax bases of the respective countries. In addition, when interest payments are deductible in some countries but not taxable in others, balance-of-payments problems arise.[19]

Inventory Purchases

Tax arbitrage can also be achieved through the purchase of inventories and resources. A firm engaged in simple purchases and sales of inventory may borrow to purchase those goods. Suppose that $100 is borrowed to purchase $100 worth of goods, that the interest rate is 10 percent, and that those goods sell one year later for $112. The real profit of the firm would be $2. Also assume that prices in general and the prices of the firm's goods increase at a rate of 10 percent. If the firm replaced its inventory and used the LIFO method of accounting, it would need to report only the $2 return on the sale of the inventory, while it could deduct $10 in interest cost. Although its real income equaled $2, its taxable income would be −$8. The problem is not caused by LIFO

17. Space does not allow an adequate discussion of this complex issue. For further detail see Thomas Neubig and C. Eugene Steuerle, "The Taxation of Income Flowing through Financial Institutions: General Framework and Summary of Tax Issues," Office of Tax Analysis Paper 52 (Treasury Department, September 1983).

18. U.S. Department of Commerce, Bureau of Economic Analysis, *The National Income and Product Accounts of the United States, 1929–76, Statistical Tables,* a supplement to the *Survey of Current Business* (GPO, 1981); and *Survey of Current Business,* vol. 64 (July 1984), tables 1.1 and 8.7.

19. See Vito Tanzi and Mario I. Blejer, "Inflation, Interest Rate Policy, and Currency Substitutions in Developing Economies: A Discussion of Some Major Issues," *World Development,* vol. 10 (September 1982), pp. 781–89.

accounting—which effectively adjusts for inflation—but by the lack of an inflation adjustment in the statement of interest paid.

Cash-and-Carry Transactions

In the commodity market a similar game is played, although without the use of LIFO. Increases in value of existing commodities generally are not subject to taxation until sold by investors. When there are low costs of storage, as in the case of silver, and interest rates are low enough relative to expected gains in price of commodities, some investors will engage in so-called cash-and-carry transactions. Money will be borrowed to purchase an asset, and the interest payments on debt will be immediately deducted. Increases in the price of the commodity will not be taxed until the commodity is actually sold. This income receipt is therefore deferred from taxation and may be allowed capital gains treatment. This type of transaction is useful not only to many speculators, but also to those who face a high tax rate in the given year (when the interest deductions would be most valuable) and expect a lower tax rate in future years.

Dividend-Received Deduction

Corporations currently receive a deduction for 85 percent of dividends received from other corporations even when they incur additional debt to purchase such stock. The original theory of the dividend-received deduction was that corporate income was already subject to a double tax—once when earned, and then again when paid out as dividends. If the receiving corporation paid the full tax on dividends received and then paid those dividends to its own shareholders, there would be a triple tax. In some cases, however, the receiving corporation may have purchased the stock with debt. In that case, interest deductions would more than offset any income that would have been includable because of the dividends received. Moreover, no dividends need be paid to stockholders of the receiving company, or some of that income may be essentially nontaxable, as in the case of payments to pension plans. Thus the combination of the dividend-received deduction plus the interest deduction can convert the triple tax into almost no tax at all. In some cases, less tax is collected than if a single corporate tax had been paid on the original company's income.

Capital Gains and Losses

We have stressed that interest income is conspicuous because it is one of the few forms of capital income in which all nominal returns are reportable for tax purposes. The difference between the rate of inclusion for this item of income, and the rate applying to the returns from almost all other investments, is the primary source of tax arbitrage opportunities. There is actually one other type of income for which all nominal income is included in income subject to tax: income from assets that are sold short-term so that yield plus all nominal gains and losses are recognized currently. Because the choice to recognize both losses and gains generally belongs to the taxpayer, a somewhat similar story about tax arbitrage can be told using these sources of income.

In the extreme, capital gains and losses can be used to bring about a result similar to the pure tax arbitrage achieved with interest payments and receipts. One can purchase a pair of capital assets that fluctuate in value in opposite directions. The negative correlation of returns means that one asset can be expected to increase when the other decreases in value. The taxpayer then sells those that decrease in value and recognizes the losses short-term while taking the gains long-term. If the change in value of the assets is known to move by the same amount but in opposite directions, there is virtually no risk from this manipulation of the tax system.

In the late 1970s, for instance, the use of paired commodity straddles became popular. Using future contracts, a person would effectively promise to buy one commodity at a given date in the future (he would purchase a futures contract and take a "long" position), while promising to sell the same commodity or an almost identical commodity on a similar date (he would sell a futures contract and take a "short" position). The increase (decrease) in the value of the promise to buy would be matched by an opposite decrease (increase) in the value of the promise to sell. The loss would be recognized in the current year, and a similar futures contract would be negotiated to eliminate the risk on the unsold one. In the next year both those contracts would be sold for a net gain approximating the loss recognized in the previous year. In some circumstances the loss could even be declared at a 100 percent rate, while only 40 percent of the gain would be included.[20]

20. The long position should decrease in value and the short position should increase,

Certain laws have been written to prevent the most outrageous cases of capital gains arbitrage, but they have limited effect on many sophisticated taxpayers. Futures contracts, for instance, are now required to be accounted on a mark-to-market basis, which effectively forces recognition of all nominal gains and losses on a daily basis. This method thereby prevents accounting for losses differently from gains—the essential source of tax arbitrage using capital gains and losses. This rule can sometimes be avoided, however, by turning to foreign forward markets, which operate similarly to futures markets but do not have mark-to-market accounting. Moreover, losses can still be recognized on many other types of assets, while corresponding gains are deferred.

Summary

These examples of tax arbitrage have included borrowing for purchasing everything from houses and consumer durables to business investment assets, and interest-bearing assets held in pension and life insurance accounts, and inventories and commodities. Tax arbitrage is an important aspect of tax shelters, international financial flows, commodity straddles, and other arrangements in which capital assets are both purchased and sold. Tax arbitrage is clearly a potential element in the investment and saving decisions of most taxpayers.

Limits on Tax Arbitrage

The opportunities and incentives for tax arbitrage are so great that one might wonder why even more of it does not take place. Returning to the basic theory of normal tax arbitrage, a related question is why so many taxpayers pay higher marginal tax rates than any realistic estimate of the breakeven point at which borrowing to invest in tax-preferred securities would be profitable. Certainly, for instance, no one should pay a tax rate in excess of the implicit tax rate on municipal bonds (or in excess of what appear to be even lower tax rates on other assets).

There are a number of reasons, not totally separable, why taxpayers do not engage in more tax arbitrage. I list these below in what I believe is their reverse order of importance.

---

or else certain short sale rules would apply. The taxpayer could get around this problem through multiple straddle purchases.

First, certain tax rules limit the obvious and egregious tax arbitrage opportunities. When cases arise in which a taxpayer is buying and selling the same asset, or borrowing and directly purchasing certain tax-exempt assets, Congress will generally step in with limitations. Thus a taxpayer technically cannot borrow to purchase tax-exempt bonds. This provision, however, is difficult to enforce. Unless the tax-exempt bonds are used directly as collateral for the loan that finances their purchase, it is almost impossible to trace the connection between their purchase and an increase in borrowing. Another provision limits individual itemized interest expenses substantially in excess of investment income. With capital gains and losses, there are also limits on recognition of a loss on the sale of an asset if the identical asset is repurchased immediately, or if a commodity futures straddle is attempted. Each of these rules, of course, is easily avoided, as none of the restrictions essentially applies when one's home or business is used as collateral. For gains and losses, one needs merely to find a substitute asset that is nearly identical to the one sold, or find assets whose movements are negatively correlated. If futures contracts are no longer viable for such purposes, forward contracts might be used. While these legal limits do not prevent tax arbitrage, they do make it more complex, increase the cost of transactions, and, therefore, make it less worth the time and effort when only small amounts of tax reduction can be achieved.

Second, as noted in chapter 4, the income tax is in part a tax on those who avoid complex transactions or lack knowledge of the tax laws. Many taxpayers do not take advantage of a variety of opportunities for reducing taxes, including mechanisms that are virtually riskless. Even when taxpayers do adjust, there are often long lags before they will manipulate their portfolios or make other behavioral adjustments to governmental laws and rules. The literature contains numerous related examples where individuals forgo opportunities to increase their income by billions of dollars: they fail to file for food stamps, to average their income for tax purposes, to reduce overwithholding of taxes, and to move deposits from lower- to higher-yielding accounts of equal value. Some taxpayers simply do not enjoy playing games no matter what the certainty of the return; the U.S. tax system is designed to insure that such individuals pay a greater share of the tax burden than those who are not so hesitant. Adjustment does come eventually, however, especially if the law is not changed over time.

Third, the model of normal tax arbitrage did not address the important

[handwritten: risk]

issue of risk. When taxpayers borrow to purchase an asset, they increase their debt-to-equity ratios and the riskiness of the total investment. Such an investment involves risks on both the asset and debt side. Especially as interest rates have risen with inflation, the riskiness of both buying and selling long-term debt has increased enormously. Financial institutions may consider risky assets to be insufficient collateral, thereby limiting a taxpayer's borrowing opportunity. The markets do try to adjust to this situation by making available new types of instruments through which the risk of the debt can be negatively correlated with the risk of the asset. In the case of pure tax arbitrage, for instance, some savings institutions have offered borrowing at rates that move with the rate promised on an IRA account. These adjustments, however, also take time and increase the complexity of the transaction.

Fourth, many taxpayers are simply averse to creating a situation in which recognized income differs substantially from their economic income. The principal assets involved in tax arbitrage are those that generate increases in value that need not be recognized for tax purposes. However incorrect their beliefs may be, many individuals do not view capital gains in the same way as they do flows of cash income. Thus one often hears investment advice to buy bonds and stocks with high dividend yields when income is needed for consumption—almost without regard for the total return from alternative investments with lower current yields.[21] Even if all risk and transaction costs were eliminated, many individuals would pay more for a dollar of cash than for a dollar of capital gains. They simply have not adjusted their accounting to a world of both inflation and taxes.

[handwritten margin note: not adjust to world of inflation ? taxation.]

In the case of corporations, of course, the value of the stock in the market may be related to reported financial income. Corporate managers are often reluctant to reduce stated earnings by deferring gains for long periods of time or take large interest deductions against unrecognized income. Engaging in tax arbitrage would reduce income reported on the financial statement. Far preferable to the corporate manager are tax subsidies (such as investment credits), which allow financial income to

---

21. If the total return from the bond or dividend-paying stock were higher than the total return elsewhere, or the risk were less, such a move may be desirable. Portfolio theory and the simple theory of normal tax arbitrage would even support an argument that an investment with greater portions of income subject to tax would give a higher before-tax yield. Nonetheless, the investment advice is much more simplistic in nature, and the point here is that many individuals do not treat all forms of cash and noncash income equally.

remain high and taxable income or taxes paid to be kept low. Even if this constraint did not exist, corporate tax arbitrage can only be used to offset income from capital. Since corporate losses cannot be carried over to individual tax returns, corporate tax arbitrage is not a viable mechanism for reducing taxable income from labor.

Given all these constraints, there is still a huge reservoir of tax arbitrage opportunities that can and likely will be taken in the future. People constantly become aware of these opportunities, even if lags in response are great. Financial institutions adjust their types of lending and borrowing to accommodate new demands. Risk can be reduced both through these accommodations and through new types of direct insurance, as well as through short sales, options, and futures contracts. Some corporations become more willing to sell assets to generate the income needed for financial statements, and corporations not taking advantage of their opportunities become merged into larger firms. Other corporations are spun off to the noncorporate sector.

Since the incentive for tax arbitrage remains strong, it is highly likely that tax arbitrage is also limited by a final factor: the supply of loanable funds. Tax arbitrage investors are no different than many other investors in demanding loanable funds to achieve their investment objectives. Monetary policy, on the other hand, is able to influence the amount of such funds that will be available in society. These funds are then allocated through financial institutions according to established rules and operating procedures. The loans may be restricted because of the riskiness of the investment, as discussed above. In addition, one common rule of lenders is to require adequate cash flow to service a particular investment, regardless of the expected economic income from the investment or the potential increase in value of collateral because of capital gains. This interaction between lending rules and tax arbitrage is examined in more detail in chapter 7. For now, I simply note that arbitrage opportunities can also be limited by the amount, and method of distribution, of loanable funds in society.

CHAPTER SIX

Financial Arbitrage

In the discussions of normal tax arbitrage it was noted that the demand for loanable funds by those wanting to purchase preferred assets tends to either exert upward pressure on the price of preferred assets or drive a wedge between the interest rate and rates of return on (relatively) preferred assets. This chapter examines some of the forces that tend to prevent those types of adjustments from taking place, especially between interest rates and returns to preferred assets sold in liquid markets. Among the consequences are a large remaining demand for tax arbitrage investment and financial markets in which long-run stability of prices and rates of return is not possible.

Reverse Arbitrage

Up to this point, the emphasis has been on tax arbitrage in which there were negative holdings of only one type of asset—the interest-bearing asset. Most debtors can be considered as holders of these negative assets. There is no theoretical reason, however, why there cannot be financial arrangements that provide the equivalent of negative holdings of almost any asset—that is, provide for a rate of payment by a "debtor" to approximate or equal the rate of return expected by the asset holder.

In practice the financial markets have become increasingly sophisticated in recent years in providing just such opportunities. A short sale of a stock, for instance, makes the seller indebted to pay back that asset at some point in the future. The effective rate of payment on that indebtedness includes the rate of appreciation or depreciation in the value of the stock itself. Similarly, a short position in a futures contract obligates the seller to deliver a particular commodity or financial asset at a given point in time and at a predetermined price. Increases or decreases in the value of that asset are paid by or to the seller on a daily basis under a system known as mark-to-market. Thus a short position in a Treasury-bill future obligates a seller to pay the effective interest due on that bill (plus any other change in its market value if the future is sold before maturity).[1] If the short position is in a commodity, the seller would need to cover any change in the price of the underlying commodity. Technically in a futures contract the seller holds both a negative amount of one asset (a promise to deliver a commodity) and a positive amount of another (the promise of the buyer to pay cash). While short sales and futures contracts are not provided for many types of assets and commodities, the financial markets are evolving rapidly. When incentives are sufficient, alternative mechanisms become available for holding the equivalent of negative amounts of assets.

As more financial instruments are developed, there are additional opportunities for pure tax arbitrage when the payments or losses on the negative holdings are recognized, while corresponding receipts or gains are deferred or excluded from tax. Here, however, the discussion focuses on examining the effect of negative holdings of assets on normal tax arbitrage itself. Recall that in the simple theory of normal tax arbitrage, taxpayers are expected to bid for available supplies of loanable funds and thereby to raise the interest rate relative to the rate of return on assets with greater tax preference (and equal risk). In examples of tax arbitrage presented so far, the interest rate, i, was shown to exceed the rate of return, r, on other assets. If r was nontaxable and i was deductible, for instance, the theory was followed to its logical conclusion: i would rise or r would fall until after-tax income became equilibrated at a breakeven tax rate, $1 - r / i$, and tax arbitrage was demanded by all taxpayers with marginal tax rates above that point.

Below this breakeven marginal tax rate, taxpayers tend to hold only interest-bearing assets. After all, for the low-bracket taxpayer, the after-tax return on interest-bearing assets would be greater than the after-tax rate of return on other assets.

What happens in this model if taxpayers are allowed to hold other assets in negative amounts? The behavior of low-bracket taxpayers should be just the reverse of that of taxpayers in higher brackets. These

1. All interest from Treasury bills is subsumed into the total change in market value. Thus a Treasury bill will rise in value as it approaches maturity even with no change in market interest rates; if market rates decrease (increase), however, the bill will further increase (decrease) in value.

low-bracket taxpayers may be expected to engage in arbitrage in order to maximize their own after-tax rates of return by increasing their negative holdings of other assets and using those funds to purchase additional amounts of interest-bearing assets. I refer to this particular type of behavior as *reverse arbitrage*.

Suppose that the rate of return on the preferred nontaxable asset equaled 7 percent, while the taxable interest rate was 10 percent. As before, all taxpayers with rates above 30 percent would borrow and purchase the preferred asset until their marginal tax rate was reduced to 30 percent. In addition, taxpayers with rates below 30 percent would increase their negative holdings of the preferred asset and purchase additional interest-bearing assets. For instance, if short sales of the preferred asset were possible, that asset might be sold short and the proceeds invested in money market accounts. If these taxpayers were subject to a progressive rate schedule, they would continue this process until their taxable income increased enough to put them in a 30 percent marginal rate bracket. The shaded section in figure 5-1 shows the area in which this reverse arbitrage takes place.

In theory, reverse arbitrage extends the effective tax-rate structure shown in figure 5-1 to low-bracket taxpayers. Both portfolio reallocation toward interest-bearing securities and reverse arbitrage would mean that low-bracket individuals would pay tax dollars to the Treasury even though their net implicit tax was negative. The simple model therefore shows that a rise in the interest rate relative to the rate of return on other, more preferred, assets would encourage low-bracket taxpayers to change their holdings into interest-bearing securities and to engage in reverse arbitrage by holding negative amounts of preferred securities.

Asymmetric Tax Treatment

If the interest rate exceeds the rate of return on preferred assets, U.S. tax laws provide many taxpayers in all tax brackets—not just those in brackets below the breakeven point—with an incentive to hold negative amounts of preferred assets and to purchase interest-bearing assets.

This seems to contradict previous statements that normal tax arbitrage discourages taxpayers in high tax brackets from holding interest-bearing assets. The difficulty with the simple model results from an important asymmetry in the tax treatment of capital income. While positive receipts of income, including gains in value, will usually be forgone or avoided, payments or negative receipts, including losses in value, will usually be recognized. Reverse arbitrage does not fit neatly into the model of normal tax arbitrage because the lower tax rate or inclusion rate associated with the tax preference is discretionary, not mandatory. Taxpayers would engage in strict reverse arbitrage only if the preference were to operate symmetrically with respect to both receipts and payments or both gains and losses. In the latter case, losses would need to be recognized with the same frequency as gains, and losses would need to be excluded from deduction as frequently as gains were excluded from taxation. Current tax rules, however, almost never require the exclusion of the losses and deductible payments even though gains and receipts are excluded on the opposite side of the ledger.

When voluntarily recognized, losses or other payments on negative holdings of assets will be exactly like interest payments: the entire nominal loss in income—all cash payments plus change in value—will be recognized in full and deducted on tax returns. For instance, many losses on assets are recognized in the short term and thus are neither deferred from recognition nor partially excluded from deduction. It follows that the tax inclusion rate and marginal tax rate for *each* taxpayer will be exactly the same for both interest payments (or receipts) and payments on negative holdings of other assets. In deciding whether or not reverse arbitrage between interest-bearing and other assets is profitable, a taxpayer need only compare before-tax rates of return. In effect, by recognizing all payments and receipts over short periods of time, the taxpayer is in a world in which profitable before-tax arbitrage among assets in the financial markets can be made to result in profitable after-tax arbitrage. This world is consistent with many financial models in which it is generally assumed that all taxpayers face the same tax rate on all sources of income or that there is no tax at all. If one before-tax rate of return is higher than another, each person has an incentive to sell short the asset with the lower rate of return and buy the asset with the higher rate.

Unlike tax arbitrage, this financial arbitrage places taxable investors and nontaxable investors on about the same footing. The taxable investor's tax on positive interest income is offset mainly by a tax reduction on the negative income. Only the clear arbitrage profits, or differences in before-tax rates of return, are subject to tax. The nontaxable investor, on the other hand, receives no deduction for losses, but pays no tax on offsetting gains. Total income, both positive and negative,

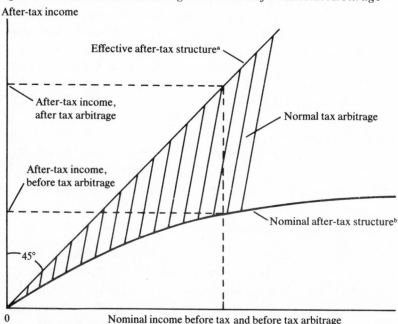

Figure 6-1. *Normal Tax Arbitrage in a World of Financial Arbitrage*

After-tax income

Effective after-tax structure[a]

After-tax income,
after tax arbitrage

Normal tax arbitrage

After-tax income,
before tax arbitrage

Nominal after-tax structure[b]

45°

0   Nominal income before tax and before tax arbitrage

Source: Author's calculations.
a. Slope equals 1.0, which equals *r* divided by *i*.
b. Slope equals 1.0 minus the marginal tax rate.

is recognized currently. Therefore, if financial arbitrage is profitable for the nontaxable investor, it is profitable for the taxable investor. When the profit is negative, it is negative for both. With normal tax arbitrage, on the other hand, receipts had a lower tax rate than did interest deductions; the profitability of normal tax arbitrage depended upon the marginal tax rate of the investor.

In this simple model in which investors could sell preferred assets short and buy interest-bearing assets long, financial arbitrage would prevent interest rates from rising relative to rates of return on preferred assets. Thus the profits from tax arbitrage would remain for all taxpayers with marginal tax rates above zero. The breakeven point would move to the zero tax rate, and figure 5.1 would look like figure 6.1

Financial Arbitrage in the Real World

As in the case of tax arbitrage, financial arbitrage is not merely a theoretical proposition; it is quite common in the real world. Financial arbitrage is most likely to take place in highly liquid and sophisticated markets like stock and commodity futures markets and least likely in less liquid markets for investment goods such as local real estate. Unlike tax arbitrage, however, the players are often governments, nonprofit institutions, or traders and brokers handling large sources of money, and these players have either a special ability to issue nontaxable securities or have knowledge of and access to the most sophisticated parts of the financial markets. So although tax arbitrage through borrowing and paying back interest on debt is common to most taxpayers who purchase preferred assets, only a few taxpayers are engaged in the issuance of preferred securities or in short sales of assets and commodity futures.

State and Local Governments

A well-known example of financial arbitrage is provided by state and local government issuance of nontaxable bonds, combined with the purchase of taxable securities. Because these governments can issue preferred securities at lower-than-market rates, they have a powerful incentive not only to finance projects through borrowing, but also to borrow and directly use arbitrage to trade off between taxable and nontaxable rates of return. When the government participates in this activity for its own purposes, it essentially engages in financial arbitrage because both the payment of interest and the interest received are nontaxable (in effect taxed at the same rate).

In practice, state and local governments hold significant amounts of taxable securities, many in pension and similar types of reserves for workers or constituents. In some cases bond funds are established as reserves for contingency expenses of projects or as sinking funds from which future expected expenses will be paid. Often excess reserves are held in these funds solely, or at least primarily, for the purpose of engaging in arbitrage between taxable and untaxable rates of return.

State and local financing has become so lucrative that it is done not only for the governments' own accounts, but for private firms and individuals also. State and local bond financing is used to support mortgage loans, private hospital loans, education loans, loans to private industry, and a host of other private purposes. The government borrows at a tax-exempt rate and relends to the private taxpayer. As the taxpayer pays off a loan to the government, the government in turn uses this to pay off its debt to bondholders. In doing this, the government directly competes with other private financial intermediaries. Given its pure competitive advantage, the government sometimes generates money for its own coffers through a generous spread on the rate that it charges and the rate that it pays. Regardless of the government's spread, private borrowers generate the rest of the financial arbitrage profit, and they additionally deduct (on federal returns) the interest payments to the state or local government.

Because federal taxpayers bear the cost of these efforts, each individual project generates profits for the state or local government and the private firm without imposing much expense on local taxpayers. It is no wonder that such projects are extremely popular. One result, of course, is a "beggar thy neighbor" type of effort in which each federal taxpayer loses from the efforts of other jurisdictions, but not his own.

Nonprofit Institutions

For nonprofit institutions, both financial arbitrage and simple portfolio shifts toward interest-bearing assets are profitable whenever the interest rate rises above the rate of return on alternative taxable assets. It is generally recognized that a nontaxable institution has a clear advantage over taxable businesses and persons because it can achieve an equal or higher after-tax rate of return on any asset held. In fact, its relative advantage is greatest for the asset that has the highest inclusion rate for the taxable investor—in other words, the least tax-preferred asset. If taxpayers bid up the prices of assets relative to the amount of preference given each, the highest rate of return available to a nontaxable institution comes from owning the least tax-preferred asset.

What a nonprofit institution might do in practice is shift its portfolio toward those assets for which taxpayers face the highest tax rates, sell short tax-preferred assets, and use those funds to purchase less preferred assets such as interest-bearing securities. If fiduciary responsibilities limit net negative holdings of any asset, the institution might still sell and lease back assets such as real estate that it currently owns and uses for its own functions. Sale and lease-back arrangements are in many ways similar to short sales of assets held in one's own portfolio. This type of activity became increasingly popular in the early 1980s, especially with the increased preferences given to real estate because of accelerated cost recovery and with the rise in the interest rate. At one point several private colleges and governments attempted to negotiate or engage in a variety of sale and lease-back arrangements.[2] Even though such arrangements have been partially restricted by Congress, pure portfolio shifts toward ownership of interest-bearing and other taxable securities and away from direct ownership of buildings can be expected whenever interest rates rise above expected before-tax rates of return on buildings.[3]

Traders and Brokers

The business of traders is to engage in financial arbitrage in order to take advantage of differences in rates of return among assets. When the before-tax return on asset A rises relative to asset B, traders begin to sell off stocks of asset B and purchase asset A. When stocks of asset B are insufficient, they sell it short and use the funds to purchase asset A. Because traders and brokers are allowed to treat purchases and sales of assets essentially as if they were inventory (and, thus, gains and losses represent ordinary rather than capital gains income), the tax rate or inclusion rate for income paid is the same as that for income received. In general, traders need not worry about differences in the tax treatment of different assets, and financial arbitrage will almost always be profitable when the before-tax rates begin to differ.

Suppose, for instance, that the interest rate began to rise above the rate of return on corporate stock. The trader could then hold the equivalent of negative amounts of stock in a variety of ways. He may sell particular stocks short and purchase interest-bearing assets. Or he may simply sell a stock market future and buy a bond future.

Some traders are also very adept at avoiding any tax on the profit from this financial arbitrage. Since they can also buy stocks and other assets for the personal accounts, they can effectively use normal tax arbitrage to offset much of the income from their inventory accounts. Their knowledge of the financial markets is often sufficiently sophisticated so that many have been able to reduce their taxable income to close to zero by taking advantage of pure tax arbitrage schemes such as commodity straddles, or their equivalent, in the forward markets.

2. Harvey Galper and Eric Toder, "Owning or Leasing: Bennington College and the U.S. Tax System," *National Tax Journal*, vol. 36 (June 1983), pp. 257–61.

3. At the same time, these shifts will be limited by the need of many institutions to guarantee a constant location and not to turn that choice over to a group of lessors.

Limits on Financial Arbitrage

As in the case of tax arbitrage, there are a number of limits on the extent to which individuals and businesses engage in financial arbitrage.

First, tax rules do limit somewhat the extent to which some entities can benefit from financial arbitrage. State and local governments theoretically would become the only financial intermediary if it were not for occasional congressional limitations on their activity. Certain federal limits are placed on mortgage lending by state and local governments. Industrial development bonds are supposedly limited in amount and purpose. The size of reserves for student-loan bond funds are restricted, and so on. Each new restriction has been only partially effective, and new methods are continually found to engage in arbitrage to obtain lower tax rates for both the governments and different groups of clients in the private sector. The conservative financing habits and rules of states and localities (some constitutionally imposed) has also limited the supply of tax-exempt bonds.

There are also legal restrictions on the extent to which ordinary persons can engage in normal tax arbitrage and financial arbitrage at the same time. For instance, it is not possible to borrow, buy a stock, sell the stock short, invest in interest-bearing assets, and generate tax savings. The loss on either the stock purchase or the short sale cannot legally be recognized until the corresponding gain is recognized. For taxpayers in the aggregate, however, the restriction does not apply. If one person performs the first two transactions, and a second person the last two, total income, savings, and change in net worth in the economy will equal zero. As before, one taxpayer will still be able to recognize the loss while the other defers or excludes tax on the gain. Because of these restrictions, high-bracket taxpayers often find themselves divided into groups of financial arbitragers or tax arbitragers, but not both simultaneously.

Second, financial arbitrage is fairly complex and only made more so by the additional rules of those who regulate the tax system and the financial markets. Financial arbitrage would not be profitable for many taxpayers once they took account of the cost of learning the system or the possible high costs of transactions and legal expenses. Economies of scale, however, will lower such costs for persons and institutions with a large volume of transactions.

Third, financial arbitrage can be risky. Purchases of preferred assets often involve risk, but the taxpayer's maximum loss is the cost of the asset. With negative holdings of preferred assets, on the other hand, the limit on the potential loss is often infinite, especially if the value of the asset itself has some possibility of skyrocketing in value. Many individuals and businesses do not want to incur such risk; even if they do, their activity will likely be limited by brokers or others who could be saddled with the responsibility to cover the losses of bankrupt customers.

Both the complexity and riskiness of financial arbitrage lead to its use by a small portion of the population, especially when the amount of potential gain is considered. Suppose that the return from a given asset has fallen 2 percentage points below the interest rate. If $100,000 worth of the asset were sold short and the proceeds were invested in interest-bearing assets, the expected annual profit from the financial arbitrage would only be $2,000, assuming the spread was expected to remain constant. Of course, if the spread narrowed or increased, there could be speculation gains and losses over a much shorter period of time. To make this type of activity highly profitable, therefore, millions of dollars of transactions would be necessary—a deterrent for most taxpayers.

Interest Rates and Returns from Real Assets

As noted, all taxpayers with tax rates below the breakeven point are given incentives to hold interest-bearing assets. As interest rates rise, the breakeven point also rises—fewer people benefit from holding preferred assets, and the inducement for low-bracket taxpayers to hold interest-bearing assets increases even more.

Other pressures prevent tax arbitrage from driving interest rates above the rates of return on other assets. One group with large potential for purchasing interest-bearing assets—as well as engaging in financial arbitrage—is composed of investors in both domestic and international securities, including foreign individuals, banks, and governments. Many of these investors are effectively nontaxable for a variety of reasons, including treaties and problems of enforcement. The market for arbitraging differences in interest rates on obligations issued in different countries has become enormously efficient. The financial markets, including bond, forward, and futures markets, have become quite sophisticated, and many international investors are able to respond almost instantaneously to changes in prices of financial assets. Over longer periods of time it is also possible for investors to sell foreign real assets, and financial assets, to purchase domestic interest-bearing securities. All these pressures work to prevent the interest rate from rising well above the before-tax rate of return on other assets.

One might even question how stable a long-term situation could be in which the interest rate was above the rate of return on most other domestic assets. Increased foreign investment in domestic financial securities would aggravate balance-of-payments problems as foreigners lowered the price of exports to obtain funds to buy interest-bearing securities. Moreover, even if foreign purchases of domestic bonds increased domestic investment, domestic income could be reduced when the value of the product made possible by the investment equals the rate of return on the investment, which in turn is less than the interest payments made abroad.

Tax Arbitrage versus Financial Arbitrage

A fundamental conflict exists between the results of a model of tax arbitrage and one of financial arbitrage. This conflict has serious implications for the efficiency of the economy as a whole.

Normal tax arbitrage drives up the demand for preferred assets relative to interest-bearing assets. Since loans are necessary to obtain the full benefit of tax arbitrage, the demand for loanable funds is also increased, leading to potential increases in the rate of interest. Pure tax arbitrage also drives up the demand for loanable funds, but the taxpayers in this case effectively provide the loans to themselves. If monetary authorities limit the supplies of loanable funds—offsetting the increased deposits of the pure tax arbitrager with government sales of its own bonds—pure tax arbitrage could indirectly push up interest rates also.

While there is good reason to believe that tax arbitrage does drive up the price of preferred assets sold in less liquid markets—in particular, real estate—financial arbitrage is a major force that prevents the interest rate from rising *relative* to rates of return on many preferred assets. Whenever rates of return on assets of equal risk begin to depart from each other, traders, governments, nontaxable firms, individuals, and foreign investors increase the share of their portfolios in interest-bearing assets and sell short their preferred assets. Financial arbitrage, however, restores the profitability of tax arbitrage. Thus there is no marginal tax rate (other than zero) at which the incentives of tax arbitrage and financial arbitrage are brought into stable long-term equilibrium. The implications are not merely domestic in nature, nor do they apply only to financial markets. For instance, differences among countries in the tax treatment of returns from assets—including differences caused by inflation—may prevent the simultaneous achievement of both equal interest rates across countries (interest-rate parity) and equal prices of consumer goods across countries (purchasing-power parity).[4] This in turn implies unstable international markets in which there are nonoptimal flows of capital and labor.

The only possible short-run solution to this conflict is one in which no income taxes are collected or one characterized by increased riskiness of investment, large transaction and information costs, and limits on the supply of loanable funds, which together channel investment in inefficient ways. The conflict between tax and financial arbitrage creates a quite unstable capital market, and the economy suffers as a consequence.

4. See David H. Howard and Karen H. Johnson, "Interest Rates, Inflation, and Taxes: The Foreign Connection," *Economic Letters*, vol. 9, no. 2 (1982), pp. 181–84; and International Monetary Fund, Department of Fiscal Affairs, "Interest Rates and Tax Treatment of Interest Income and Expense," June 1, 1983.

CHAPTER SEVEN

The Effects of Inflation

THE EFFECTS of inflation on capital allocation are the focus of this chapter. An explicit examination is given of how inflation causes capital income to be treated less uniformly by the existing tax structure and also by certain nontax rules that influence the allocation of loans in society.

Inflation Neutrality

In many simple models of the economy, expected inflation plays a neutral role. At its core, the neutrality assumption states that when actual inflation equals expected inflation, all variables adjust to the real values that would prevail in the absence of such inflation. While inflation might technically affect the accounting for income or well-being of persons and businesses, decisionmakers demand and supply goods and services on the same real basis that they would in the absence of inflation. They make identical decisions in real terms based upon essentially identical information.

While this treatment of inflation is useful in drawing out the implications of certain models, it is highly unrealistic for other purposes. To be more precise, inflation theoretically can be neutral if people interpret it in a certain manner, and accounting systems effectively, if not actually, adjust in a prescribed way. It might also be possible to design the institutions of an economy so that inflation has less impact on real activity. The premise here, however, is that a blanket neutrality assumption masks the way in which high rates of inflation affect various accounting systems and cause real adjustments that lead to lower growth rates in the economy.

To gain a preliminary understanding of the magnitude of the problem, some numbers can be examined. I begin with the assumption of an increase of 1.0 percentage point in both the expected and actual inflation

93

rate and look at the effect of that increase on some accounts of the private sector.

Measured at current cost, total private tangible assets of corporations in the private sector at the beginning of 1982 equaled approximately $14.5 trillion; private liabilities of households and nonfinancial businesses and farms were about $4 trillion; and gross national product was $3.2 trillion.[1] At that level of wealth and income, I next assume that real, before-tax rates of return on assets and liabilities are unaffected by inflation. Then each rise of 1.0 percentage point in the rate of inflation increases the nominal value of assets—and thereby increases nominal income, which includes nominal, not just real, changes in value—by about $145 billion a year, or 4.5 percent of GNP. Interest payments on debt simultaneously rise by about $40 billion, or 1.3 percent of GNP. By contrast, compensation of employees goes up about $18 billion, or 0.6 percent of GNP. Although the real income of all persons and sectors is the same, nominal cash payments on private debt go up by more than twice the increase in total wages, while nominal measures of total income from capital, including purely inflationary gains in value, increase by four and one-half times the inflationary increase in current dollar GNP.

The presumption that inflation does not affect the real activity of the economy is therefore predicated on the notion that these changes in accounts "wash through" the system. All relative measures in all accounts stay the same. No one is confused by these changes—not the borrower whose cash payments must go up to pay off new debt, not the lender who receives income in the form of interest and consumes with current income. The changes are not a problem for financial institutions that make loans based on the ability of the borrower to make payments, consumers who see greater inflationary gains in the value of their houses, corporations that lower their statements of financial income, tax accountants who find that tax arbitrage profits initially go up with a higher rate of inflation, and so forth. If there is confusion, it is either confined to the very short run or assumed to be random in such a way that it does not bias aggregate behavior. I believe this is a fundamentally incorrect view of how people behave.

Inflation separates the measures of economic income, financial income, taxable income, and cash flow. The remainder of this chapter demonstrates how this separation induces nonoptimal saving and investment decisions by households, nonfinancial businesses, and financial

1. Board of Governors of the Federal Reserve System, *Balance Sheets for the U.S. Economy, 1945–83* (The Board, 1984); and *Survey of Current Business*, various years.

intermediaries. The confusion induced by inflation may be sufficient by itself to generate an inefficient pattern of capital allocation. Attention is concentrated, however, on two principal effects: the allocation of investment under a tax system that allows tax arbitrage, and the allocation of loanable funds under a lending system based upon cash flow.

Inflation and Tax Arbitrage

Perhaps the simplest way to comprehend why inflation exacerbates problems of tax arbitrage is to begin with the perception that inflation increases the tax wedge between fully and partially taxable assets. At higher rates of inflation, asset shifts and borrowing to purchase tax-preferred assets increase the levels of tax savings.

For many real assets, as noted above, much nominal income comes from capital gains, gains that can be recognized on a discretionary basis by the taxpayer. Even when recognized, a fraction of the inflationary income is often excluded. For preferred assets in general, the amount of total nominal income (cash flow plus change in value) subject to tax does not increase dollar for dollar with inflation. For interest income, however, the full inflation component is included. Although at maturity the real value of debt declines with inflation, the nominal value remains the same. Neither lender nor borrower is allowed to claim this inflationary source of real gain or loss for tax purposes.

Since inflation is fully deducted by most interest payers and fully included (when recognized) by interest recipients, higher inflation inevitably means that the real receipts or payments of both lenders and borrowers are increasingly overstated. Arbitrage involves the taxation of the receipt at a lower rate than the payment, and so a higher rate of interest implies greater gains from arbitrage even if the tax rate differential stays the same. A historical example of this phenomenon is shown in the interest flows examined in chapter 4. Higher interest rates in the postwar period continually increased the amount of real dollars of interest deducted in excess of the amount taxable as receipts.

Pure Tax Arbitrage

Inflation generally increases the amount of tax arbitrage profit per dollar of borrowing. This can be seen quite readily in the case of pure tax arbitrage. If, for example, inflation raises the nominal interest rate from 10 percent to 15 percent, a taxpayer in the 50 percent bracket who borrows and deposits the borrowings in an IRA will experience a jump in arbitrage profits from $50 to $75 for each $1,000 borrowed. Because the taxpayer is both a debtor and a creditor in this transaction, and because inflation will affect both sides of the transaction equally, the taxpayer's real wealth will not be eroded by inflation. The taxpayer's 50 percent increase in arbitrage profits is a pure windfall.

Normal Tax Arbitrage

A similar story can be told in the case of normal tax arbitrage. However, the profits from normal tax arbitrage at least theoretically may be shared with lenders in low tax brackets if real rates of interest increase. The final distribution of the profits from portfolio shifting and tax arbitrage, therefore, depends in part upon what happens to the rate of return on preferred assets relative to the rate of interest.

Inflation exacerbates problems of normal tax arbitrage no matter how the market readjusts the balance of asset ownership among different taxpayers. To understand why, one can assume for a moment that the real rate of return from a preferred, nontaxable asset stays constant, while its nominal return increases with the rate of inflation. In the model of normal tax arbitrage, other variables cannot remain the same.[2] The difference between the interest rate and the rate of return on the preferred asset must increase, the breakeven marginal tax rate must decrease, or both.

If the differential between before-tax returns stays relatively constant, the breakeven tax rate falls, and tax arbitrage becomes profitable for persons in lower tax brackets. In higher brackets the profit per dollar of borrowing and purchasing preferred assets also increases.

If, on the other hand, inflation requires that each person be induced to hold exactly the same assets at the same breakeven tax rate, there must be an increase in the differential between the interest rate and the rate of return on the preferred asset. If the latter return rises in step with

2. Technically $r = i (1 - t)$, where r equals the nontaxable return on the preferred asset; i, the interest rate; and t, the breakeven marginal tax rate. If r increases in line with inflation, there must be some adjustment on the right-hand side of the equation also.

inflation, the interest rate rises by a multiple of the increase in the rate of inflation—that is, by inflation divided by (1 − marginal tax rate).

Note that this result can produce inflation neutrality only under the strictest of assumptions. In particular, within the context of a model of normal tax arbitrage, all taxpayers—including foreigners, tax-exempt organizations, corporations, brokers, and traders—must have engaged in tax arbitrage and reverse tax arbitrage to the point that they are all at the same marginal tax rate. Only in that case does a rise in the rate of inflation have no effect on marginal incentives among taxpayers.

Other Considerations

The question of whether total borrowing for tax arbitrage actually increases with inflation cannot be determined from theory itself. For tax arbitrage borrowing to increase, the supply of loanable funds must be available—either from savers making deposits or from government efforts to build up the money supply. Real risks of undertaking long-term borrowing may also go up with inflation, thus lowering the demand for loans. On the other hand, higher rates of inflation mean higher nominal rates of return on most assets and hence more nominal income to arbitrage, at least if some of those inflationary gains tend to be realized. An inflation rate of 10 percent, for instance, results in several hundred billion dollars of additional nominal income from assets.[3]

The Postwar Era

Despite the theoretical plausibility of different responses to inflation, the empirical data tend to show sizable increases in the amount of tax arbitrage during the postwar era. It is known, for instance, that the household sector increasingly deposited dollars in pension funds and then borrowed those dollars back in private loans. Households stopped trying to pay off mortgages and instead began to believe that too much equity in a home was an evil to be avoided. The markets became increasingly sophisticated in finding financial arrangements to allow taxpayers to engage in tax arbitrage.

While tax arbitrage activity increased, it is less certain that it induced

3. At the same time, because tax arbitrage is more profitable per dollar of borrowing, it takes less borrowing and tax arbitrage investment to produce a given amount of reduction in taxable income or in the marginal tax rate.

Table 7-1. *Private Capital Expenditures, Household Flows of Funds,*
Various Periods, 1946–81
Percent of GNP

Period	Total	Consumer durables	Residential construction
1946–51	13.6	9.1	4.2
1952–57	14.0	8.9	4.7
1958–63	12.8	8.4	4.0
1964–69	12.6	9.0	3.0
1970–75	12.5	8.9	3.2
1976–81	13.0	8.8	3.9

Source: Derived from unpublished data provided by the Flow of Funds Section, Board of Governors of the Federal Reserve System. Figures are rounded.

net increases in investment, including the principal investments of the household sector—housing and consumer durables. Indeed, the tax savings may simply have financed other forms of consumption. During the postwar era, housing and durables maintained a constant zero tax rate on equity investment. Higher inflation increasingly subsidized borrowing, no matter to what purpose it was eventually put. Thus at the beginning of the postwar era, mortgages were being let to households at a rate of about 2 percent of GNP, while household investment in residential construction was at a rate of about 4 percent (see table 7-1). By the 1976–81 period, new mortgages were being let at almost double their earlier rate, yet new investment in housing had declined as a percent of GNP. Mortgage loans were actually in excess of new investment in housing. In a similar, although less striking way, expenditures on automobiles and other consumer durables declined slightly (for example, from 9.1 percent in 1946–51 to 8.8 percent in 1976–81), while consumer credit went up (from 1.3 percent to 1.5 percent during the same period; see table 7-2).

Tax arbitrage also seems to have been encouraged by the failure of the interest rate to rise sufficiently to hold breakeven tax rates constant. Until the early 1980s, interest rates in general hardly compensated for the rate of inflation, much less for any tax rate above zero.[4] During most of the postwar era, therefore, tax arbitrage was profitable for most taxpayers in all tax brackets.

4. Vito Tanzi, "Inflationary Expectations, Economic Activity, Taxes, and Interest Rates: Reply," *American Economic Review*, vol. 72 (September 1982), pp. 860–63; and Lawrence H. Summers, "The Non-Adjustment of Nominal Interest Rates: A Study of the Fischer Effect," in James Tobin, ed., *Macroeconomics, Prices, and Quantities: Essays in Memory of Arthur M. Okun* (Brookings, 1983).

Table 7-2. *Financial Sources of Funds, Household Flows of Funds,*
Various Periods, 1946–81
Percent of GNP

Period	Total	Credit market sources	Mortgages	Consumer credit
1946–51	3.2	3.4	2.1	1.3
1952–57	3.8	3.6	2.5	1.1
1958–63	3.9	3.7	2.6	1.0
1964–69	3.9	3.7	2.2	1.2
1970–75	4.3	4.2	2.8	1.1
1976–81	6.3	6.0	4.2	1.5

Source: Same as table 7-1. Figures are rounded.

Interest rates were kept low for a number of logical reasons. Financial arbitrage was always possible if interest rates rose too much relative to the other rates of return. Until the mid- to late-1970s, there was a relative decrease in the demand for borrowing by the government, and the stock of government debt relative to GNP generally declined.[5] An increased supply of loanable funds thus may have been available at low rates for all private purposes, but tax arbitrage investors certainly received their share.

Technically these are ex post results. Whether taxpayers intended ex ante to engage in tax arbitrage would depend upon their expectations about the inflation rate, the interest rate, and the rate of return on preferred assets. Although no one can measure expectations well, much less with certainty, there is widespread belief that people's expectations of inflation increase, perhaps with a minor lag, with the rate of inflation itself. Surveys tend to confirm that expectations of inflation are closely in line with the most recent experiences of inflation.[6] If these results are correct, taxpayers who engaged in both pure and normal arbitrage generally had high expectations for profit throughout the postwar era. These expectations help explain why the prices of assets that sold in less liquid markets—in particular, real estate—tended to rise as people anticipated higher inflation rates and as homeowners, farmers, and noncorporate business persons increasingly used arbitrage.

5. Board of Governors of the Federal Reserve System, *Balance Sheets for the U.S. Economy, 1945–83.*
6. See F. Thomas Juster and Robert Comment, "A Note on the Measurement of Price Expectations," rev. ed. (University of Michigan, Institute for Social Research, April 1980).

A Case Study: Farms and Small Businesses as Tax Shelters

In the inflationary postwar era most assets of farms and small businesses became especially good tax shelters.[7] Perhaps no asset has proven better in meeting the required shelter characteristics, especially in an inflationary environment, than real estate. For both land and buildings, only the yield from each asset is subject to taxation. All gains in value, including those due to inflation, can be deferred or excluded from taxation.[8] Real estate has also served as an especially good form of collateral for the securing of loans.

Real estate is by far the principal asset of the noncorporate business and farm sectors. For the beginning of year 1984 land alone had a value equal to almost 60 percent of the total net worth of noncorporate businesses and 79 percent of net worth of farms. This contrasts with a figure of 19 percent for the nonfinancial corporate sector (see table 7-3). Moreover, while the postwar era has seen an increasing percentage of the reproducible business assets held by the corporate sector, no such shift has taken place in the case of land.

The tax shelter aspect of farms and small businesses leads to a familiar story about the distribution and allocation of resources in society. Because the assets of the small business and farm sectors make good tax shelters, they tend to be purchased by persons with substantial income from other sources. Persons with less income and lower marginal rates of tax are induced to invest their savings elsewhere. They are put at a substantial competitive disadvantage relative to those who can make full use of the tax deductions and losses.

At the same time, real estate is not sold in highly liquid markets, or markets for which sales are likely. Land is also fixed in quantity. Therefore, the theory of normal tax arbitrage states that the prices of these preferred assets are liable to rise, and their yields fall, relative to the interest rate.

If a farm is for sale, a likely purchaser today is a nearby farmer whose

7. For a thorough summary of the many tax provisions affecting American agriculture and an argument that tax policy has led to upward pressure on farmland prices, see Charles Davenport, Michael D. Boehlje, and David B. H. Martin, *The Effects of Tax Policy on American Agriculture,* U.S. Department of Agriculture, Agricultural Economic Report 480 (USDA, 1982).

8. Land will also increase in real value over time because of increased scarcity due to population growth. Fluctuations in value, however, can be large both by area and through time.

income is currently substantial or a person who also works in a nearby community and obtains income from other sources. In the early postwar era farm owners generated most of their income from farming itself; by the mid-1970s farm owners had outside sources of income in excess of the returns from farming. For many small businesses, especially those requiring ownership of land and buildings, purchases of business assets are also favored among those who already are successful in generating income in other small businesses or in salaried employment elsewhere.

The tax shelter advantage is reflected in the amount of losses reported on tax returns. In 1982, for instance, reported losses (on returns with losses) as a percentage of reported net income (on returns with positive net income) were as follows: farms, 118 percent; rents, 126 percent; and partnerships, 88 percent. In contrast, for active corporations, deficits were only 44 percent of net profits, while for other noncorporate businesses and professions, the ratio was 53.5 percent.[9] This last category, of course, includes many labor-intensive small businesses such as legal, medical, and other service-oriented organizations.

The consequences of land becoming a tax shelter, by the way, are the subject of many complaints by farmers: problems of liquidity, increased borrowing to deal with cash-flow problems, and the tendency for the children of farmers to be deterred from becoming farmers themselves because they are often not the optimal owners of tax shelters.

The Profitability of Unproductive Investment

In a world with zero inflation, almost all investment by taxpayers, regardless of their tax brackets, is generally in assets with expected real rates of return above zero. Since the interest rate is above zero and has no inflationary component, the after-tax rate of interest is also positive in real terms for taxpayers in all tax brackets. Different real rates may be faced by different investors, but for any investment to be profitable, the after-tax return from the investment or use of the funds must also itself be positive in real terms. Unless the tax rate on the equity

9. Corporation statistics for 1982 are preliminary. See Sandra Byberg and Victor Rehula, "Corporation Income Tax Returns: Preliminary Income and Tax Statistics, 1982," *SOI Bulletin,* vol. 4 (Winter 1984–85), p. 36. Individual statistics are from Internal Revenue Service, *Statistics of Income—1982, Individual Income Tax Returns* (Government Printing Office, 1984), table 1.4.

Table 7-3. *Balance Sheets of Nonfinancial Corporations, Unincorporated Businesses, and Farms at the Beginning of Year, 1947, 1962, 1984*[a]

	Amount (billions of dollars)			Distribution (percent of net worth)		
Assets and liabilities	1947	1962	1984	1947	1962	1984
Nonfinancial corporations						
Reproducible assets	130.3	377.0	2,782.8	86.7	93.9	98.7
Land	33.3	85.0	538.2	22.2	21.2	19.1
Financial assets	67.4	194.6	1,214.7	44.8	48.5	43.1
Liquid assets	33.6	54.8	287.1	22.4	13.7	10.2
Consumer and trade credit	25.9	97.9	580.0	17.2	24.4	20.6
Other (including U.S. foreign investment)	7.9	41.9	346.7	5.3	10.4	12.3
Total liabilities	80.8	255.3	1,715.2	53.8	63.6	60.8
Credit market instruments	49.5	165.0	1,144.9	32.9	41.1	40.6
Trade debt	20.0	67.8	427.0	13.3	16.9	15.2
Other (including foreign investment in the United States)	11.3	22.5	143.3	7.5	5.6	5.1
Net worth	150.3	401.3	2,819.5	100.0	100.0	100.0
Net worth excluding land	117.0	316.3	2,724.8	⋯	⋯	⋯
Unincorporated businesses (nonfarm noncorporations)						
Reproducible assets	80.0	156.3	1,023.5	63.7	65.5	68.2

Land	39.7	90.5	896.6	31.6	37.9	59.8
Financial assets	19.8	35.1	71.4	15.8	14.7	4.8
Liquid assets	9.7	12.5	12.5	7.7	5.2	0.8
Consumer and trade credit	9.2	19.4	52.9	7.3	8.1	3.5
Other	0.9	3.2	31.6	0.7	1.3	2.1
Total liabilities	13.9	43.0	491.7	11.1	18.0	32.8
Credit market instruments	8.4	28.2	489.6	6.7	11.8	32.6
Trade debt	5.5	14.8	27.6	4.4	6.2	1.8
Net worth	125.6	238.8	1,499.8	100.0	100.0	100.0
Net worth excluding land	85.9	148.3	603.2	...	...	...
Farms						
Reproducible assets	44.2	74.4	330.3	46.5	43.7	42.2
Land	51.3	113.3	618.6	53.9	66.6	79.1
Financial assets	7.2	7.7	29.5	7.6	4.5	3.8
Liquid assets	6.4	5.8	7.8	6.7	3.4	1.0
Other	0.8	1.9	21.7	0.8	1.1	2.8
Total liabilities	7.6	25.3	196.4	8.0	14.9	25.1
Credit market instruments	7.0	21.6	184.2	7.4	12.7	23.6
Trade debt	0.6	3.8	12.1	0.6	2.2	1.6
Net worth	95.1	170.2	782.0	100.0	100.0	100.0
Net worth excluding land	43.8	56.9	163.3	...	...	...

Source: Board of Governors of the Federal Reserve System, *Balance Sheets for the U.S. Economy, 1945–83* (The Board, November 1984), tables 703 through 705. Figures are rounded.
a. Beginning of year is equivalent to the end of the previous year.

Table 7-4. *The Profitability of Unproductive Investment for a Taxpayer in the 46 Percent Tax Bracket*[a]
Percent

Tax treatment of return from preferred asset	Breakeven interest rate to prevent investment in unproductive asset	Breakeven real return at interest rate of 14 percent
Nontaxable	18.5	−2.4
Real return taxable	18.5	−4.4
Real return taxable with tax preferences granted[b]	23.7	−9.6

Source: Author's calculations.
a. With a 10 percent inflation rate.
b. Tax preferences given to offset taxes on a real return of 6 percent.

investment would itself be negative, no amount of borrowing or tax arbitrage could induce a business or household to purchase an investment with a before-tax real rate of return that was expected to be negative in a world without inflation.

For the purposes of this discussion, I refer to assets with negative real rates of return, or depreciation rates greater than real yields, as unproductive assets. As the inflation rate rises, there is an increased probability that persons will gain from investments in these unproductive assets. How does this happen? The tax subsidy for the deduction of the inflationary component of the interest rate may compensate for the loss in real income. To be more precise, borrowing and investment in an unproductive asset may be profitable whenever the interest rate is less than the inflation rate divided by $(1 - t)$, where t is the taxpayer's marginal tax rate. Unless the interest rate rises so much that it becomes positive in real after-tax terms for taxpayers in even the highest tax-rate bracket, at least some taxpayers can borrow at negative after-tax rates, invest in unproductive capital, and still profit from tax arbitrage.

As an example, suppose the inflation rate is 10 percent. Unproductive investment in nontaxable assets is profitable for a taxpayer in a tax bracket of 46 percent unless the interest rate rises to 18.5 percent or higher (see table 7-4). At nominal before-tax rates below 18.5 percent, the effective real after-tax interest rate is negative, and it may be profitable to borrow at the negative real after-tax interest rate and invest in the unproductive asset with a less negative return. If the interest rate is only 14 percent, for instance, the taxpayer profits from any nontaxable investment that produces a nominal return of 7.6 percent or more. At a 7.6 percent nominal return, the real social return is −2.4 percent even though the private after-tax returns of the taxpayer are zero.

While high rates of inflation almost inevitably lead to investment in unproductive assets, the extent to which unproductive investment is encouraged will actually depend upon the nature of the tax preferences given to assets. If an asset is taxable on almost all of its nominal return, there is not a large tax wedge between its rate of return and the rate of interest that will be paid. If the asset is nontaxable, as in the example above, the interest rate must rise substantially to deter the unproductive investments.

As it turns out, nontaxability of the return from a preferred asset may be less distorting than taxability! If the tax system imposes negative taxes on negative real income from an asset, the after-tax profit from unproductive investment may be even greater than it would be if the real return were nontaxable. Suppose, for instance, that the tax system was indexed for the preferred asset, and only its real return was taxable. This would occur if the depreciation rate on an asset was accurately calculated and indexed for inflation. In this case, the breakeven before-tax rate necessary to prevent unproductive investment would not change from the case of the nontaxable investment; however, when the interest rate was below that breakeven rate, assets could have even more negative real returns and yet remain profitable. Repeating the assumptions of a 10 percent inflation rate and a 14 percent interest rate, the breakeven real return falls to −4.4 percent for the investor with a marginal tax rate of 46 percent, as seen in table 7-4.

Now suppose that in addition to taxing only real returns—thus allowing tax refunds for negative real returns from unproductive assets—other tax preferences are given in the form of additional credits and deductions that are independent of the rate of inflation. This type of preference is quite common to the tax system. Investment tax credits and accelerated cost-recovery allowances, in fact, are currently designed to operate in almost exactly this manner: first the tax on returns due to inflation is offset at some assumed rate, and then a further tax reduction is provided. In this case, the investor in unproductive assets has the best of all worlds—tax preferences, further tax reductions, or negative taxes on the negative returns from unproductive assets, and even further tax reductions because of the allowed deduction of the inflationary component of the interest payment. This can be seen within the framework of the previous example, with the addition of an allowance for a nontaxable investment credit of 2.8 percent of the value of the asset each year, that is, a credit sufficient to offset tax due on real returns of 6.0 percent. Then the breakeven interest rate rises to 23.7 percent, while the breakeven real before-tax return required for after-tax profitability falls to −9.6 percent at an interest rate of 14 percent.

Cash Flow and Inflation

inflation, taxes, distribution of loan -

Higher rates of inflation and higher interest rates affect the distribution of investment in society not only through tax-induced portfolio shifts and tax arbitrage. Most financial markets are organized in such a way that inflation brings about a large and inefficient redistribution of lending in society even in the absence of any income tax effects. Individuals and businesses deterred from socially productive investment by the loan markets are in many cases prevented from making optimal investment because of tax-induced variations in "hurdle" rates of return—that is, the rates of return at which investments first become profitable. The tax and financial effects thus reinforce one another.

A simple example may demonstrate how inflation affects the distribution of loans in society. Compare a world with a real interest rate of 6 percent and an inflation rate of zero percent with an identical world having the same real interest rate and an inflation rate of 8 percent. If the average price of a house was $80,000, the annual interest costs associated with that purchase would be $4,800 in the first case and $11,200 in the latter. If the median income of persons wanting to purchase a home was $20,000, the cash flow necessary to make interest payments would equal 24 percent of income in the first case and 56 percent in the second. If an inflation rate of 8 percent also implied that the value of the house could be expected to increase by 8 percent more than in a world with zero inflation, the net economic return from the investment in housing would be identical to that for each household in each world. Yet it is obvious that with inflation the $20,000 household would either be denied or would deny itself the loan; without inflation the loan might be readily made and received.

Accounting Systems

Recall that inflation has a different effect on various accounting systems. Here I examine the difference between accounting for economic income and accounting for cash flow. For an investment in a real asset, inflation alone is not likely to change the relation between the cash flow from an asset (or implicit cash flow if one "rents" to oneself) and its real economic return. Excluding any tax effect, cash flow will be greater than the real economic return by the real rate of depreciation regardless of the rate of inflation.[10]

The separation of the measures of economic income and cash flow arises primarily in accounting for returns from financial interest-bearing assets or liabilities and in comparisons of their returns with the returns on real assets. As inflation rises, the measures of the economic return and the cash-flow return from an interest-bearing asset increasingly diverge. In fact, the difference between the cash flow and the real interest rate is exactly equal to the rate of inflation.

For a borrower, such as a financial institution hedging an interest-bearing debt with ownership of an interest-bearing asset, net cash flow may not differ greatly from net economic income.[11] This is not true, however, if the debt is hedged by ownership of a real asset. As inflation increased, the real return from the asset would maintain the same approximate relation to cash flow, while the cash payment on the debt would equal the real payment plus the rate of inflation. If the real rate of return on the asset and the real interest rate remained constant, therefore, the net rate of cash flow (as a percentage of the value of the investment) on an investment financed entirely with debt would be decreased almost exactly by the rate of inflation.[12]

In summary, the accounting method used for assessing the cost of debt leads to a measurement of the soundness of an investment according to whether it can produce a cash flow sufficient to cover interest costs (and certain principal repayments) on associated loans. At higher rates

10. Increases or decreases in the value of the asset because of inflation technically cause the nominal income from an asset to differ further from its cash flow, but those increases or decreases are recognized if the asset is sold. Recognized returns from the asset normally maintain the same relation to cash flow. Inflation may raise the measure of the current value of cash flow and economic income, but this implies no change in the real or constant value differential between the two measures.

11. If the debt and asset are of different maturities, a higher expected rate of inflation may imply an increase in risk because of potential losses from changes in the actual rate of inflation.

12. Let r equal the real rate of return and cash flow on a real asset of value R and i be the real interest rate. If inflation rises instantaneously from a rate of zero percent to a rate π, and all real rates of return stay constant, the net cash flow from the investment financed entirely with debt is decreased by π from $(r - i)$ to $[r - (i + \pi)]$. There is no loss in real income, however, because the real asset also rises in price by π, but this is not reflected in cash flow.

of inflation there is a greater disparity between accounting for cash flow and for economic income from a leveraged investment.

Market Attempts to Restore Balance

Such disparities in accounting systems leave the capital markets in a state of imbalance. Some economists are reluctant to recognize that accounting systems can affect real activity, primarily because market forces such as financial arbitrage by traders work to redirect investment back toward those assets with the highest economic rates of return. Put simply, market participants attempt to find ways to get around institutional rules, although not without significant costs.

In the U.S. economy the principal mechanism for allowing loans to go toward investments with positive economic returns, but inadequate cash flow, is what one might call "averaging." That is, both lenders and borrowers do not require that the marginal investment provide adequate cash flow to cover the marginal loan, but only that the average investment do so. The potential lender or borrower often compares the total cash receipts of the borrower with the cash payments necessary to cover debts (and other costs). As long as total cash flow is sufficient to meet total payment on debts, the "return" from the new investment will be of lesser importance in determining access to loan markets.

In many ways, of course, this is merely an extension of the requirement that loans be backed by sufficient collateral. If net worth or collateral is high enough relative to the size of the new loan, there is also more likely to be adequate cash flow from other assets to support payments on new loans. There is a crucial distinction: in a world without inflation, the new asset was more likely by itself to produce sufficient cash flow to cover payments on the debt used to acquire it. With inflation, the purchase may still be economically profitable, but its cash yield will not rise with the increased cash payments due on debt. Thus the lack of alternative sources of cash flow will be much more likely to prevent suppliers from making a loan in a world of inflation.

The second mechanism allowing loans to be made based on economic returns is provision for the renegotiation of loans and additional lending to cover interest payments. As interest becomes due and cash flow of the borrower is inadequate to cover payments, additional loans can be made to cover the interest payment.

Suppose, for instance, that inflation was 5 percent a year; the interest rate, 10 percent; and the real interest rate, 5 percent. If investment in a nondepreciating piece of land or in a building would produce a cash yield of 5 percent and an increase in value (net of depreciation) of 5 percent, its economic return would equal the economic rate of interest. For investors financing an investment entirely with debt, however, the cash flow would only be adequate to cover a 5 percent rate of payment on the debt, implying that the nominal debt must itself be allowed to rise by 5 percent or by the rate of inflation. This increase in nominal debt, of course, is exactly what is needed to keep the real debt constant, or to make the real amortization of the debt invariant to the rate of inflation.

Many institutions and lenders frown on lending to cover interest payments. If economic income and cash flow are loosely equated, this additional lending appears to involve the pouring of more money into a bad investment.

The confusion once again results because the same effect—inadequate cash flow—is the consequence of two very different phenomena: over-extension of loans for bad investment and the mismeasurement of the true economic return from the investment. In the latter case, if a financial institution was willing to increase the face value of the loan, or to continually renegotiate loans according to the true economic income of the borrower, it would recognize the identical riskiness of any two projects that had equal expected returns but differed in the amounts of their cash flow.

Although lending institutions have made more provision for relending and renegotiation of loans over the years, such modifications have been few and incomplete. While loan renegotiation is not uncommon, it is still more the exception than the rule. Some new types of lending instru-ments—graduated-payment loans and original-issue discount bonds—also "relend" the borrower some of the interest due at various stages of the loan period. These new types of lending instruments, however, compensate in only crude ways for the effect of inflation, and the flow of such instruments is still small.

Cash Flow and Corporate Investment

This analysis of the cash-flow behavior of lenders does not imply that there is necessarily a decrease in the total amount of loans made available for investment. It does imply that the distribution of those loans will differ from that of an economy in which loans are directed to their highest and best use through correct measurement of economic rates of return.[13]

For corporations, new loans are most available to those with cash flow in excess of the amount needed to cover interest due on outstanding debts and loans. Corporations without such access generally do not hold instruments that adjust for the effects of inflation. Corporate bonds, for instance, generally are not designed to relend the inflationary portion of the interest payment back to the borrower.

It is fortunate for many businesses that the cash-flow requirement really applies to the total activity of the business, not to a specific investment. At the margin, therefore, many businesses are able to negotiate loans for new investments based upon the cash flow from all activities, not the potential returns from new investments. Thus the existing cash flow may already be sufficient to cover new loans as well as outstanding loans. The business is recognized as a creditworthy customer and one that has a fairly good access to the market for loans.

Contrast this business with a new or potential business that has no existing cash flow. Lending institutions, being cautious and necessarily conservative, will be much more reluctant to lend to this enterprise (and will normally demand a higher rate of interest if loans are made available). Note how this third strike against new businesses adds to the two strikes thrown by the tax system—the new business is unable to take advantage of tax incentives and to make use of the extra deduction allowed by the deductibility of the inflationary component in the interest rate. Some preferential treatment of existing business is only natural, even in the absence of inflation. The problem of differential treatment, however, is greatly compounded when the accounting system used to determine soundness of loans is based upon cash flow from an activity.

In practice, many executives of successful corporations, as well as division heads with the power to make investment decisions, are constrained from taking advantage of their preferred status by the need to maintain growth in their statements of financial income. When interest rates are high because of inflation, loans decrease cash flow and financial income far more than they decrease real income. Unlike the noncorporate

13. With inflation, the central bank may also restrict the supply of loanable funds. Rationing to those with low risk may be a consequence. See Alan S. Blinder and Joseph E. Stiglitz, "Money, Credit Constraints, and Economic Activity," *American Economic Review*, vol. 73 (May 1983), pp. 297–302. If cash flow is used as a measure of risk, a misallocation of loanable funds will result.

business sector and the household sector, corporations also cannot turn to wage income as a source of cash flow. These constraints on lending are another reason why the ownership of real estate and other assets with large inflationary gains components (and large tax arbitrage possibilities) tend to be more concentrated in the noncorporate sectors.

Cash Flow and Household Investment

In the household sector the cash-flow method of accounting for loans has had similar distributional effects. For the purchase of a house or a consumer durable, of course, there is no measured return from the investment but rather a flow of services to the owner, which eliminates the need to make cash rental payments elsewhere. A lender's requirement for adequate cash flow is then related primarily to the question of how much of the existing cash flow from other sources can, in the absence of rental payments, be used to make payments on the loan.

The postwar era witnessed a major shift in the attitude of financial institutions in favor of the use of human capital as collateral for loans. The successful household found itself actively solicited by financial institutions as a borrower. Again, however, the safety of the loan was measured by cash flow from other sources, except wages were now considered as one source of that cash. The means of measuring adequacy of cash flow was usually through such rules of thumb as expenditures of a household on mortgages should be no more than one-third of income (as measured essentially by cash receipts), or loan payments for non-mortgage purposes cannot exceed 15 percent of income. These are more than just rules of thumb; they are the actual cash-flow rules by which loans were made to households.

Households usually adopted rules very similar to those of lending institutions and set their own internal limits on payments as a percent of income. Many, if not most, households operate almost purely on the basis of an accounting system that measures income essentially on the basis of cash flow. As one example, households often cut back on consumption loans or automobile loans when the interest payments become large relative to other income—calculating not the economic return from the purchase of an automobile or a durable good, but their own cash-flow limitations.

Lenders and households eventually adjust the rules under which they operate as the rate of inflation or the supply of loanable funds changes.

The percentage limitations imposed by lenders, for instance, were liberalized throughout the postwar era; at the same time, household borrowing and interest payments rose relative to income. The problem with these cash-flow rules is not that they will prevent a financial institution from lending available funds, but rather that they have distributional effects that cause misallocation of resources. Loans will be distributed on a basis other than the potential economic income that can be generated by the user of the loan.

There is the simple example of mortgage loans. The postwar era saw a sizable increase in the amount of mortgage lending relative to the amount of new residential construction. Secondary loans increased relative to the amount of primary mortgage loans. These trends partially reflected the tendency of both borrowers and lenders to make loans on the basis of adequate cash flow rather than actual demand for housing or even the economic rate of return that could explicitly or implicitly be obtained by those using the loans. Tax considerations obviously were likely to compound this effect.

Other Cash-Flow Distortions

Although the emphasis here has been on the effect of cash-flow accounting on the distribution of loans within the business and household sectors, other distortions in the economy surely have arisen because of the connection between cash flow and economic income. Persons who consume out of existing returns from savings, for instance, are often misled by the amount of their cash flow from interest-bearing assets. The common advice to investors is to conserve principal, but this advice would bring about very different rates of consumption out of real income with different levels of inflation. Technically the saver should reinvest the entire inflationary component of the interest return if that saver's goal is to preserve real capital. By the same token, investors who borrowed to purchase housing or other assets may have been led to pay off equity at a much faster rate than they anticipated or desired because of the continual decline in the real value of their debt (or the increase in the nominal value of the asset relative to the nominal value of the loan). While these types of behavioral responses will not be examined in more depth, it can be seen that the equation of interest cash flows with income will have additional distortionary effects in an inflationary economy.

PART TWO

Interpreting Some Current Events

CHAPTER EIGHT

Limitations of Macroeconomic Policy Initiatives

MACROECONOMIC initiatives per se are not the subject of this book. Indeed, previous chapters have failed even to treat such important issues as the initial causes of inflation, the importance of cost-push versus demand-pull inflation, and optimal levels of budget surpluses or rates of monetary growth during periods of underemployment. Also ignored, for the most part, are cyclical changes in demand and supply and the responses of labor and consumers to differences between actual and expected rates of inflation. Most of the discussion of the taxation of capital income, historical changes in flows of interest, and tax arbitrage and cash-flow problems was presented from an intermediate- or long-run rather than short-run perspective.

The previous analysis, nonetheless, has significant implications for macroeconomic policy. As is shown below, macro policy has found itself on a seesaw; it offers excess incentives to those with least need for them and then dampens total demand in the economy by restricting those with least access to such incentives in the first place. Indeed, an important part of the low growth in productivity of the 1970s is likely due to the resulting misallocation of scarce savings to less than optimal investment, a misallocation that became worse as rates of inflation increased.

These conclusions will not be satisfying to those who ignore the individual or microeconomic foundations of macro policy or to those who believe that macroeconomic analysis needs to focus on a single variable, such as aggregate money supply, a full-employment budget deficit, or the average marginal tax rate. Instead, these results will be important to those who seek to understand why inflation causes problems in the economy and to those who search for ways to make macro policy more effective. If the analysis so far has been correct, it offers the strong possibility that future bouts of inflation can be made to have a less stagnating effect on the economy, and that monetary and fiscal policy designed to correct for that inflation can be made less costly.

The Assumption of Inflation Neutrality

[handwritten: macro assumption — inflation has no real effects if anticipated]

In chapter 7 it was noted that many theoretical economic macro models have followed an assumption that, except for initial surprises, the rate of inflation per se has no effect on the size or distribution of total output in the economy.

This type of neutrality argument has often been used to support very different policy conclusions. Many persons who believed in active fiscal and monetary policy used the argument to show that in a simple trade-off between unemployment and inflation, the former involved costs, whereas the latter (at least initially) was neutral. If expansionary government policy could lower unemployment, and the only related cost was a higher rate of inflation, then most benefit-cost calculations would tend to favor fairly active policy. Many monetarists and opponents of fluctuating government policy used a neutrality argument in supporting government policy that held constant the rate of expansion of the monetary supply and, by implication of their models, the long-term inflation rate.[1] It was not inflation that was opposed, but a monetary or other policy that fluctuated so much that it led (among other things) to changing expectations of long-run or core inflation and to economic cycles that were caused by and followed the expectations cycles. Advocates of the new classical macroeconomics or rational expectations theory have in turn used the neutrality argument in designing models in which inflation has no effect on real quantities, relative prices, and market equilibrium. Because the economy is also assumed to have continually clearing markets, their conclusion is that stabilization policy is essentially impotent.[2] Note how opposed each conclusion is to the other! Also note the difference between these schools of thought and the more public discussion that recognizes inflation, even at a constant rate, as a threat.

[left margin handwritten: inflation → employment | macro policy ? Keynesian vs, rational expectation]

1. Milton Friedman, *A Program for Monetary Stability* (Fordham University Press, 1959).

2. Robert E. Lucas, Jr., "Econometric Testing of the Natural Rate Hypothesis," *The Econometrics of Price Determination, Conference* (Board of Governors of the Federal Reserve System, 1972), pp. 50–59.

[handwritten: Is inflation a threat?]

The concern here is not with resolving the debate about differences among these schools of thought—a debate that centers on how individuals and businesses form expectations—but rather with the realism of the inflation-neutrality assumption itself. If the inflation rate started at either 2 percent or 10 percent and then remained at that level for a decade, most of the simple macroeconomic theories would at least be united in finding no difference in the real product of the economy and the efficiency of its investment. In a world such as ours with structures of taxation and financial intermediation, that basic macro conclusion cannot be sustained.[3]

Inflation neutrality generally requires that at least two factors be treated as inconsequential: the tax system and the misleading information provided by inaccurate accounting for income.[4] One reason these two factors are ignored is that many theoretical models that do account for inflation operate primarily within the markets for labor and consumer goods. Even if inflation is not correctly anticipated within these markets, its interaction with taxes and accounting sources of information can safely be assumed to have little effect on the level of demand and the supply of labor or consumer goods.

First, with respect to taxes, the real income tax rate on labor income or excise tax rate on consumer goods will change little or not at all because of inflation. Even with substantial inflation, at most there would be some bracket creep in income taxation not offset by statutory change, but this would not involve a large adjustment in the rate of take-home pay, nor an adjustment for which major disruptions could be expected as they became recognized. In any case, inadequate labor supply has hardly been the problem to be explained during recent periods of stagnation.

3. I want to distinguish here between the simple theories and the theorists. Theorists generally add qualifications and footnotes to their models and assumptions, and there is no doubt that an economist otherwise noted for belonging to a school of thought would still find reasons to oppose too high a rate of inflation.

4. While many macro models do have misleading information as a major source of economic cycles, the misleading information is essentially incorrect knowledge of or incorrect anticipation of the rate of inflation. Disequilibrium can occur, for instance, as a result of a temporary difference between expected and actual inflation. After a period of adjustment of debated length, however, equilibrium will be restored at a higher rate of inflation. See, for instance, Edmund S. Phelps, *Inflation Policy and Unemployment Theory: The Cost-Benefit Approach to Monetary Planning* (W. W. Norton and Company, 1972); and Milton Friedman, "The Role of Monetary Policy," *American Economic Review*, vol. 58 (March 1968), pp. 1–17.

Second, inflation does not greatly distort information in the labor and consumer goods markets. Even in the absence of knowledge of future inflation rates, all methods of accounting for income or cash flow in these markets are fairly accurate. Prices are still correctly stated at any point in time, and the consumer generally is not misled for long about real prices or the ability of current cash wages to cover current cash purchases.[5] The cash wage will still equal the real economic wage, as well as the amount of wages subject to taxation. Thus while workers and consumers may find themselves disappointed with the information they eventually receive, most accounts will still provide them with fairly accurate information.

It is in the capital markets that these assumptions become unrealistic. Taxes and the misleading information provided by income accounting systems are affected much more dramatically by inflation here than in labor and consumer goods markets.

First, real tax rates—and real after-tax rates of return—begin to vary significantly, depending on the asset, the tax bracket of the investor, and the amount of loans associated with the investment. These real effects occur regardless of whether the inflation is anticipated.

Second, differences in the measures of economic income, financial income, taxable income, and cash flow become quite pronounced at high rates of inflation. Even in the presence of correctly anticipated inflation, individuals and businesses often change their behavior on the basis of the measures used in existing accounting systems. While correct anticipation of actual inflation would eliminate the smaller distortions in the labor and consumer goods markets, distortions created by the association of economic income with financial income, taxable income, and cash flow would remain in the capital markets.[6] In summary, the capital markets retain significant distortions regardless of whether persons anticipate or respond with a short lag to inflation. Only if all individuals completely see through the veil of various accounting systems will these additional distortions be avoided.

Although I object to the assumption of inflation neutrality in many

5. If consumers incorrectly estimate the inflation rate, their primary error is more likely to be in setting a forward price such as a future wage that is inadequately hedged against other future prices.

6. Durable goods are in part consumer goods and in part investment goods. Although inflation does not affect the zero tax rate on returns to such goods, it does affect relative tax rates on returns to all investments. Moreover, durable goods are likely to be financed by borrowing in the capital markets.

Accepts partially
R.e. model

Re possibility of distortions in capital mkts. with inflation

macro models today, it would be more correct to state that I disagree with the extent to which it is employed. Differences between nominal and real values have long been accepted as causes of economic cycles.[7] Because unemployment is the variable of most concern in recessions or depressions, however, too much emphasis can be placed on differences between nominal and real wages in the labor markets, and not enough to what is going on in the capital markets. Although the capital base is smaller than the labor base, the differences between nominal and real values in the former case are of a far greater magnitude. If workers or employers can be deceived by relatively minor differences between nominal and real values in the labor market, why cannot savers and investors and also lenders and borrowers be deceived by much greater differences between nominal and real values in the capital markets? Moreover, one of the effects of differences between nominal and real values—greater distortions in relative measures of capital income from different sources—has real effects even in a world of perfect knowledge because of related changes in real, after-tax rates of return.

Current Limitations on the Effectiveness of Macro Policy

In this section I summarize some of the ways in which the operation of the tax system and the loanable funds markets have limited the effectiveness of macro policy in recent years. Many of the capital allocations and related problems presented in the first part of the book would be present regardless of the macro policy being pursued. The concern here is to show how these problems interact with macro policy to limit policy effectiveness.

Long-Run Distortions in the Allocation of Capital

When macro policy leads to higher levels of expected inflation, it creates substantial long-run distortions in the allocation of capital. A higher rate of inflation may be a short-run means of increasing output and employment or overcoming false expectations about wage levels and prices. If wages are sticky and tend to be low or declining, for

7. See Kenneth J. Arrow, "Real and Nominal Magnitudes in Economics," in Daniel Bell and Irving Kristol, eds., *The Crisis in Economic Theory* (Basic Books, 1981), pp. 139–50.

instance, a deflationary economy may lead to higher real wage rates than can otherwise be supported. Similarly, an unexpected increase in the rate of inflation may lead to temporary reduction in real wage demands, perhaps increasing profits from sales and spurring further output.

If the rate of inflation is increased on a more permanent basis, however, it will lead to substantial distortions in the way capital is allocated. Effective tax rates will vary more across assets, significant portfolio shifts will be encouraged by tax arbitrage, and unproductive investment may even become profitable. Within the loan markets, cash restraints will limit access of new businesses and households to funds.

A macro policy that continually allows the rate of inflation to creep upward from one economic cycle to the next is therefore doomed to long-run failure. A corollary of this proposition is that the existing economic structure cannot continually tolerate a macro policy that considers the economy almost always to be growing at a slow rate, to be in a recession, or to be in the early recovery from a recession—and therefore in constant need of additional stimulus.

Coping with Instability

[handwritten margin note: Macro policy cannot solve financial instability problem]

Macro policy cannot by itself solve the problem created by the conflict between tax and financial arbitrage and therefore must cope with instability in financial markets. Because tax and financial arbitrage effectively set different relative prices or returns for the same real and financial assets, there is no stable, long-term equilibrium possible in the financial markets.[8] Short-run balance or market clearing is essentially maintained through limits on the supply of loanable funds; reluctance of taxpayers to allow cash flow and economic income to differ greatly; and increased risk, complexity, and limits placed in the tax laws on the simplest forms of tax and financial arbitrage. If one goes through this list, however, it becomes apparent that any current balance is unstable from one period to the next. New ways can be found to create money and loanable funds; and taxpayers' reluctance can be changed, even if slowly, to accord with economic incentives. Riskiness can be reduced

[handwritten margin note: financial instability, different prices, rates of return on same assets]

8. Macro models often avoid this problem of different prices or returns from the same asset by assuming that some average marginal rate applies to most or all potential savers and investors, both domestic and foreign. In effect, these models eliminate the problem by converting the existing tax structure to hypothetical structures that are tractable within the models themselves.

through the creation of new forms of financial instruments, new means of hedging, and greater ability to borrow against different parts of one's portfolio. Complexity is reduced by service providers such as lawyers and accountants, as well as by any constancy in policy. The simplest forms of arbitrage are replaced by other mechanisms that serve the same purpose.

This instability makes it difficult to establish long-term macro policy rules. If the natural tendency of tax and financial arbitrage is to reduce the tax base to zero (or at least keep it far below current levels), fiscal policymakers may respond in many different ways to regain those revenues, including the development of new forms of taxation. Changes in the rules of the game may even be necessary for an indirect revenue effect: unpredictable changes in tax rules do limit tax and financial arbitrage by increasing the complexity, cost, and riskiness of arbitrage transactions.[9]

By the same token, suppose that monetary policymakers have as their goal an increase in loanable funds or a decrease in interest rates in order to spur increased real investment in productive equipment and plant. The intermediate goal may be much higher than otherwise necessary if much of that increase in loanable funds is used for other purposes. For instance, investment in unproductive assets may be encouraged by normal tax arbitrage. Loans used for pure tax arbitrage may also be increased. Moreover, the first persons to make use of the expanded supply of money may be those who were most constrained by cash-flow considerations, including many with pent-up demand for housing. In effect, the total amount of loanable funds in the economy must be increased by a multiple of the originally planned increase in level of investment-related loans, especially if the investment is in equipment and plant.

The Costs of Macro Policy

Under current tax and loan rules, macro policy will be unnecessarily costly regardless of whether it is used to expand or contract the economy. The relation between the interest rate and the real rate of return on assets is quite tenuous. Different taxpayers face significantly different after-

---

9. For other arguments related to random tax collections see Joseph E. Stiglitz, "Self-Selection and Pareto Efficient Taxation," *Journal of Public Economics,* vol. 17 (March 1982), pp. 213–40.

tax interest rates and rates of return on assets. Fiscal and monetary policy designed to correct distortions for one group of taxpayers will inevitably add to the distortions faced by other groups. For instance, if during a period of rising inflation the after-tax rate of interest is kept constant for high-bracket borrowers, it will be increased for low-bracket taxpayers who do not receive the same tax benefits.

Macro policy faces an unavoidable dilemma. Monetary policy that expands the supply of loanable funds and lowers interest rates, for instance, would initially increase both the number of persons who demand loans for tax arbitrage and the reward per dollar of loan used for tax arbitrage purposes. Given the amount of potential tax arbitrage that can still take place, it is likely that this policy would increase the amount of loans actually spent for tax arbitrage purposes.[10] A secondary effect would be an increase in the price of land, real estate, and certain other preferred assets. Increases in such asset prices fuel inflation through feedback effects on the prices of goods and services.

Attempts to slow the economy have their own undesirable costs. First, they have a disproportionate effect on new businesses and on the cash-flow parts of the economy, such as the housing and automobile sectors. Increases in nominal interest rates result in greater increases in real, after-tax interest rates for borrowers in lower brackets, including new businesses, new homeowners, and purchasers of automobiles—taxpayers who often do not itemize deductions. Even when after-tax returns from borrowing and investment are still positive, higher interest rates deter investment and purchases most for those with inadequate cash flow from other sources.

A contractionary policy that has disproportionate effects on different parts of the economy entails unnecessary costs. The production sectors are often hit so hard relative to other sectors that the initial response may be one of unemployment rather than general reductions in wage and profit rates.

A restrictive policy may also be especially burdensome for those individuals and sectors where it is least desired. A good example is presented by the housing market. Tax arbitrage creates too much demand for housing by persons with high tax rates and adequate external income, while higher interest rates caused by inflation creates too little demand

10. Recall that the question is an empirical one because greater profit per dollar of arbitrage means that fewer dollars might be spent to reduce taxes to zero or some breakeven point.

by those with inadequate cash flow to service loans. A contractionary monetary policy shrinks much of the demand for housing by those who most need housing and is much less restrictive for those who have the greatest tax incentives to invest in excess amounts of housing.

Contractionary policy also requires increases in interest rates beyond the increases necessary in a world without tax arbitrage. The after-tax interest rate will rise by only a portion of the increase in the interest rate itself. Thus if monetary authorities want to counter the effect of inflation by keeping real, after-tax interest rates constant, they must try to increase nominal rates by more than the increase in the rate of inflation. In addition to the effect on new businesses and unnecessary sectoral effects mentioned above, this means that monetary authorities must be willing to accept the increased risk inherent in higher interest rates, especially with respect to long-term borrowing. These authorities must also face the consequences of pushing up the exchange rate and paying potentially higher real rates of return to foreign investors in domestic securities—a "beggar-thyself" type of trade policy.

CHAPTER NINE

Limitations of Existing Incentives for Saving and Investment

Incentives to spur the economy

MANY PROVISIONS in the tax code that relate to capital income are believed to operate as incentives for saving and investment. Some of these provisions were enacted in times of relative prosperity, others during stagnation. In either case, it was often argued that the incentives were cheap mechanisms to spur the economy. By not being extended to the largest source of income—labor income—they were less costly than other forms of tax reduction or expenditure increase. Many incentives were designed in a way to minimize their original cost; for instance, by applying only to "new" capital investment or "new" deposits in savings institutions.

As an approach to solving the problems of stagnation, the use of saving and investment incentives has been second in popularity only to changes in monetary and fiscal policy. Saving and investment incentives involve direct revenue reductions of several hundred billion dollars. In many cases the reductions merely offset tax "penalties" on the inflationary component of capital income. Nonetheless, these incentives must, for the most part, be judged failures. The question addressed here is, why?

The answer cannot be found in an examination of the economic inefficiencies that may exist if there is inadequate saving and investment or if there are improper allocations of consumption expenditures over time. Saving and investment may not be adequate regardless of the efficacy of incentives to increase household saving and business investment.[1] Nor can the answer be found in the use of structural tax policy to increase investment and saving (assuming the responsiveness of the

---

1. For an examination of the responsiveness of saving to changes in tax rates or after-tax interest rates, see Barry P. Bosworth, *Tax Incentives and Economic Growth* (Brookings, 1984). Even if there was a high rate of response (or elasticity) of saving to such changes, existing incentives would be found to be poorly designed.

private sector to changes in after-tax rewards). Even many expenditure tax advocates—those who favor zero tax rates on returns to capital—recognize the failure of existing incentives. The answer instead lies in the design of existing incentives.

In many ways, current saving and investment policies aim at the creation of new wealth in society primarily by promising people with current wealth a means to maintain or increase that wealth. Excluded from this subsidized market are many new market participants and new businesses (including young families looking for their first homes and young graduates with new ideas or inventions). Both groups are put at a competitive disadvantage in the creation of new wealth.

This discrimination is achieved primarily through two related conditions. First, saving and investment incentives are almost always associated with acts of purchase, deposit, or retention that can be easily identified. Second, a necessary condition for receiving the subsidies is that they must be used to reduce taxes on other income, that is, be attached directly to the income from other sources. The first condition allows certain acts to be labeled as investment or saving even if they are not, and the second ensures that even when saving and investment do occur, the rate of subsidy will be a positive function of the amount of old wealth or income from that wealth.

Incentives for Saving

For any tax proposal or provision to be accurately labeled a saving incentive, three criteria must be met.[2] First, tax benefits should not go to taxpayers who simply switch assets from one form of saving (or one kind of account) to another. The shift of assets into a tax-preferred form permits taxpayers to achieve tax reductions with no increase in their saving.

Second, no tax provision can be labeled a true incentive if it does not apply at the margin. A deduction with a cap—that is, one with a limit on the amount or exclusion permitted—provides little marginal incentive for a person already receiving income in excess of the maximum. For example, a cap of $500 on the amount of interest or dividends that can

2. Much of this discussion of saving incentives is taken from work done in collaboration with Harvey Galper. See Harvey Galper and Eugene Steuerle, "Tax Incentives for Saving," *The Brookings Review,* vol. 2 (Winter 1983), pp. 16–23.

Table 9-1. *Distribution of Returns and of Interest and Dividend Income Reported on Income Tax Returns, 1981*
Cumulative percent unless otherwise specified

Amount of interest and dividend income (dollars)	All returns	Returns with interest and dividend income	All interest and dividend income
1–100	56.8	24.2	0.3
1–200	62.8	34.7	0.8
1–300	66.9	41.9	1.3
1–400	69.6	46.7	1.8
1–500	71.8	50.5	2.4
1–1,000	78.1	61.5	4.8
1–1,500	81.8	68.1	7.3
1–2,000	84.2	72.3	9.5
1–3,000	87.5	78.0	13.8
1–6,000	92.6	87.1	25.6
6,001–10,000	95.7	92.4	38.0

Source: Data derived from the tax model of the Department of the Treasury, Office of Tax Analysis. Figures are rounded.

be received tax-free would have only a very modest marginal incentive effect, since taxpayers who receive more than $500 of dividend and interest income have accounted for as much as 97 percent of such income (see table 9-1).

Third, a tax incentive for saving must provide symmetrical treatment of positive saving on the one hand and negative saving or borrowing on the other. If a taxpayer can borrow and deduct the costs of interest, while at the same time acquire an asset-yielding income that is partially or fully tax-exempt, the taxpayer may achieve a tax reduction with no increase in net saving.

In the case of pure tax arbitrage the taxpayer effectively borrows and lends an interest-bearing asset at the same time. It is as if he had borrowed from himself and then obtained a tax reduction for that activity. In the case of normal tax arbitrage, tax reduction may also be attained without any increase in net saving in the economy, but the process is more complex because both lenders and borrowers are involved.[3]

3. For instance, an arbitrager may borrow to buy a preferred asset and generate tax reduction through the difference between the after-tax returns on the asset and the liability. At the same time, there may be some initial holder of the preferred asset who has moved in the opposite direction by selling the preferred asset and purchasing an interest-bearing asset. In this case, there is zero net saving and zero net investment.

There is an appropriate treatment of borrowing and interest expense that prevents tax arbitrage. Where saving incentives allow deductions for positive saving or deposits, there should be a corresponding inclusion of negative saving or borrowing in taxable income. Thus if deposits are deductible, proceeds of loans should be taxable when received. Such is the normal treatment prescribed in an expenditure or consumption tax that determines the taxable base by subtracting net saving from income. When the saving incentive allows the exclusion of interest, dividends, or other capital income from the tax base, it should also disallow the deduction of interest payments. Finally, partial incentives of either type should require a corresponding inclusion of borrowing or a disallowance of interest expense. In all cases, it is simply recognized that borrowing is negative saving and interest payments are negative interest receipts. The same incentive rule that applies to positive saving and capital income must also apply to negative saving and capital income.

In summary, for a saving incentive to be effective, it must meet three criteria: have little or no inducement to shift forms of asset ownership, provide a positive incentive to save at the margin, and not offer opportunities for tax arbitrage. I next turn to an examination of the extent to which these criteria are met by current tax provisions that are believed to act as incentives for saving.

As discussed in chapter 2, existing tax provisions that favor saving include exclusions of income from most durables and owner-occupied housing; special exclusions for capital gains realizations, and complete exclusion of gains accrued until death; deferral of taxation for gains on most assets appreciating in value; special treatment of deposits to and earnings from pension funds and IRAs; and partial dividend and interest exclusions. These preferences more than offset any tax raised by inflation, such as the tax collected on the inflationary component of capital gains realizations.

Because about 80 percent of all assets of individuals are eligible for one or another of these tax preferences, it may appear at first glance that the tax structure has moved toward some version of a consumption tax. This view is quite misleading, however, because it ignores the question of whether the existing incentives actually are incentives at all in light of the three previously noted criteria for a saving incentive to be effective.

Because the latter's increase in taxes will normally be less than the decrease in taxes attained by the arbitrager, there will still be a net tax reduction.

Although existing incentives are examined here, the last part of this book treats broad changes in the tax laws that do meet all these criteria.

Criterion 1: Prevention of Asset Shifts

Saving incentives adopted on a piecemeal basis and applying only to certain forms of saving will almost certainly encourage households to reorganize their portfolios. Because each investment decision will be based partly on tax considerations rather than exclusively on true economic productivity, the overall efficiency and productivity of investment will decline.

Some of these welfare losses are captured by general equilibrium models, which attempt to allow for differential tax rates for broad categories of investment assets.[4] It should be stressed once again that the actual welfare losses or inefficiencies will be far greater than the estimates produced by simple models that assume some average marginal tax rate for holders of assets in different sectors of the economy or that measure efficiency losses by shifts in aggregates—total investment, total investment in housing, total output of the automobile sector, and so forth. Each asset can be of different value to each *individual decision-maker* who makes use of the asset.

In this regard, one especially important aspect of the efficiency losses induced by asset shifts has been generally overlooked. The exclusion of interest income and payment from most incentives means that individuals are charged the highest effective tax rate for direct lending to others and a much lower tax rate for holding their saving in other forms. Lower-income individuals and new businesses are discouraged from borrowing in order to invest, while higher-income individuals and established businesses with current flows of income are encouraged to borrow and to leverage their investments even further or to retain earnings for investment in their own projects. The resulting loss in efficiency occurs not because of changes in the aggregate level of saving, but because the saving is not made available to those whose potential investments could yield the highest return.

4. See, for instance, Don Fullerton, John B. Shoven, and John Whalley, "Replacing the U.S. Income Tax with a Progressive Consumption Tax: A Sequenced General Equilibrium Approach," *Journal of Public Economics*, vol. 20 (February 1983), pp. 3–23.

Table 9-2. *Estimated Utilization Rate of Individual Retirement Accounts, by Income Class, 1982*

Adjusted gross income (dollars)	Number of returns reporting salary and wages (millions)	Number of returns reporting IRAs (millions)[a]	Utilization rate (percent)[b]
0–5,000	15.0	0.1	0.7
5,000–10,000	13.9	0.4	2.9
10,000–15,000	12.2	0.7	5.7
15,000–20,000	9.3	1.0	10.8
20,000–30,000	15.1	2.7	17.9
30,000–50,000	13.7	4.5	32.8
50,000–100,000	3.3	2.1	63.6
100,000 or more	0.6	0.5	83.3
All income classes	83.1	12.0	14.4

Source: U.S. Internal Revenue Service, *Statistics of Income—1982, Individual Income Tax Returns* (U.S. Government Printing Office, 1984), pp. 44, 53. Figures are rounded.

a. Excludes the effect of self-employed persons who are also eligible to invest in IRAs.

b. Defined as the number of returns reporting IRAs (second column) as a percentage of returns reporting salary and wages (first column).

Criterion 2: Marginal Effectiveness

Current tax preferences for capital income provide no incentive for increased saving at the margin if a cap has been placed on the amount of income eligible for a tax reduction. The current exclusion of $100 of dividends for each taxpayer ($200 for a joint return) is a prime example. The tax provisions regarding IRAs include both a cap and an inducement to shift assets into tax-preferred accounts. IRAs may provide some saving incentive for persons whose current rate of saving places them below the cap amount, but inevitably those who can most easily obtain the tax reductions that IRAs offer are those who need only to change the form of their saving, rather than those who actually must increase net saving. Accordingly, it should come as no surprise that in 1982 two-thirds of the eligible taxpayers with incomes over $50,000 made deposits in IRAs, but less than 5 percent of those with incomes under $20,000 did so (see table 9-2).

Criterion 3: Tax Arbitrage

All the existing incentives are found to be deficient in terms of this criterion; none of them effectively disallows tax arbitrage through borrowing. Indeed, much of the interest paid on the $2.7 trillion of individual financial liabilities (see table 2-4) is deducted immediately even though it is likely that many of these borrowed funds are used to acquire assets—such as pensions, annuities, land, housing, and corporate stock—for which income is deferred.[5]

One further question needs to be addressed. Is it possible that the various preferential tax provisions discussed here, although sources of sectoral and portfolio misallocations when taken one at a time, largely cancel each other out when treated in aggregate? Several considerations argue against such an outcome. Interest income received by households is conspicuously absent from the list of items for which tax preferences are allowed. The provisions are so varied in their approach and subject to so many caps and limits that the differentials among rates of taxation (or subsidy) for different types of assets are still quite significant. Finally, the ability to engage in tax arbitrage undercuts any possible incentive since the tax benefits can be obtained without increasing saving at all.

Incentives for Investment

Investors incentives — to those with existing wealth.

Like saving incentives, investment incentives have been designed in such a manner that the greatest incentives are given to owners of existing wealth. There has been little variety in these investment incentives, however. During the postwar era almost all have been designed in much the same way. First, each offers a tax reduction that can be used only to offset taxes or taxable income, including income from other sources. Second, the value of the incentive is available almost immediately. Third, each incentive has applied primarily to expenditures on plant, equipment, and to a lesser extent, buildings. Finally, the incentive or the effective rate reduction has applied only to "marginal" or new expenditures, but not to old investments or returns from old investments.

Many authors have emphasized the extent to which the differential tax rates implicit in these incentives have caused distortions among different types of equity investment.[6] Students of investment tax policy

5. The problem of tax arbitrage has been recognized in the tax laws but, as discussed in chapter 6, only in ways that have little impact.

6. See *Economic Report to the President, February 1982*, pp. 109–33; and Jane G. Gravelle, "Effects of the 1981 Depreciation Revisions on the Taxation of Income from Business Capital," *National Tax Journal*, vol. 35 (March 1982), pp. 1–20.

are quite aware that such distortions have been present for some time, and that the problems are not caused only by recent changes in cost-recovery allowances. The premise here is that much of the failure of investment incentives can be understood by examining some problems created as more and more incentives were added. The focus is on three problems that are inherent in the common design of postwar investment incentives: the creation of entry barriers for new businesses, the emphasis on plant, equipment, and buildings as items of investment, and the failure to address tax arbitrage.

Barriers to Entry

Barriers to entry are commonly associated with investment. Where they exist, an existing firm needs a lower rate of return than a new firm to make a new investment. Put another way, a new firm must be able to achieve a higher-than-normal return from an investment in order to compete in either an old or a new market. Note that existing firms do not necessarily have to make the investments in order to limit competition from new firms. The threat of new investment by established firms is by itself sufficient to increase the risk and decrease the investment made by new firms. The failure of new firms to enter a marketplace may simultaneously lessen the incentive for old firms to take advantage of new technologies and methods of production. Even when the older firms do undertake the investment, they may simply be less capable of integrating the new investment with the necessary labor and ideas to produce the maximum value of output for the lowest cost.

The function of financial markets is to channel scarce savings through competitive forces to those persons or firms capable of achieving the maximum rates of return in the use of those savings. Financial markets are deterred from performing this efficiently, however, because existing investment tax incentives create substantial barriers to entry. These barriers are not created by the preference given to investment per se, but rather by the particular way in which the incentives are designed. Recall two of the features of all postwar incentives: they are available only as a tax reductions, and they are almost entirely available immediately. These features ensure that the incentives will be of maximum value only to firms and individuals who have substantial income from other sources.

Take the case of a piece of equipment purchased by a corporation with loan dollars. For a $1,000 investment, about $720 (undiscounted) will be returned in tax reduction—investment credits and the value of depreciation allowances—within the first four and one-half years of the investment. To take maximum advantage of the credits and deductions, the firm would need to have taxable income (undiscounted) of almost $1,570 over the same period, yet the flow of output from a typical piece of equipment would yield less than one-half of the necessary receipts. For the beginning firm that has no external income or cannot carry back credits and deductions, the inability to use all the tax savings may well make the investment prohibitive.[7]

The differences among firms can become even greater when the investment is financed through borrowing. For purchases of equipment, for instance, tax rates are almost always negative when leverage is involved. The after-tax cost of debt has been found to vary significantly among firms and industries.[8]

Perhaps as important as differences in tax rates are differences in cash flows related to investment. The existing firm already has an advantage in the sense that its external income helps ensure the lender against loss, and its other assets are available as collateral. The tax incentives, however, increase this advantage considerably by making the cash flow from the tax reductions available immediately for the firm that can fully use them. Another factor is that the cash flow from the tax reductions is more certain than the receipts from sales of eventual output.

This is most easily explained in the case of expensing, but the general results apply in any case where the tax reduction is immediate. A corporation that has sufficient taxable income and expenses will receive 46 cents in immediate tax reduction for every dollar of its investment. Assuming no borrowing, its net outflow of cash in the first year will then be only 54 cents, less any receipts from goods sold by reason of the investment. A corporation with no other income, on the other hand, will acquire almost no cash flow from the tax savings. It needs a full dollar of cash flow in the first year to make a dollar's worth of investment.

7. The debate about leasing is in large part a consequence of these differences in tax savings for equal equity investments by different firms. The opportunity to lease, however, may be considerably greater for the firm that is temporarily unprofitab゙ ﾗ than for the new firm. The new firm has had little chance to build the necessary goodwill or reputation as a reliable producer and creditor; it therefore has minimal access to the leasing market. See chapter 12 for more details on leasing.

8. See Joseph Cordes and Steven M. Sheffrin, "Estimating the Tax Advantages of Corporate Debt," *Journal of Finance*, vol. 38 (March 1983), pp. 95–105.

Alternatively, the firm with existing income has 46 cents of additional cash flow with which to make other investment or to help secure additional loans.

Expenditures on Plant, Equipment, and Buildings as the Measure of Investment

Optimal investment policy could channel investment expenditures toward those items that produce the maximum value of future output per dollar of expense. True economic investment includes expenditures on such items as research and development, training of employees, acquisition of know-how, and education. Plant, equipment, and buildings represent only a moderate portion of total investment in the economy.

The initial application of investment incentives only to plant, equipment, and buildings may have created no more distortion than many other governmental attempts to identify certain items for special treatment. Some view investment tax incentives as offsetting other distortions, such as those caused by the taxation of capital income in the first place. As more incentives became tacked onto old ones, however, the new distortions created by selective incentives became more severe. With too many incentives, there was in all likelihood an increase in the amount spent on preferred assets that provided a negative total value added or a negative value of output less cost. This was especially likely to occur for assets whose net rates of subsidy (less tax) became positive— as is the case under current law for purchases of equipment when interest rates are low or when borrowing finances the investment.

The fascination with plant and equipment and, to a lesser extent, with buildings as the measure of investment, the source of growth, and the item to be preferred is the result of several factors. In a historical sense, the harnessing of energy and the industrial age meant enormous growth in national output and in the stock of investment goods. While plant and equipment were complementary goods to ideas, technology, and labor, there was still a high correlation between observed growth and observed investment in plant and equipment. It was quite logical that many persons treated plant and equipment as the cause of the growth, rather than only a component. Especially in the "take-off" stage, moreover, plant and equipment may indeed have been the component in least supply and therefore may have been capable of generating the most return. Denison and Bosworth make a convincing case, nonetheless, that recent variations in economic growth cannot be attributed to changes in the rate of expenditure on plant and equipment.[9]

The increasing historical importance of plant, equipment, and buildings show why incentives to purchase these assets have been appealing, but they do not necessarily explain why investment incentives have been applied only in that area. Certainly more neutrality among different types of investment could have been achieved through a lowering of corporate tax rates, greater integration of corporate and personal taxes, or some similar method of lowering tax rates on returns from capital on a broader scale.

As noted, all these postwar investment incentives were efforts to increase returns only on the margin. Neutrality across sources of capital income would have required that rates be lowered equally for capital income from all new investments. The marginal contribution of new ideas, inventories, training, and so on would have been almost impossible to assess or measure. Income from new capital could not be separated from income from old capital. Since marginal income could not be measured, the advantage of focusing on new investment in plant, equipment, and buildings, it was argued, was that here at least measurement could be made at the margin—or so it appeared.[10]

Marginal incentives defer the long-run cost of any tax reduction into future years. As in so many other cases of government expenditure and tax policy, politicians like to support changes that over the long run may be significant, but whose costs are hidden in the early years. Economists were also in the forefront of those supporting this marginal approach, believing it was a way to achieve maximum "bang per buck." Since the tax reduction applied only to new investment, the full-incentive effect would take place immediately, but the revenue costs would be forestalled as old investment continued to be taxed in the old way.

Implicit in the theory that this type of strategy would work was the

9. Edward F. Denison, "The Interruption of Productivity Growth in the United States," *Economic Journal*, vol. 93 (March 1983), pp. 56–77; and Barry P. Bosworth, "Capital Formation and Economic Policy," *Brookings Papers on Economic Activity*, 2:1982, pp. 273–317.

10. Note the difference between saving incentives and investment incentives in the attempt to be marginal. Saving incentives often apply only to the *first* dollars of saving and are not marginal because they do not apply to all saving, including the last dollars saved. Investment incentives are applied to the *last* investments made but, for various reasons, it is questionable whether this approach is preferable to a general reduction in the rate of taxation of all capital income.

notion that the costs would be low relative to the benefits. Some of the costs have already been noted: large barriers to entry; distortions between investments in plant and equipment and other investments; possible investment in assets with negative rates of return when the tax rate was negative.

Other effects on the cost-benefit ratio must be taken into account. First, the tax incentive did not really apply to all investment that would not otherwise have taken place; it did not even apply to net new investment. Instead, because of measurement problems, it was applied to all expenditures on plant and equipment, gross of depreciation. Second, costs of administration and organization increased as established firms with negative taxable income and insufficient ability to carry back current losses sought to overcome limitations in the law by means of leasing, mergers, or other techniques.[11] Finally, the ability of the government to make the incentive marginal by imposing a lump-sum tax on existing capital must have lessened over time. After all, if the after-tax cost of new capital is lowered from one dollar to ninety cents or sixty cents, the value of old capital must also be reduced in the process of adding a new investment tax incentive. If, however, this tax on old plant, equipment, and buildings is not paid in a lump sum, the incentive is no longer strictly marginal in effect. One does not have to accept a theory of rational expectations to recognize that the fear of arbitrary future changes in tax policy can affect current decisions to invest even if the exact nature of those changes cannot be fully anticipated.

Existing types of investment incentives may still be useful short-run countercyclical tools in certain economic circumstances.[12] Regardless of whether short-run gains are present from "marginal" incentives, however, in the long run all expenditures on plant, equipment, and buildings will have received the investment credits and accelerated cost-recovery allowances.[13] Thus there are no long-run revenue gains from

11. Leasing may, at the same time, lessen barriers to entry and reduce costs if it is made available to new firms.

12. If the marginal incentive is applied as an effective countercyclical tool, the lump-sum tax may be more than offset by the increased value of previously underutilized capital.

13. Although I have faulted macro models for their failure to deal with the effect of tax policy on taxpayers facing different marginal tax rates, even these models show little gain from "marginal" incentives. Amerkhail, for instance, investigated the impact of investment tax incentives using econometric models developed by Data Resources, Inc., and Chase Econometrics. She finds that "gains in business fixed investment from

the attempt to be marginal. The costs associated with these marginal incentives, however, are permanent. Once investment incentives, as designed in the postwar era, were turned from a temporary countercyclical tool into a permanent policy for promoting growth, the cumulative long-term costs rose considerably relative to the possible one-time political and economic gains.

Tax Arbitrage

Investment incentives in the postwar era have continually ignored the problem of tax arbitrage. Tax arbitrage is of course possible with the purchases of physical, as well as financial, assets. For new purchases of plant and equipment the combination of the investment tax credit and accelerated depreciation more than compensated for the understatement of depreciation because of inflation. Current law investment credits, along with accelerated cost recovery, provide at least the equivalent of expensing for particular categories of investment. If equity investments are essentially nontaxable, then it becomes even more important to deal with the taxation of interest income and the allowance of interest deductions.

It is unfortunate that the design of investment incentives reduces the extent to which the wedge created by the different tax treatment of different types of income could be lowered with a decline in the rate of inflation. While lower inflation will eliminate some of the subsidy inherent in deductions of the nominal interest rate, at the same time it will increase the subsidy for expenditures for plant, equipment, and buildings. If proper income accounting had been adopted for equity investment, the tax rate on returns from that investment would not have varied with the rate of inflation. Accelerated recovery allowances, however, were stated in nominal terms and made independent of inflation; as the rate of inflation declines, therefore, the real value of the recovery allowances will increase. In many cases the effective tax rate on equity investment will therefore turn decidedly negative.

---

a targeted tax cut are minimal, and come largely at the expense of housing investment, foreign trade, and a larger federal deficit, not from reduced consumption." See Valerie Amerkhail, "The Effect of Recent Corporate Tax Changes on Aggregate Investment and Real Growth," paper prepared for the 1983 annual meeting of the Allied Social Science Associations.

CHAPTER TEN

Effects on Organizational Structure

THE lack of uniform treatment of income from capital has been shown to create an enormous spur for businesses and individuals to rearrange their affairs. In this chapter the focus is on the ways in which firms organize and operate. The interactions among taxes, loans, and inflation create incentives for firms to combine, separate, and rearrange their asset holdings and to seek alternative mechanisms for financing invest-ment. Although many organizational efforts are a response to economic incentives other than those created by the tax system, the loan markets, and inflation, almost no major organizational or financing effort can be made today without placing a large, sometimes dominant, weight on these latter factors.

Mergers, Conglomeration, and Divestitures

One effect of the nonuniform treatment of income within the tax and loan markets is to encourage the merger of corporations. If a corporation has current losses of income in excess of taxable income that can be carried forward from past years or faces limits on the amount of its investment credits, it will not be able to use its tax deductions and credits fully. Similarly, if a corporation has a probability of losses, there likely is some probability of being unable to achieve the full tax reduction available for those losses. While many deductions and credits can often be carried forward and used in future years, the measured value of those deductions and credits are not increased by any interest rate. Their present value therefore decreases with the passage of time.[1]

1. Tax policy affects industrial concentration through a variety of other means that are not discussed here. Important in this respect are the slight progressivity in corporate tax rates and rules regarding the treatment of reorganization exchanges and distributions resulting from capital divisions of firms. These issues have only begun to be analyzed. See Alan F. Feld, *Tax Policy and Competition*, U.S. Federal Trade Commission, Bureau of Competition and Office of Policy Planning and Evaluation (FTC, 1979).

A similar problem arises in loan markets. Whenever a firm suffers from a downturn, whether firm-specific or industrywide, it will likely have a much greater need to borrow funds. Yet a firm's best access to loan markets is when it is generating profits, not losses. Losses make a firm appear less secure and give it less access to the capital markets often at the time when loans are most needed.

The actual or potential loss of tax benefits and reduced access to capital markets can be alleviated by the merger of firms. When a firm with losses combines with a firm with positive taxable income, their combined tax liability will be lessened. As a result, the value of the merged firms often will be greater than the sum of their values as separate companies. By the same token, the merged, or combined, firm is liable to have greater total access to capital markets. The increased access is partly the result of a greater diversification of products and sources of profitability. The pooling of conditional losses or liabilities reduces the risk of lending or providing insurance to the merged firm. As one example, suppose firm B has access to the loan markets in a given year, but does not need a loan, while firm A lacks access. By using B's assets as collateral and B's income as proof of future ability to make interest payments, the merged firm may be able to obtain a loan to expand A's activities.

The incentive for one firm to merge or buy up another firm is not confined to the situation in which the buyer has taxable income and the purchased firm has losses. Two firms with current income but some probability of losses from partially independent events may also merge as a form of insurance against the probability of not being able to use all future losses for tax purposes. In addition, firms with losses may find that they can pay a premium for firms with current income.

These tax and loan incentives encourage reorganizations other than mergers. Many managers of smaller companies may not want to become part of larger conglomerates, but they may still have divisions that generate taxable losses for which current deductions are unlikely. Those loss divisions, if expected to provide economic profit over the long run, will often be sold to other companies that are better able to use the loss deductions.

Organizational efforts to ensure against both the inability to use tax deductions and the lack of access to capital markets are not unique to the current era. What is unique is the extent to which these problems are compounded by both inflation and the current design of tax incentives for investment. Once again, it is possible to trace a set of seemingly unrelated events in the economy—in this case, various reorganizations of firms—to the same set of causes outlined in chapters 2 through 7 of this book.

Inflation raises the nominal interest rate on loans and decreases the probability that nominal financial or taxable income will be measured as positive even when real economic profits are present. The real rate of profit, moreover, will be understated most for those firms with the greatest ratios of debt to equity. At the same time, the higher rates of interest will increase the need of corporations to return to the loan markets merely to finance the payments on their debt, or to keep the real value of their debt constant, much less to meet other costs.

For nonfinancial corporations the importance of interest, both as a deductible expense and as a use of funds, is reflected in the increase in net interest payments from 0.38 percent of net national product in 1948 to 2.36 percent in 1983, or from about one-ninth of real retained earnings to about 1.4 times real retained earnings (see figure 3-2).[2] Because investment incentives in the postwar era have all been realizable immediately, the possibility has greatly increased that their full value cannot be gained except by the firm with sufficient current taxable income. The incentives have given even greater relative access to the loan markets to firms that can take advantage of them. For these firms the tax reduction in the first years equals a sizable portion of the total value of an investment and a multiple of the interest payments on loans used to finance the investment.

Although mergers will be a frequently used mechanism for minimizing tax liabilities, the past few years have also seen an enormous increase in the number of partnerships and trusts sold as tax shelters. These partnerships often own the assets used by corporations and include freight cars, films, real estate, and oil and gas properties.[3] As has been noted, the principal advantage of concentrating tax shelters at the level

---

2. See also U.S. Department of Commerce, Bureau of Economic Analysis, *The National Income and Product Accounts of the United States, 1929–76 Statistical Tables,* a supplement to *Survey of Current Business* (Government Printing Office, 1981); and *Survey of Current Business,* vol. 64 (July 1984), tables 1.13 and 1.7.

3. As one example of the many press accounts of such activities, Robert J. Samuelson ascribes a battle over the organization of Gulf Oil to a dispute about how much of the corporation's oil and gas properties should be placed in a "royalty trust" that would be owned directly by individuals. See Robert J. Samuelson, "Gulf Battle a Reflection of Society," *Washington Post,* December 6, 1983.

of the individual is that taxable losses can be used to offset wage income or income from other sources. In addition, in contrast to corporate managers, managers of tax shelters do not face the same pressure to show positive financial outcome. Future projected declines in the taxable income of the corporate sector relative to its economic income will likely have a significant effect on the way in which existing corporations operate and new corporations are formed. Some tax advisers at major accounting firms have recently suggested that the corporation may no longer be the preferred form of ownership for many traditional corporate activities.

Although there is a tendency for many tax shelters and tax arbitrage activities to take place at the noncorporate level, it should still be recognized that, in some cases, only large corporations or corporations with experience in given areas have the expertise to see the possibility of arbitrage profit. Often only large corporations have the capability of engaging in arbitrage through the buying and selling of whole companies, or subsidiaries of companies. Some conglomerates with high debt-to-equity ratios, for instance, specialize in such activity. Thus corporations have the financial power to make major exchanges unavailable to even some of the most sophisticated individual investors.

It is not always clear, by the way, whether the trading induced by various tax and loan considerations tends to increase or decrease the average size of firms in the economy. The concern here, however, is with the efficiency of firms, not with their number or size per se. As long as exchanges are motivated by the nonuniform treatment of economic income, they will result in the creation of organizational structures that are economically inefficient.

Leasing of Equipment

The inability of some firms and individuals to gain the full tax benefit from investment incentives or to generate sufficient cash flow to pay off loans has stimulated much activity in equipment leasing. Through sometimes complex transactions a leasing firm will lease equipment from a lessor who can take full tax advantage of the investment. The lessor effectively demands tax benefits plus rental payments, which in present value are equal to or slightly in excess of expected returns from other direct forms of investment. Because the lessor accrues the tax benefits, the rental rate charged the lessee will be lower. If the lessee is unable to use tax benefits directly, it will pay a smaller amount in (present value of) rental payments than it would pay if it made the investment itself.

Leases substitute transferability of various investment incentives for refundability. In effect, when tax benefits can be transferred or sold to other firms, the transfer accomplishes some of the same purposes as refunds for negative taxable income or credits in excess of allowable amounts. If the value of tax incentives were refundable, corporations would have much less reason to lease rather than purchase assets. Without refundability, transfer or sale of tax benefits to other corporations helps minimize total corporate liability. The terms of the lease are set so that the value of the tax reduction is shared between the lessor and lessee.

A Note on "Safe Harbor" Leases

Before 1981 the Internal Revenue Service limited the use of leases through some complex rules that will not be described in depth here. These rules essentially restricted leases in which the lessor had no significant risk of ownership or had no use for the asset other than leasing it to the lessee.[4] Safe harbor leasing, which was allowed by the Economic Recovery Tax Act of 1981 (ERTA), eliminated many of these restrictions and required only a minimal 10 percent investment by the lessor. These leases reduced and in many cases eliminated the risk of the investment by allowing the leases to be structured in such a way that only the present value of the tax benefits was effectively bought and sold between firms. Other nontax payments were designed essentially to cancel each other, that is, the rental payments would just cover the amortization and interest cost of the debt used to purchase the investment asset.

In the Tax Equity and Fiscal Responsibility Act of 1982 (TEFRA) the rules were tightened again for leases beginning in 1984, although with limitations that were not as strict as those that prevailed before 1981.[5]

4. Tests included required minimal profits and cash flow, primarily through lease payments, exclusive of tax considerations; a minimal equity or interest by the lessor throughout the life of the lease and at its expiration; a useful life of the asset in excess of the life of lease agreement; and a prohibition against investment or financing by the lessee.

5. Essentially, the rules legislated before 1981 will apply with some important exceptions. Property can be leased even if only usable by the lessee, and the lessee can hold an option to purchase the property at the end of the lease for a fixed price (at least 10 percent of cost).

Table 10-1. *Estimated Amounts of Equipment Leasing under Safe Harbor Leasing Rules, 1984 Levels of Income*
Billions of dollars

Type of leasing	Amount
1984 leasing that would have occurred under pre-1981 law	13.3
Additional leasing, with accelerated cost-recovery system	11.7[a]
Additional leasing, with safe harbor leasing	21.8
Total	46.8

Source: *Safe Harbor Leasing Provisions of the Economic Recovery Tax Act of 1981,* Hearings before the Subcommittee on Oversight of the House Committee on Ways and Means, 97 Cong. 1 sess. (U.S. Government Printing Office, 1982), p. 20.
a. Included in this figure is investment made by nontaxable corporations that would have been merged into taxable corporations in the absence of the safe harbor rule.

Then in the Deficit Reduction Act of 1984 the effective date for certain liberalized leasing rules was further postponed.

Safe harbor leases highlighted the way in which tax benefits were simply bought and sold. Opposition was not deterred by a Treasury Department analysis which showed that about 85 percent or more of the net benefits actually went to the leasing company, not to the lessor with the reduction in tax liabilities.[6] The lessor effectively accepted lower before-tax rates of return or rental streams in exchange for the lower taxes.

What was also ignored in many of the debates of the period on safe harbor leasing was the extent to which leasing was already encouraged under the accelerated cost-recovery system (ACRS), as shown in table 10-1. One of the primary arguments for safe harbor leasing was that the benefits of ACRS were so attractive that there would be a large increase in the number of nontaxable companies and companies that reached the statutory limit on the use of the investment tax credit. These companies would be unable to lower tax liabilities in the current year through use of credits and deductions for new investments. Such companies included both established firms with current losses and new firms with start-up costs.

The Leasing Dilemma

In an atmosphere of substantial, nonrefundable, immediately realizable tax incentives for investment, principles of tax law cannot give an

6. U.S. Department of the Treasury, Office of Tax Analysis, "Preliminary Report on Safe Harbor Leasing Activity in 1981" (Washington, D.C., March 26, 1982).

unequivocal answer to the question of how much equipment leasing should be allowed. A dilemma is unavoidable and is reflected in the diverse views of tax experts on the subject. One group, including the Treasury Department, argued that leasing was necessary so that incentives for investment would apply equally to all firms, including start-up firms and firms with current losses. A second group maintains that firms in a loss situation already are nontaxable at the margin on new investment and, therefore, should not have the added advantage of leasing to make their tax rate on marginal investment negative or more negative than the rate paid by taxable companies.[7] A third group holds that refundability or transferability is necessary even for firms with current losses because interest deductions, when combined with incentives, makes the tax rate for profitable companies negative anyway.[8] A fourth group distinguishes between the measurement of economic income and the provision of incentives.[9] This group suggests refundability or transferability as a second-best approach, which would be confined to the subsidy element inherent in investment incentives. They see no reason that one should be able to "sell" losses due to investment in equipment but not losses due to payments of wages, interest, or expenses incurred in purchasing other assets.

The choice for policymakers is difficult because they are forced to make two-way comparisons in a world in which the lack of uniformity is widespread. Equalizing the incentives between new firms and established firms, for instance, may only increase the differential in tax treatment of established firms with current income and those with losses. The difficulty is caused primarily by the design of the investment incentives themselves. In a world without total refundability for all losses and credits, almost all indirect ways of reducing some discrepancies will necessarily exacerbate others. No matter what choice is made, two-way comparisons of inefficiency and inequity will almost inevitably arise.

7. See *Analysis of Safe-Harbor Leasing,* Joint Committee Print, Joint Committee on Taxation, 97 Cong. 2 sess. (GPO, 1982); and Steven M. Sheffrin, "The Simple Economics of the Liberalized Leasing Provisions," Working Paper 180 (University of California–Davis, Department of Economics, October 1981).

8. See Alvin C. Warren, Jr., and Alan J. Auerbach, " Tax Policy and Equipment Leasing after TEFRA," *Harvard Law Review,* vol. 96 (May 1983), pp. 1579–98; and Alvin C. Warren, Jr., and Alan J. Auerbach, "Transferability of Tax Incentives and the Fiction of Safe Harbor Leasing," *Harvard Law Review,* vol. 95 (June 1982), pp. 1752–86.

9. See Donald C. Lubick and Harvey Galper, "The Defects of Safe Harbor Leasing, and What to Do about Them," *Tax Notes,* vol. 14 (March 15, 1982), pp. 643–52.

To the extent that incentives are to be made independent of other tax considerations, refundability of those incentives alone would be the most direct way of achieving that result.[10] Refunds present some difficult administrative issues, but hiding refunds in complex transactions further prevents adequate budget analysis of the effects of the policy and entails unnecessary additional transactions and other social costs.

Simply limiting leasing will not solve the basic problem. The incentives for leasing are fairly similar to the incentives for mergers. In both cases, an indirect means is created for two companies to minimize total tax liability through broad reorganization of the way they do business or finance their investments. Whatever qualms there are about complex and unnecessary leasing, they should be no less than the concern about mergers. The more that leasing is restricted, the greater is the extent to which mergers or other forms of reorganization will be used to accomplish the same purpose. Without adequate improvement of the investment incentives themselves, no good dividing line can be drawn between discouragement of leasing and encouragement of mergers.

The Cost of Human Resources

Mergers, sales-etc — have for tax reasons — high transactions costs.

Mergers, leases, divestitures, purchases, sales, and break-ups of companies are not accomplished without significant transaction costs. Although aggregate estimates of such costs are not available, the cumulative circumstantial evidence indicates that the costs for the economy are high. Tax lawyers increase substantially in numbers and on average are the highest paid of all members of the legal profession. The demand for accountants and corporate executives with financial and tax expertise inevitably increases in importance relative to the demand for persons with actual operating experience.

An understanding of taxes and finances has always been valuable, but no more so than in the modern economy. As net interest rose over the postwar era from 0.9 percent of GNP in 1948 to 8.0 percent in 1981 and deductible types of interest payments from 2.6 percent to 13.1 percent (see table 4-2), the handling of loans would have become far more important even in the presence of consistent and accurate accounting

10. For further discussion of refundability and other options see Donald W. Kiefer, "The Effect of Safe Harbor Leasing on Lessors, Lessees and the U.S. Treasury" (U.S. Congressional Research Service, June 7, 1982).

systems. The lack of uniformity both in tax rates for different assets and in accounting for income in various accounting systems only increased the value of knowledge of the tax and financial systems. The potential tax savings from proper asset shift and tax arbitrage, for instance, is on the order of tens, if not hundreds, of billions of dollars. These numbers have become so large relative to the before-tax profit from investment that tax considerations not only drive many investments, but they increase enormously the worth of tax and financial experts.

Although the complexity of the induced transactions adds to the need for tax and financial experts, the additional costs can be mitigated partly through economies of scale from learning specific tax provisions, interpreting tax laws in ways most favorable to taxpayers, lobbying Congress for new specifications, and so forth. Economies of scale, however, imply that the cost is inversely related to size. Complexity thus increases the incentive to merge and reduces the threat of competition from smaller firms.

Many tax and financial experts are among the brightest and most educated members of our society, and it would be a mistake to believe that they could not have produced many valuable services and goods in a variety of other tasks or even other occupations. There is little doubt that one of the major costs of the nonuniform treatment of income from capital for both loan and tax purposes is the deterrence of some of our best and most inventive people from activities that would more likely increase the productivity, growth, and well-being of society in general.

CHAPTER ELEVEN

Some Equity and Supply-Side Considerations

THE FOCUS of this examination of the tax system thus far has been on issues of efficiency: the allocation of capital among sectors, individuals, and organizations, and limitations of various governmental efforts to control the economy and encourage saving and investment. This chapter, which continues the description of the tax structure, provides insight into issues of progressivity, equity, and the ability of the income tax to generate revenues through "supply-side" or "feedback" effects.

Issues of Equity

Although all income is nominally subject to progressive rates of taxation, that is, increasing in rate as the base increases, in practice it is primarily in the taxation of wage income that the individual income tax achieves progression. Wage earners with equal amounts of wages can be said to be taxed in approximately the same manner on their wages and, with the important exception of employer-provided fringe benefits, there is at least some semblance of "horizontal" equity, or equal treatment of equals. On the other hand, there is little tax on income from capital at the individual level. Historically, progressivity with respect to capital income has occurred, but has been hidden. In effect, it resulted from the tendency of capital owners to hold large shares of their portfolios in corporate stock and pay a significant corporate tax on that income. When taxation does occur at the individual level, however, it is often arbitrary and random. There are three related sources of these differences between the taxation of wage and capital income: realization of income, inflation, and tax arbitrage.

146

no progressivity in capital income
due to (1) realization
(2) inflation
(3) arbitrage

Realization of Income

Accounting for income is generally associated with the realized payment and receipt of cash. Exceptions occur primarily at the business level, at which accrual accounting is the method used to keep track of such items as inventories and accounts receivable, and investment in plant, equipment, and buildings is treated differently from other expenses. At the individual level, however, income has tended to be recognized for tax purposes only when it is received as cash. Unrealized income is either deferred or permanently excluded from taxation.

Most wages are paid in cash and are recognized currently. Some serious problems do occur, nonetheless, in the taxation of labor compensation; employer-provided health insurance and other fringe benefits have been among the largest sources of the decline in the tax base during the postwar period.[1] In relative terms, however, most wages are recognized currently and are reported on tax returns as income subject to taxation.

In the case of capital income received by individuals, most returns are not recognized currently. Although capital gains are the most obvious example, I have shown that only about 32 percent of net real returns from capital is reported on individual income tax returns, and a much smaller percentage of nominal returns is reported.

Inflation

Inflation increases any difference between the taxation of wage income and income from capital by distorting greatly the latter measure, while having almost no effect on the former. Cash wages will rise with inflation, but in current dollars those wages will still be measured accurately.[2] With capital income, inflation is known to cause serious distortions in the measure of income. When recognized, interest payments and interest receipts, as well as capital gains, are overstated. Because so many interest payments are deducted on one side of the ledger but not included on the other side, inflation increases the amount of real private interest

1. Eugene Steuerle and Michael Hartzmark, "Individual Income Taxation, 1947–79," *National Tax Journal*, vol. 34 (June 1981), pp. 145–66.
2. The discussion ignores the interaction with the measurement of capital income. See the discussion in chapter 8 under the heading "The Assumption of Inflation Neutrality."

payments (net of receipts) that is deducted on tax returns. An increase in the rate of inflation also decreases the value of real depreciation allowances and increases the amount of capital gains (not necessarily recognized) on many assets.

One of the major effects of inflation, therefore, has been to greatly increase the differences in tax rates faced by individuals, not so much on the basis of their total income, but rather according to their relative tendencies to finance their investments with debt and to realize economic income. Inflation has generally subsidized borrowers; it has been more neutral with respect to the income of accumulators (who do not recognize gains); and it has penalized many retired persons and small savers who are compelled to recognize income or at least have cash available to meet consumption needs.

Tax Arbitrage

Tax arbitrage is an important means by which taxpayers take advantage of differences in tax rates on returns from capital assets, including those differences caused by the interaction between inflation and a tax base determined by realizations. Normal tax arbitrage by itself converts the effective after-tax structure into a flat-rate tax for nominal income above some breakeven point, and possibly below that point, as shown in figure 6-1. The progressive rate schedule is effectively eliminated for most returns from capital, and the top effective marginal rate is well below the highest nominal rate of tax.

Technically the theory of normal tax arbitrage does not eliminate progressivity altogether. An effective flat-rate schedule above any breakeven point implies some progressivity as long as the flat rate is greater than rates paid on income below the breakeven point.[3] The final outcome also depends in part upon the extent to which there is a reduction in the before-tax rate of return on preferred assets or an increase in the interest rate paid to low-income lenders. Recall that the tax saving from tax arbitrage may be shared between lenders and borrowers. The more that the subsidy accrues to borrowers with high marginal tax rates, the less progressive the system is. The more that the tax saving is passed on to persons at the bottom of the income distribution,

---

3. Average rates of tax will still increase with income, and other measures of progressivity can still show the individual income tax to have a progressive effect on the after-tax distribution of incomes.

the greater is the amount of progressivity that is maintained. In effect, a higher breakeven rate implies more progressivity because there are reduced opportunities to arbitrage down the top marginal rates of tax.

Once one takes into account financial arbitrage and pure tax arbitrage, the effect of the tax system becomes even more random among individuals and across time. Preceding chapters have shown both theoretically and empirically that it is unlikely that interest rates have been or, for long periods of time, can be significantly in excess of many other returns to capital sold in liquid markets. It is thus unlikely that compensation through higher interest rates or lower returns on preferred assets would be sufficient to restore much progressivity to the system. In addition, pure tax arbitrage can be used by taxpayers at all income levels. Since some persons engage intensively in this type of arbitrage, and others not at all, it adds further to the randomness and horizontal inequity of the system.

The possibility of tax arbitrage is insufficient by itself to explain why capital income is taxed differently from wage income. Technically tax arbitrage can and does offset wage income and income from capital. There are three reasons, however, why the effect of tax arbitrage is different for the two forms of income. First, tax arbitrage requires the purchase of assets. The wage earner must become a capital owner to reduce taxes, but the capital owner need not engage in labor activities.[4] Second, wage earners may be less likely to incur risk than capital owners. Third, for capital income, possibilities for tax arbitrage are supplemented by opportunities for changes in portfolios without any additional borrowing. Portfolio adjustment is not a viable means of excluding most labor income from taxation. Again, these arguments do imply that the wage earner, especially one who holds a mortgage, is not engaged in a substantial amount of tax arbitrage. Tax arbitrage has simply been likely to offset a higher proportion of capital income subject to taxation.

Taxpayer Dissatisfaction with the Income Tax

Variations in amounts of realizations, inflation subsidies, and penalties and use of tax arbitrage are so great among taxpayers that the tax rate on capital income often has only a minimal relation to the income of the taxpayer. Many taxpayers at all income levels report negative returns to

4. *Net* wealth can still be negative, but assets and liabilities must be held.

capital while receiving substantial economic returns; others with no real income from capital are taxed as if they had received substantial sums.

For those who do report positive returns to capital, the rate of inclusion will often be related to need for consumption, reluctance to take risk, desire to diversify assets, and ignorance of the tax code. To the extent that there is a correlation between income and these factors, one likely implication is that low-income persons will actually be taxed more at the individual level on their returns to capital, not less. If persons in low income brackets can bear little risk, for instance, or need a significant portion of their income and assets for consumption, then they will include in the taxable base a much greater percentage of capital income than will persons in higher income brackets.

One should not conclude from this last paragraph that there is a class distinction in the arbitrariness of the tax system: it is arbitrary for all classes. Nor does the lack of progressivity of the individual income tax imply that progressivity may not be established through some other means. At least historically, most taxes on capital income have been collected through corporate income taxes, and corporate stock has been held mainly by persons in higher income brackets.

The common perception of the income tax as unfair is due in no small measure to a partial understanding of the arbitrariness with which capital income is taxed. Most taxpayers are aware of some differentials in the taxation of returns to different types of assets, especially those differentials from which they do not benefit. Many know, for instance, that the interest that they receive has a huge inflation component for which indexing is not allowed. Most are also aware that some persons pay little or no individual income tax because of tax shelters and large interest deductions.

What these taxpayers are less likely to perceive is the tremendous tax subsidies accorded to borrowers, including those holding mortgages on homes, during a period of inflation; the generous treatment given to almost all capital owners through the rules regarding pensions, life insurance, and owner-occupied housing (independent of borrowing); the number of persons at all income levels who are engaged, often unintentionally, in both pure and normal tax arbitrage; and the extent to which corporate equity owners at least historically paid substantial taxes because of the additional corporate tax and the understatement of depreciation allowances.

In the end, most taxpayers probably do not understand many of the ways that the tax system operates, but they do understand that persons with equal incomes are taxed very unequally, that wage earners are treated differently than capital owners, and that progressivity is nowhere near that implied by the rate schedules. It is not surprising that dissatisfaction with the income tax has grown along with increasing interest payments and inflation rates, the number of special tax provisions, and other causes of tax differentials in recent decades.

Supply-Side Economics and Feedback Effects

The tax structure is perceived differently by some persons among those who label themselves "supply-side" economists. Believing that high marginal tax rates stifle the productivity of wage earners and capital owners, they proceed to assert that cuts in such tax rates will return large revenues to the Treasury Department. These "feedback" effects will reduce greatly, if not eliminate, the cost of most proposals to reduce taxes.

As evidence for these claims, they note correctly that large percentage reductions in the capital gains inclusion rate and in the highest marginal tax rates brought little reduction in Treasury revenues. For instance, preliminary evidence indicates that a significant feedback resulted from the capital gains tax reduction of 1979.[5]

Other writers, on the other hand, have shown rather conclusively that total income and production in the economy cannot be made to increase greatly simply because of the incentives of reduced marginal tax rates.[6]

5. The extent to which revenues actually decrease or increase with a given tax capital gains tax cut is discussed in Martin S. Feldstein, Joel Slemrod, and Shlomo Yitzhaki, "The Effects of Taxation on the Selling of Corporate Stock and the Realization of Capital Gains," *Quarterly Journal of Economics,* vol. 94 (June 1980), pp. 777–91; Gerald E. Auten, "Capital Gains: An Evaluation of the 1978 and 1981 Tax Cuts," in Charls E. Walker, Jr. and Mark A. Bloomfield, eds., *New Directions in Federal Tax Policy for the 1980s* (Ballinger, 1983); Gerald E. Auten and Charles T. Clotfelter, "Permanent Versus Transitory Tax Effects and the Realization of Capital Gains," *Quarterly Journal of Economics,* vol. 97 (November 1982), pp. 613–32; and Joseph Minarik, "The Effects of Taxation on the Selling of Corporate Stock and the Realization of Capital Gains: Comment," *Quarterly Journal of Economics,* vol. 99 (February 1984), pp. 93–110.

6. See, for instance, Don Fullerton, "On the Possibility of an Inverse Relationship between Tax Rates and Government Revenues," *Journal of Public Economics,* vol. 19 (October 1982), pp. 3–22.

The purpose of this section is to show how these apparently contradictory perceptions can be reconciled.[7] The main thrust of the argument is that much of the empirical evidence presented in support of both views is correct. One should not, however, draw inferences about the effects of taxing one source of income from the taxation of other sources. Despite a common statutory rate schedule, wage income is taxed very differently from capital income, and as already noted, different forms of capital income are also taxed in a variety of ways.

For capital income, the combination of a discretionary realization system and the opportunity for tax arbitrage already limits substantially the net amount of capital income that is taxed. Capital gains taxes give the best example of the discretionary nature of capital income taxation, and that is why such taxes are the most easily cited example of feedback effects. As rates of tax on capital gains are lowered, people quite rationally may volunteer to recognize more gains. They may find, for instance, that the cost of changing to an asset with a higher expected rate of return has declined enough that portfolio reallocation is now profitable.

Since most labor income is recognized currently, only a greater supply of productive effort can generate more revenues from the taxation of wages. Capital owners, on the other hand, do not need to save or invest more; they can compensate the government for the tax change simply through increased sales of assets. Indeed, for many taxpayers, the cost of consumption will go down with the decrease in capital gains tax rates. Large feedback effects from decreases in capital gains tax rates may even imply increased consumption, rather than increased saving, especially in the short run.

The cost of lowering the top marginal rates of tax that apply primarily to capital income, not just capital gains, is also small. For instance, before 1981 there was a maximum rate of tax on labor income of 50 percent, although the interaction of this regulation with other provisions of the tax code sometimes raised the effective maximum rate. The maximum rate on capital income, however, went as high as 70 percent. Yet there was little revenue cost to reducing the top statutory rate on all income to 50 percent.

The reason is quite simple. Taxpayers subject to high rates of tax on nominal returns from capital were never numerous. Much of their income

7. For a thorough discussion of many other supply-side issues, see Barry P. Bosworth, *Tax Incentives and Economic Growth* (Brookings, 1984).

may already have been excluded and deferred from taxation, and the remainder was subject to tax largely because of inadequate use of portfolio shifting and tax arbitrage opportunities. Taxes paid at the highest marginal rates of tax were likely paid by widows, widowers, and others with large amounts of risk aversion or simple lack of knowledge of the tax code.

Given the current tax structure, one significant advantage of lower tax rates on income from capital is that the benefits from tax arbitrage are reduced. Borrowing is more expensive, and the differences in tax rates on returns from different assets are lessened. In the case of transactions categorized as pure tax arbitrage, in which the net amount of recognized income is negative, a reduction in tax rates actually increases, not decreases, taxes paid. Even for persons engaged in normal tax arbitrage, a reduction in tax rates increases the taxes paid by most persons involved in private interest transfers; that is, the decline in value of interest deductions will be greater in absolute value than the increase in value of interest receipts. This net tax increase will offset some of the tax decrease on taxes paid on other, usually more preferred, assets.[8]

In summary, significant reductions in marginal tax rates on capital income may at times cost only small amounts of tax revenues because of the combination of: (1) the small amount of capital income that is currently recognized at top rates; (2) the decrease in the value of tax arbitrage; and (3) the greater recognition of income at lower rates of tax.

This analysis cannot be extended too far, however. Part of the argument can be summarized simply as saying that it does not cost much to reduce statutory tax rates on income that, for the most part, is not recognized in the first place. This logic does not imply that any lowering of tax rates—especially on labor income or capital income that is usually recognized—would have the same effect. Wages are taxed currently in significant amounts at all tax rates; tax arbitrage does not currently offset most wage income. The greater the proportion of wages in the tax bracket being considered for rate reduction, therefore, the smaller are the likely secondary or feedback effects. As another example, many corporations are engaged in the types of activities that are likely to generate current recognition of income—recall that tax shelters tend to be concentrated

---

8. These secondary effects are not feedback effects in the strict sense because they are captured through ordinary, fixed-behavior types of revenue-estimating techniques. When tax rates are lowered, tax models will show changes in taxes for all persons and sources of income, including interest paid by arbitragers and received by others.

in the personal sector—and corporations often want to recognize financial income. A lowering of the top tax rate for the individual income tax
weil below the corporate tax rate could cause significant revenue loss if
corporations changed their ownership of all or a portion of their assets
to partnership status.

PART THREE

Prescriptions for the Economy

CHAPTER TWELVE

Prescriptions for Major Tax Reform

IN RECENT YEARS the public has found itself barraged with proposals for tax reform ranging from broader-based, lower-rate income taxes to flat-rate taxes, indexing, expenditure taxes, and reductions in tax rates. This chapter focuses on the extent to which these proposals move in the direction of uniformity of treatment of income from all capital. Because such proposals are often debated on other grounds, such as equity, administrability, growth, and saving, some attention is also given to these considerations.

Efficiency Conditions

This book has argued that an efficient economy is one in which institutions are designed so that savings are channeled into the real investment that produces the highest rate of return. A corollary is that financial investments or loans should be made available to the persons with the best ideas for using capital and labor, or more precisely, to those who can produce the highest rate of return on borrowed dollars.

The first condition is met when the before-tax rates of return on investment in all real assets (of equal risk) are the same. In a world with efficient tax and loan markets, competition would induce this result by encouraging investors to increase their investment in any asset that temporarily has a higher rate of return than other investments. When taxes are imposed, therefore, for each investor the same tax rate must apply to economic returns from any real investment.[1] If the taxes are imposed in a nonuniform manner, the taxpayer may not invest in the asset with the highest social rate of return, as tax savings may more than compensate for purchasing a less productive asset and receiving a lower before-tax return. Note that this first condition does not imply that the

1. See the appendix to this chapter for a mathematical representation.

tax rate faced by each investor must be the same as that faced by other investors.

While this first condition for efficient taxation is commonly stated in much public finance literature, I will add to it a second condition that is less well known or is commonly misinterpreted. Efficiency in the loanable funds market requires that, for each investor in competitive equilibrium, the after-tax rate of return on investing in interest-bearing assets must equal the after-tax rate of return for investing in real assets (of equal risk, marketability, and so on). This rule helps ensure that loans are available to those who can best use them. In effect, regardless of tax bracket, if a person can produce before-tax returns in excess of the interest rate, that person should be able to compete for loans without being subject to discriminatory tax or lending rules.

The second condition is stated in a way slightly different from the first. Social efficiency requires that the before-tax rate of return on real assets (again, of equal risk) be the same. Under certain hypothetical conditions, such efficiency may not require that the interest rate—a measure of payments between borrowers and lenders—be equal to the before-tax rate of return on real assets. Nonetheless, for each taxpayer the after-tax rate of interest must equal the after-tax rate of return on other assets, or else some taxpayers would not efficiently decide between direct investments in real assets or making loanable funds available to others. The fact that the before-tax interest rate differs from the before-tax rate of return on real assets does not by itself affect the efficiency of real investment. In effect, while the after-tax interest rate affects the price of borrowing, aggregate income is not influenced by the level of the before-tax interest rate. Total private interest payments equal total private interest receipts, and the level of real output (although not necessarily the distribution of its proceeds) need not be changed by the amount of interest payments per se. This last point is somewhat technical and will eventually be shown to have only limited relevance. It is an argument, however, that can be used to support flatter-rate tax structures, as will be discussed below.

One can construct a world in which the second efficiency condition is unnecessary. In such a world, knowledge of ideas and technological advances would be freely accessible to all, and opportunities would be equally recognized by all. As a corollary, there would be no need for the establishment of new businesses or for entrepreneurs to take advantage of opportunities not recognized by others. Employees would not need to change jobs because their abilities were underutilized. Also assumed would be no social benefits from diffuse ownership of different forms of capital, and no costs to unnecessary transactions such as redistributions of asset ownership induced by efforts to minimize taxes. Under those conditions, efficiency in the loan markets would be unnecessary, or at least less necessary, for an economy to achieve efficiency of investment. By the same token, if it does not matter who invests, and one can be assured that investment would always be directed to its best use, the loan markets themselves would, in a sense, be unnecessary.[2] The extreme nature of these assumptions shows why an efficient economy requires a well-functioning loan market.

Just as an economy may respond to an inefficient monetary policy through the creation of money equivalents, so it may respond in part to an inefficient loanable funds market through alternative devices such as lease agreements and management positions for persons who would otherwise be independent entrepreneurs. These compensating mechanisms are incomplete, however, and those who otherwise could make best use of loans or real capital will still have significantly less access to and control of the particular resources they need.

I will now proceed to examine various tax proposals in light of these efficiency conditions. As will be shown, theoretically there are several ways in which these conditions can be made to hold and, therefore, there are several types of tax design that would improve the efficiency of both the real and financial asset markets.

Broader-Base, Lower-Rate Income Taxes

One group of tax proposals enhances the efficiency of the real and financial capital markets essentially by providing more uniform taxation of all income from capital under a progressive rate schedule. Falling in this category of proposals are many with labels such as "broad-base income tax" and "comprehensive income tax." These proposals are designed to broaden the tax base through elimination of rules allowing

2. The quality of performance in the financial sector and the effect of monetary policy would also be of no importance in a world with complete financial markets and no information or transactional costs. See Ben S. Bernanke, "Nonmonetary Effects of the Financial Crisis in the Propagation of the Great Depression," *American Economic Review*, vol. 73 (June 1983), p. 263.

for differential tax treatment of various types of income. Tax preferences, including deferrals and exclusions of income from certain sources of capital, would be discarded; by the same token, partial or full integration of corporate and personal income taxes would reduce disparities between corporate income and other income from capital and between retained corporate income and corporate income paid out as dividends. At the same time, lower rates would offset any net expansion of the tax base. In many revenue-neutral proposals, the distribution of tax burdens among income classes would be kept the same. Within classes, however, those who made the best use of existing preferences and paid the least tax would take advantage of tax incentives and would pay more tax, and those who paid the most taxes would benefit from tax decreases.

If the reform is truly comprehensive, for each individual all income from capital would be subject to the same tax rate.[3] The broader base would improve the allocation of capital by directing saving to its most efficient use rather than favoring some forms of capital or some sectors of the economy over others. Even when the reform is not fully comprehensive and some differentials are retained, lower tax rates would still improve efficiency by reducing the value of a tax-preferred asset relative to an asset that is not preferred. Since lower tax rates automatically reduce the wedge between before-tax returns and after-tax returns for fully taxed assets, such assets become more competitive with tax-preferred securities. By the same token, base broadening—even in the absence of lower rates—would reduce disparities, especially between nontaxed items currently excluded from the tax base and currently taxable items.

One seldom-noted, but important, aspect of broader-base, lower-rate tax proposals is the way in which they address the interest deduction and the tax arbitrage problems. Even in the absence of indexing for interest income, a reduction of tax rates would at the same time reduce the tax subsidy for borrowing or making interest payments. Meanwhile, preferences on many assets would be eliminated. Both these changes would move the tax rate applying to interest income closer to the rate on other forms of income from capital.

Although the extent of potential reductions in the tax rate depends on the degree of base broadening, even modest efforts toward a broader base could represent an improvement in current law. More uniform and

---

3. See the mathematical expression for this in the appendix to this chapter.

comprehensive inclusion of capital income in the tax base, offset by a reduction in the corporate tax rate, would be likely to make more uniform the treatment of all income from capital and reduce many of the inefficiencies and problems discussed throughout this book. Similarly, removing exclusions of certain forms of labor income, such as employer payments of health premiums on behalf of employees, would move in the direction of uniform treatment of capital income if the revenues were used to finance a rate reduction for all forms of income.

One objection to broader-base, lower-rate proposals comes from those who fear that the broader base may increase taxes on income from capital more than they are reduced through lower rates. In a revenue-neutral proposal, for instance, much of the rate reduction could apply to wages and salaries, as opposed to income from capital. Whether capital income faces a higher average rate of tax depends on the exact nature of the proposal and on the particular tax preferences or penalties elimi-nated—on capital or labor—in order to better measure the tax base.

There are reasons to discount the worth of this objection. First, it often leads to the types of "saving incentives" provisions that exist today—provisions that are of such poor design that they cost revenue, create a number of inefficiencies and distortions, and at the same time have an uncertain effect on the total amount of savings. Second, if one believes that saving is highly responsive to tax rates, the reform proposal can always be designed to ensure that at least a proportionate share of base broadening occurs with respect to labor income and that the taxation of capital income is not increased. Indeed, a truly comprehensive income tax would involve several reductions in tax on income from capital, such as indexation of the base by which depreciation is measured and elimination of the double tax on corporate income paid as dividends.

A more uniform definition of the tax base, accompanied by a flatter tax-rate schedule, would have mixed results in terms of simplicity. On the one hand, flatter rates would decrease the need for, and reduce the use of, provisions such as income averaging, deductions for a second wage earner, and other provisions designed to compensate for unin-tended effects of a progressive rate schedule. At the same time, base broadening would allow elimination of alternative minimum taxes, limitations on tax credits, and other provisions designed to compensate for the failure to define income comprehensively. On the other hand, base broadening would require a more elaborate depreciation schedule, and many fringe benefits would need to be evaluated for tax purposes.

A number of problems also remain in measuring capital income, such as determining when the deferral of business receipts should increase the current measure of taxable income.

Although broader-base, lower-rate taxes would bring about a substantial improvement in efficiency, such taxes are challenged or supported primarily on the basis of equity. It is often difficult, however, to lower taxes for some persons who do not really expect such reductions, while raising taxes for others who take maximum advantage of existing tax preferences. Because tax preferences really redistribute greater shares of the total tax burden to those more ignorant of complex tax rules, traditional tax reform often increases shares of tax burdens for those who understand the changes, and decreases shares for those who are least cognizant of the benefits they receive.

Flat-Rate Taxes

Some broader-base, lower-rate tax proposals call themselves "flat taxes" while maintaining progressive, rather than flat, rate schedules.[4] The reason that the label is adopted is partly because the term *flat tax* became temporarily popular in the early 1980s and partly because the proposals do envision flatter-rate schedules. Other proposals, while actually designed to be a type of consumption tax, have also been labeled flat tax because they envision a single, flat-rate tax rate on much of the taxable base.[5]

This discussion is limited to flat-rate tax proposals that truly attempt to impose a flat rate of tax on income. Suppose first that a pure flat-rate tax system could be designed. It would clearly meet the efficiency conditions defined above by providing uniform treatment of different

4. See, for instance, *The Treasury Department Report to the President, Tax Reform for Fairness, Simplicity, and Economic Growth* (U.S. Government Printing Office, 1984); and bills proposed by Sen. Bill Bradley, Democrat of New Jersey; Rep. Richard A. Gephardt, Democrat of Missouri; and by Rep. Jack Kemp, Republican of New York, and Sen. Bob Kasten, Republican of Wisconsin.

5. See, for instance, Robert E. Hall and Alan Rabushka, *Low Tax, Simple Tax, Flat Tax* (McGraw-Hill, 1983); and Hall and Rabushka, *The Flat Tax* (Hoover Institution Press, 1985). Hall and Rabushka do obtain some progressivity via a low-income exemption on wage income. Their proposed tax might even be viewed as an "unusual form of value-added tax." See George N. Carlson and Charles E. McLure, Jr., "Pros and Cons of Alternative Approaches to the Taxation of Consumption," paper prepared for the 1984 annual meeting of the National Tax Association.

forms of capital income for each taxpayer. Each taxpayer would face equal tax rates on the real returns from all real assets because there is only one tax rate for all returns. In addition, after-tax rates of return would be the same for both interest and returns from real assets because the tax rate on each would be the same. Competition would influence the before-tax returns for assets of equal risk. Thus, as for uniformity of treatment of different types of capital income, there is no doubt that a pure flat-rate tax would meet that objective.

Second, assume that one assumption about the purity of the flat tax is relaxed. Suppose that the same flat-rate tax can be imposed in a closed economy on all real income with one exception: interest payments and receipts continue to be included in the tax base in nominal terms. If the flat-rate tax is otherwise pure, there need be no efficiency loss. Interest rates would rise relative to the stated return from other assets until the point that the after-tax interest rate equaled the after-tax rate of return on those other assets. Note, however, that the second efficiency condition is still met. Because the after-tax rate of return is the same for all assets and all persons, there is no incentive for some taxpayers to borrow to purchase real assets of equal risk, nor for other taxpayers to avoid purchase of those assets because the interest rate has been bid upward or other rates have been bid downward relative to the interest rate.

This argument can be restated in terms of the model of normal tax arbitrage. Borrowing to purchase (relatively) preferred real assets generates no tax savings to be shared between borrower and lender. The tax reduction on the interest payment will be equal to the tax paid on the interest receipt. Regardless of the amount of borrowing that takes place, the total amount of taxes collected on income from capital will not be affected. (Here it is assumed, of course, that no pure tax arbitrage is possible.) No excess amount of normal tax arbitrage would be encouraged in such a world.[6]

In the absence of indexing of interest income for inflation, therefore, an otherwise pure, flat-rate tax is superior to an otherwise pure, broad-base, progressive tax by the previously defined efficiency criteria. Although both taxes may establish equal after-tax rates of return on noninterest-bearing assets—the first criterion—only a pure, flat-rate tax eliminates tax arbitrage and thereby meets the second efficiency criterion of setting equal after-tax rates of return for interest-bearing and non-

6. In a graphical presentation such as figure 5–1, the nominal after-tax structure and the effective after-tax structure would be the same.

interest-bearing assets of each taxpayer. At first this may appear to be a powerful argument in the favor of the flat-rate tax. There are several related difficulties with this argument, however.

First, the comparison is unfair because a pure (nonflat rate), broad-base tax would require the indexing of all income, including interest, for inflation. It is the absence of correct measurement of all income, including interest payments and receipts, not the inherent superiority of a flat tax, that weakens the case for a progressive tax.

Second, it is unrealistic to assume that a flat-rate tax could ever be imposed on all real noninterest income of all persons. There will always be numerous foreigners and tax-exempt institutions that are given zero tax rates. Moreover, there has never been any serious consideration of imposing a flat-rate tax without allowing for a zero tax rate for the first few thousand dollars of income. Thus all realistic flat rate proposals are in fact progressive to some degree.

With zero-rate taxpayers, particularly foreign investors, financial arbitrage may prevent interest rates from rising, or rates of return on preferred assets from falling, to compensate for relatively greater rates of taxation on interest income. In addition, in a tax system based upon recognition, many taxpayers subject to positive rates can engage in financial arbitrage by recognizing losses and taking deductions for payments, while deferring recognition of accruals of income and other positive receipts. As is discussed in the next section, the recognition principle has resulted indirectly in the indexing of the returns from most real assets. In essence, both a progressive tax and a flat-rate tax need indexing of interest so that all income from capital is measured on a more equal real basis. Or both need accrual accounting so that all income from capital is measured uniformly on the same nominal basis.[7] In the absence of indexing of interest or accrual accounting of other capital income, the conflict between tax arbitrage and financial arbitrage cannot be avoided by turning to a flat-rate tax.

Administrative Simplicity

Imposing a flat-rate tax on income would have some administrative advantages over other types of income taxes. In particular, some income

7. Presumably if income from capital were measured on a nominal basis in a period of inflation, there would be some adjustment in the aggregate capital income measure (or in the tax rate) to avoid taxation of the inflationary component. Otherwise, tremendous amounts of purely inflationary gain would be subject to tax (see chapter 2).

could be taxed at the source rather than at the level of the taxpayer. If the same amount of tax were owed on income regardless of the recipient, no accounting would be required by those recipients for whom tax has already been collected at the source. Recipients of income would find that their "withheld tax" would equal exactly their tax liability on that income. As an aside, this is one of the arguments used to support the notion that tax returns could be reduced to postcard size.[8]

The issue of administrative simplicity, however, cannot be carried too far. Once one allows for zero tax rates for the first dollars of income received, or for the income of some tax-exempt foreigners and domestic institutions, accounting is again required by many taxpayers. There are compromises that can be made, but only at a cost. For instance, some proposals would essentially disallow the use of personal exemptions and zero bracket amounts to offset anything but wage income. These proposals essentially distinguish taxpayers by the sources, rather than the amount, of their income.

Progressivity

Despite these arguments with respect to both the uniform treatment of income and simplicity of the tax system, the principal debate about flat-rate taxes centers on the issue of progressivity. There is no doubt that progressivity introduces some complexity to the tax system, but the problem is often overstated. The principal question is whether society wants to maintain progressivity. Treasury Department testimony shows the type of redistribution of tax burdens resulting from the adoption of a tax that is flat except for a standard deduction and a personal exemption for the first dollars of income (see table 12-1).[9]

Under the flat-rate tax system shown in table 12-1, there are substantial tax increases in lower income classes and large tax decreases in the highest income classes. Some increases in tax burdens at the bottom can be mitigated by the allowance of zero tax rates on more dollars of income, as are achieved with higher levels of personal exemptions. Even then, there would be substantial tax reductions for upper-income taxpayers and tax increases for middle-income taxpayers. As may be obvious, this

8. See Hall and Rabushka, *Low Tax, Simple Tax, Flat Tax.*

9. *Flat-Rate Tax,* Hearings before the Senate Committee on Finance, 97 Cong. 2 sess. (Government Printing Office, 1983), pt. 1, pp. 173–202.

Table 12-1. *Total Liability and Average Tax Rates under a Flat-Rate Income Tax, 1981*[a]

Uniform income class (dollars)	Tax under 1984 law[b]		Tax with a single flat rate of 16.27 percent		Change in tax	
	Amount (millions of dollars)	Percent of uniform income	Amount (millions of dollars)	Percent of uniform income	Amount (millions of dollars)	Percent change from present law
Less than 0	3,507	n.a.	. . .	0.0	−3,507	−100.0
0–5,000	1,775	2.9	3,080	5.0	1,305	73.5
5,000–10,000	8,200	5.0	15,402	9.4	7,202	87.8
10,000–15,000	14,611	7.2	22,563	11.2	7,952	54.4
15,000–20,000	19,754	9.4	25,792	12.2	6,038	30.6
20,000–30,000	48,208	10.9	57,444	13.0	9,236	19.2
30,000–50,000	76,339	13.0	80,574	13.7	4,235	5.5
50,000–100,000	47,068	18.1	37,557	14.5	−9,511	−20.2
100,000–200,000	23,874	25.5	14,282	15.3	−9,592	−40.2
200,000 or more	25,223	33.6	11,908	15.8	−13,315	−52.8
Total	268,558	13.0	268,602	13.0	44	0.0

Source: *Flat-Rate Tax*, Hearings before the Senate Committee on Finance, 97 Cong. 2 sess. (U.S. Government Printing Office, 1983), pt. 1, p. 198.

a. Assumes a $3,000 deduction per joint return ($2,000 per single return), with a $1,000 exemption per dependent.

b. Includes the attributable share of the corporation income tax.

type of redistribution is favored more by potential gainers than potential losers.

Indexing   *Taking out the effects of inflation*

Indexing of capital income for inflation under the income tax is often ignored in many proposals for tax reform. Yet indexing moves toward uniform treatment by making the tax system more impervious to inflation and to the nonuniform or differential treatment of assets that inflation otherwise causes.

Many existing preferences for capital income either have been adopted as crude forms of indexing or have had the effect, whether intended or not, of reducing or eliminating the tendency for inflation to change real effective tax rates among assets. Although such ad hoc indexing operates in an imperfect, uneven, and haphazard way, distinctions can be drawn between those assets that are shielded from inflation, in whole or in part, and those that are completely exposed.

Income from depreciable assets has had a form of ad hoc indexing through various provisions enacted over the past thirty years to accelerate depreciation or capital recovery, in addition to the investment tax credit. For long-term capital gains, deferral has always been allowed and exclusions have been granted for 50 percent, then for 60 percent, of realized gains, and for 100 percent of gains realized at the death of a transferor. At a 100 percent exclusion rate, of course, the indexing is perfect in the sense that there is no change in taxable income due to inflation. For sales of inventory, the last-in, first-out method of accounting (LIFO) allows profits on sales of inventory to be realized only for the difference between the selling price of the good and the most recent purchase price of a similar good; in effect, LIFO provides a means of indexing or deferring inflationary gains on sales of inventory of a stable or growing firm. Returns from housing and durable consumer goods are not subject to income tax and, therefore, their zero tax rate is unaffected by inflation. As for dividends, if a corporation earns the same real return on its assets and retains the same amount of real income, its dividend rate will be unaffected by inflation. In contrast, among sources of capital income, interest stands out as the most exposed to the effects of inflation; and the higher the inflation rate, the more the interest rate is misstated. The same degree of error applies to both lenders and borrowers.

In one sense, basing the tax system on realizations has been the principal means through which such ad hoc indexing has been provided. Most of the increase in the nominal income from capital in an inflationary period is reflected in accruals of inflationary gains in the value of land, real estate, and corporate stock. Most of these returns are never recognized for tax purposes, and of those that are, the value of deferral significantly reduces any inflation tax.[10] Once statutory adjustments compensated crudely for inflation's effect on the measures of depreciation, inventory change, and realized gains, the interest receipts and payments were left as the only major form of income for which there was no form of indexation.

In these circumstances, two changes in the existing system of ad hoc indexation meet the efficiency conditions. First, improvements could be made in the indexing of particular forms of income. For instance, the current method of accelerated depreciation could be replaced with an inflation adjustment of the depreciable basis of assets. Such a change would restore neutrality among depreciable assets, eliminate much of

10. In the case of corporate stock, the issue is more complex. While the recognition system also defers or excludes tax on individuals' capital gains due to corporate retentions of real retained earnings, those retentions are already subject to a corporate tax.

the existing bias against new business, and reduce the need for complex mergers and leasing agreements. The tax rate on equity investments in depreciable capital would not vary with the rate of inflation. The advantage of many tax shelters would be reduced as immediate deductions became less available.

Second, some change could be made in accounting for interest payments and receipts. So many of the problems of tax arbitrage discussed in this book result from the difference between the tax treatment of interest income and the treatment of income from most other assets. If real or ad hoc indexing is to apply to the income from these other assets, it must also apply to interest income. At a minimum, limits must be placed on tax arbitrage opportunities created in large part by this indexing differential. Partial or full indexing of interest income or even more limited approaches could reduce significantly the existing tendency toward asset shift and limit the tax-induced tendency for some taxpayers to borrow, invest in tax-preferred assets, and not provide loans to others. Similarly, indexing would help eliminate some of the barriers to entry for many new businesses by making their after-tax cost of funds more equal with the cost faced by established businesses. Other advantages are that persons in low-income brackets would become more competitive in purchasing farms and small businesses; existing savings incentives, if maintained, would at least become more efficient; and so forth.

*more equitable —
more closer to
real income level*

Other Indexing Issues

In addition to the uniformity of treatment of capital income, three other issues are important to the discussion of indexing. First, the fairness or equity of the tax system is clearly improved as the tax base is moved closer to a measure of real income. Taxing persons with 5 percent passbook interest rates in a period of 10 percent inflation, for instance, can hardly meet anyone's standard of fairness. By the same token, few would argue that a fair system would be one in which the effective tax rate declined as leverage increased. These inequities are compounded when financial arbitrage or institutional rules prevent implicit compensation for high tax rates on interest from being provided through higher relative interest rates.

Second, while indexing of interest would eliminate the bias against lending, it would also eliminate much of the favorable treatment given to borrowers. Because the nonreal or inflationary component of the interest rate is deducted from taxable income, some observers might favor retention of an unindexed measure of interest as an indirect means of subsidizing investment financed by borrowing. The analysis in this book of savings incentives, as well as of the fungibility of loans, certainly calls into question whether subsidization of borrowing is a spur, much less an efficient spur, to investment. Even if it were, any reduction in the rate of inflation would tend to eliminate the subsidy just as surely as would indexing of the interest rate. It is inconsistent to oppose elimination of this particular subsidy only when it is done directly rather than hidden in some other policy, such as a monetary policy designed to reduce the rate of inflation.

The third issue is, can an administrable system for indexing capital income can be achieved? If the system were to be completely accurate, the answer would probably be no. Accounting, however, is at best an imprecise science. Measures of depreciation rates, for instance, will always be subject to large errors, but no one seriously suggests that the measure of income would be improved through elimination of all depreciation or cost-recovery deductions for purchases of depreciable capital. Neither can the inaccuracy of the depreciation measure be a reason for allowing the real value of that measure to vary so much with the rate of inflation.

The same claim can be made with respect to indexing for other forms of income. In the case of interest income, completely accurate indexing would technically require knowledge of the rate of inflation between the starting date and ending date during which each interest-bearing asset was held by each lender and each corresponding liability was held by the borrower. There are millions of transactions daily involving interest-bearing assets and liabilities. It would be impossible to make separate price adjustments for all these transactions, including loans taken out with credit-card purchases and payments made with interest-bearing checking accounts.

It is possible, however, to provide a system in which indexing could be applied more accurately to all income flows. For instance, interest payments and receipts could be deducted or included only on a fractional basis, with the same fractional rate applying to all interest. Thus if a rate of 20 percent were applied, taxpayers would include only 80 percent of interest receipts in gross income and would be allowed to deduct only 80 percent of interest payments. If necessary, an exemption could be made for interest payments of a modest amount so that only individuals who pay large amounts of interest would be affected.

Limitations on Artificial Losses

In the absence of indexing for interest payments and depreciation, it would be more crucial that the tax law contain various mechanisms to limit deductions for artificial losses when real economic gains are likely to have occurred. Interest payments would remain overstated relative to returns from most assets. Depreciation allowances would remain accelerated if investment in depreciable capital were not to be overtaxed because of understated depreciation allowances. The presence of overstated expenses, especially in the early years of investment, would in turn imply that the tax-shelter problem would remain significant.

Various techniques could be used to limit artificial losses. First, there could be a significant expansion of the restriction in current law limiting interest income used to finance certain investment and consumer good expenses.[11] Because the interest used for mortgages, businesses, farms, real estate, and partnerships is not counted in the calculation, the existing limitation has little practical impact. If the fungibility of money were recognized, and all interest payments were limited relative to recognized income from business and capital, a much greater amount of tax arbitrage could be restricted.[12] Second, if partnerships had limited liability and were sold through public offerings, or reached a certain size, they could be required to pay taxes as corporations. (Recall that corporations cannot pass through net losses to individuals.) Third, interest deductions could be limited to the amount of income that is deferred or received tax-free through pension and insurance accounts. These and similar

11. For a further discussion of some issues surrounding limitations on interest deductions see *Symposium: Canadian and American Perspectives on the Deduction for Interest Payments*, special edition, *Wayne Law Review*, vol. 30 (Spring 1984). Because of the fungibility of money, I have generally opposed more narrow attempts to limit deductions for mortgage or consumer interest deductions here.

12. Richard Goode has suggested that all property income and interest payments be pooled and that interest payments be deductible only up to the amount of receipts of income from property. See Richard Goode, *The Individual Income Tax* (Brookings, 1976), pp. 148–52. His primary concern seems to be with itemized interest deductions taken by individuals receiving nontaxable income from owner-occupied housing and durables. It is only logical, however, to extend that idea to a world in which there is rapid growth in the number of tax shelters that produce large negative amounts of taxable income.

types of limitations become much more crucial the further that the measure of taxable income is allowed to deviate from economic income.

Comprehensive Expenditure Taxes

A comprehensive expenditure tax may be thought by many to be the antithesis of a broad-base income tax.[13] In terms of the efficiency conditions defined above, however, both taxes operate in much the same way. A comprehensive income tax moves toward uniform treatment of all income by providing uniform treatment of income for each taxpayer, no matter what the source. A comprehensive expenditure tax achieves uniformity but in a different way. Since ideally all forms of consumption are subject to tax, the source of funds for consumption does not affect its taxability. Most important, there is a full deduction from the tax base for all saving. Thus savings are treated uniformly; neither the source of the saving nor the type of investment financed by the saving will directly affect the tax rate.

The deduction for saving applies throughout the tax system. The corporate income tax is effectively repealed. Only withdrawals from an account or from a corporate or noncorporate business add to the tax base of the individual; these withdrawals, obviously, may be offset by redeposits (savings) elsewhere.

In discussions of both tax arbitrage and saving incentives, it was noted that many problems could be solved if there were reciprocal treatment of interest receipts and payments, or lending and borrowing. A comprehensive income tax tackles this issue by looking to see where receipts are understated because of exclusions and where payments are overstated because of inflation. A comprehensive consumption tax, on the

13. Among the many articles examining the expenditure or consumption tax are the following: Nicholas Kaldor, *An Expenditure Tax* (London: Allen and Unwin, 1955); William D. Andrews, "A Consumption-Type or Cash Flow Personal Income Tax," *Harvard Law Review*, vol. 87 (April 1974), pp. 1113–88; U.S. Treasury Department, *Blueprints for Basic Tax Reform* (GPO, 1977); *The Structure and Reform of Direct Taxation*, report of a committee chaired by J. E. Meade for the Institute for Fiscal Studies (London: Allen and Unwin, 1978); Michael J. Graetz, "Expenditure Tax Design," in Joseph A. Pechman, ed., *What Should be Taxed: Income or Expenditure?* (Brookings, 1980), pp. 75–113; and David F. Bradford, "The Possibilities for an Expenditure Tax," *National Tax Journal*, vol. 35 (September 1982), pp. 243–51.

(consumption tax)

Sales

tax

arbitrage

problem

other hand, treats borrowing as negative lending. Each dollar borrowed by the taxpayer adds a dollar to the taxable base.[14]

Both normal and pure tax arbitrage problems are thus solved. A dollar borrowed to purchase an asset will involve zero net saving and will be treated by the tax system as no change in the tax base. (The dollar saved will be offset by the dollar dissaved.) Although there is quite generous treatment of investment and saving, that benefit cannot be increased through higher ratios of debt to equity.

One way to understand the workings of an expenditure tax is to recognize that, under certain assumptions, an expenditure tax is equivalent to a zero rate of tax on all income from capital and a tax on labor income only. It is the zero uniform rate of tax on income from capital that effectively allows a comprehensive expenditure tax to meet the criteria for efficiency. Just as in a pure, flat-rate tax, the tax rate is the same for the real returns from all assets and for the real return from interest. In this case, however, it does not matter for tax purposes whether the income is measured properly since the same effective zero tax rate applies regardless of the measure used.

Administrability of an Expenditure Tax

(Cons. tax — easy to administer)

Many supporters of an expenditure tax favor it on grounds of simplicity or administration. The argument is that rules regarding depreciation, corporate taxes, capital gains, indexing, and so forth are not required. Only withdrawals from accounts or businesses need to be added to the tax base, so it does not matter to what extent income is accruing or depreciating in those accounts. An effective zero rate of tax applies in any case. The argument is only partly correct, however, because simplicity in one area is paid for by additional complexity elsewhere.

One reason is that, although accounting for income becomes unnecessary for tax purposes, it is still desired and required for most financial purposes. Thus tax authorities may not need to worry about the accuracy of income accounts, but businesses and corporations still need to assess the success of their business through income measurement. Stockholders, for instance, would not be indifferent to whether dividends are paid out of current income or out of capital even though the tax treatment of

14. Alternatively payments on loans may be treated as consumption in special circumstances.

those distributions would be the same; bank regulators would not be indifferent to whether there is a positive or negative flow of income in banks; and so forth. Rather than attempt to improve an existing accounting system, an expenditure tax would require the development of an additional accounting system for federal income tax purposes only.

A second reason that complexity remains is that income accounting, even for tax purposes, would still be required by foreign governments and state and local governments that maintain income taxes. Even assuming that a change was also desirable in these cases as well, many nonfederal laws would have to be modified and the entire international tax treaty structure would have to be revamped. For many governments, a change to a consumption-base tax would mean abandonment of income taxation of foreign-owned companies that operate in their jurisdictions, yet repatriate earnings to be consumed abroad.

A third and perhaps the most important reason is that an expenditure tax requires comprehensive and detailed wealth accounting or, more precisely, accounting for transactions in wealth accounts.[15] All or almost all savings must effectively be required to fall within registered accounts or businesses. Otherwise a taxpayer could change assets from unregistered to registered accounts and be measured as increasing net saving when no saving has taken place. Income in those accounts does not have to be measured for tax purposes, but all transactions into and out of the accounts must be reported to the government.

Actually the requirement for more elaborate wealth accounting is in many ways common to both an effective income tax and an effective expenditure tax. In the case of the income tax, gaming is easily achieved when many items of income (from wealth) fall outside the accounting of the tax system. With a good system of wealth accounting, such gaming could be restricted, and it would be much easier to approximate income from wealth and to tax that income when there was little relation between real economic income and cash flow. In the expenditure tax, too, it is the placement of most assets in registered accounts that allows for uniform measurement and elimination of much gaming. Thus one should

15. This wealth accounting is necessary to measure not only net saving but also transfers to other generations. See the discussion below. Also see Eugene Steuerle, "Equity and the Taxation of Wealth Transfers," *Tax Notes*, vol. 11 (September 8, 1980), pp. 459–64; and Henry J. Aaron and Harvey Galper, "Reforming the Tax System," in Alice M. Rivlin, ed., *Economic Choices, 1984* (Brookings, 1984), pp. 87–117.

not view entirely negatively the more elaborate accounting of wealth transactions required by an expenditure tax. With all wealth in wealth accounts generating information reports to the government, both systems could be made to function more effectively.

One way to reduce the complexity of recording transactions in an expenditure tax is to allow a prepayment of taxes for some or all investments. In this scheme savings are initially taxed, but then all consumption out of earnings or depletion of those savings goes tax-free. The difficulty here is that any person who is able to achieve a higher-than-normal rate of return on savings (a common reality, but one ignored in most models of expenditure taxes) would pay substantially lower tax rates on consumption. The prepaid option is often best confined to certain consumer durable and housing purchases.

Other Issues

transition problem

There is a major transition problem in changing tax accounting systems. If consumption out of existing wealth is taxed, many persons who have paid income tax on past earnings would be taxed again when those earnings are consumed. Some would argue that the transition problem can be mitigated by excluding consumption out of existing wealth. In the extreme, however, that would imply that trillions of dollars of consumption by existing holders of wealth could go tax-free. For wealthy families a tax on expenditures might not be assessed for generations.

The proposal for comprehensive expenditure taxes, like all previously discussed proposals for tax reform, is debated primarily on the basis of equity. In this regard, two issues stand out. First, advocates of the expenditure tax argue that it is unfair to impose different (present value of) taxes on those with equal wages but different saving patterns. For example, these advocates state that a person who earns $10 today, earns $1 in interest, and consumes $11 tomorrow, should pay no more tax than another person who earns and consumes $10 today. This is a variation on the "double tax" argument that a dollar saved is first taxed when earned and then taxed again when it generates additional earnings.

Second, if people are to be taxed equally on the basis of lifetime endowments but regardless of when they actually consume, unconsumed endowments—that is, those transferred to other tax units—should not be allowed to escape taxation. In the same vein, there is a question of

cons. tax
1)
favors saving

lifetime horizon — have to make sure you include gifts & bequests.

whether large accumulators of wealth should be allowed to go essentially tax-free, as would occur under many proposals for an expenditure tax. That problem can be mitigated if transfers to other generations are made subject to tax, but again, a good administrative system is needed. All transfers out of accounts must be checked to ascertain if they are transfers to others. If so, the recipients cannot be allowed to treat them as additions to saving, while the transferors must be taxed on the transfers as if they were consumption.

Another important issue relates to what would happen to saving and capital formation. A consumption tax would clearly lower the tax rate on income from capital, although some or all of that decrease could be offset by a tax on wealth transfers.[16] Whether this change would result in a net increase in saving is uncertain.[17]

Other issues relate to a proposed expenditure tax. Persons would pay their greatest tax when they withdrew funds to pay for education or other large expenditures, expected or unexpected. A withholding system on withdrawals from accounts would need to be set up, but its accuracy— given the frequency of deposits and withdrawals from accounts—would not be great. Serious compliance problems could develop with respect to transactions in foreign accounts. These and similar problems are obviously weighted differently by the proponents and opponents of an expenditure tax.

Reductions in Tax Rates

Simple reduction of tax rates, as exemplified by the tax cuts enacted in 1981, is another proposed reform of the tax system. Reductions of tax rates, however, are seldom advocated or discussed on the basis of the efficiency conditions defined above. If disparities in tax rates among different types of income were the problem being tackled, rate reduction

16. If the tax rate on capital is to be reduced to zero, an expenditure tax is clearly preferred to a zero tax on flows of capital income. It is difficult to distinguish between income from capital and income from labor, especially for many small non-corporate businesses. By only subjecting withdrawals from businesses to taxation, an expenditure tax neatly gets around this administrative problem.

17. For a recent discussion of this issue see Joseph J. Minarik, "Income Versus Expenditure Taxation to Reduce the Deficit," *Tax Notes*, vol. 22 (March 19, 1984), pp. 1257–62.

proposals would quickly be expanded to include base broadening and the further rate reductions made possible by such broadening.

Regardless of intention, rate reductions do reduce disparities among assets by reducing the *range* of tax rates. This influence was mentioned in the discussion of broader-base, lower-rate tax proposals. In addition, rate reduction is an efficient means of providing saving incentives. It reduces asset shift, provides incentives at the margin, and by applying to both receipts and deductions, cuts back the advantages of tax arbitrage.

In the absence of an indexed system, another aspect of rate reductions makes them even better at reducing the advantages of tax arbitrage than is commonly recognized. The percentage reduction in the tax rate on the real component of interest income is much larger than the percentage reduction in statutory tax rates. That is, in an inflationary economy in which interest rates rise with inflation, a reduction in tax rates provides a much greater percentage reduction in the tax on real interest income than it does in the tax on real wages or on the real return from partially taxable assets. For instance, suppose inflation is 7 percent and the interest rate is 12 percent. A reduction in a taxpayer's marginal tax rate from 33 percent to 25 percent will initially increase the real after-tax rate of return for holding interest-bearing assets by 100 percent. (An increase from 8 percent to 9 percent in the nominal after-tax yield is equal to an increase from 1 percent to 2 percent in the real after-tax yield.) The rate reduction will increase the after-tax wages by only 12 percent (from 67 cents to 75 cents for each additional dollar earned).

Value-added and Other Excise Taxes

Value-added taxes, national sales taxes, and selective excise taxes do not really fall into the list of comprehensive proposals that move toward more uniform taxation of capital income in the process of reforming the tax structure. Logically, however, these taxes can be viewed as mechanisms through which a reduction in income tax rates, or the avoidance of increases in such rates, is attained. Under a given revenue constraint, the greater the amount of revenues collected through such consumption-based taxes, the smaller is the amount that likely would be collected through personal or corporate income taxation.

All taxes by their very nature must be considered distorting: their justification is the public goods or expenditures that are financed. The choice between income taxation and consumption taxation is a choice between distortions that should be allowed. Many who view income taxation favorably may still prefer adoption of a value-added tax to an increase in income tax rates. Some who favor value-added taxation stand to benefit from current distortions in the income tax and do not want to see more uniform taxation of various sources of income, regardless of the rates that would apply. In the context of this book, however, value-added taxes and other excise taxes can best be viewed as devices to attain or maintain lower income tax rates.

Incentives

Direct rate reductions are often advocated on the basis of supply-side incentives or as a means of reducing the size of the government. As supply-side incentives, they are most effective—that is, they achieve maximum reduction in average marginal rates for the least cost—when the majority of the revenue loss is used to reduce the top rates of tax in the rate schedules. The lower the tax rate that is reduced, the more likely it is to be inframarginal for affected taxpayers. As an example, reduction of the bottom tax rate from 11 percent to 10 percent provides average tax reductions not only to those whose marginal rate is 11 percent, but also to the majority of taxpayers who have higher marginal rates. The majority is unaffected at the margin by this change. A reduction of the top rate of 50 percent, on the other hand, achieves a marginal reduction for all taxpayers who obtain some average tax reduction. The most effective rate reduction from a supply-side viewpoint is one that is an regressive as possible—with marginal tax rates reducing to zero percent in the top brackets.[18] One of the primary arguments against tax cuts with unbalanced supply-side orientation, therefore, is that they reduce progressivity.

A crucial issue is whether or not any tax reduction is offset by expenditure decreases. If not, a tax reduction today may be met by an even larger tax increase tomorrow. The rise in government debt and interest payments may actually cause average marginal tax rates, at least as measured over time, to increase rather than decrease.

As a generalization, persons who label themselves "supply-siders"

18. This is another way of saying that the ultimate supply-side income tax is a head tax that has no relation to the economic activity of the taxpayer.

are more likely to oppose increases in excise taxes, adoption of a value-added tax, or an increase in tax rates on labor income. There are, however, many who favor lower taxes on income from capital but who are more willing to finance government expenditures through a variety of other means. This latter group is also likely to stress the supply-side argument with respect to capital income but not labor income. In dealing with the problem of deficits, the two groups often split ranks.

Summary

Despite the seeming disparity among major proposals for tax reform—broad-base, lower-rate income taxes, flat-rate taxes, an indexed income tax, an expenditure tax, and reductions in tax rates—each proposal can and usually does provide a more uniform tax treatment of income from capital. None can therefore be totally discounted as unreasonable by those who favor alternative approaches to tax reform but are willing to consider ways to reduce some of the causes of the gross misallocation of the nation's capital.

Mathematical Representation of Efficiency Conditions for Taxation of Capital Income

SUPPOSE that there are two real assets, A and B, and two investors, x and y. Let t stand for marginal tax rate, and r denote rate of return. As long as the assets are not fixed in supply, an efficient economy requires that

(A-1) $$r_A = r_B.$$

In general, this cannot hold unless

(A-2) $$(1 - t_A^x)r_A = (1 - t_B^x)r_B; \qquad (1 - t_A^y)r_A = (1 - t_B^y)r_B.$$

This in turn implies the first condition:

(A-3) $$t_A^x = t_B^x; \qquad t_A^y = t_B^y.$$

Efficiency in the loanable funds market requires that, for each investor in competitive equilibrium, the after-tax rate of return on investing in interest-bearing assets must equal the after-tax rate of return for investing in real assets. If one denotes interest-bearing assets as I and the interest rate as i, this second condition can be written as

(A-4) $$(1 - t_I^x)i = (1 - t_A^x)r_A = (1 - t_B^x)r_B;$$
$$(1 - t_I^y)i = (1 - t_A^y)r_A = (1 - t_B^y)r_B.$$

What distinguishes this second condition from the first condition is that only real assets produce real output. Because i does not have to equal r (the interest rate does not represent the rate of return from a real asset), the combined requirement

(A-5) $$t_I^x = t_A^x = t_B^x; \qquad t_I^y = t_A^y = t_B^y$$

cannot yet be derived.

179

If a pure, flat-rate tax were imposed on income, it would be expressed as follows in terms of the two efficiency conditions:

(A-6) $$t_A^x = t_B^x = t_I^x = t_A^y = t_B^y = t_I^y.$$

If a broad-base or comprehensive income tax were used, it would be represented in the same way as equation A-3; if interest were indexed, the expression would be the same as that in equation A-5.

CHAPTER THIRTEEN

Other Prescriptions

MANY PRESCRIPTIONS for the economy, other than proposals for major tax reform, are not usually viewed as mechanisms to bring more uniform treatment of the economic income from capital. Yet a number of these prescriptions address the uniformity issue in one of several ways: by making loans available on a more uniform basis, by attempting to control inflation (and the nonuniform treatment that accompanies it), or by making financial markets impervious to the effects of inflation. By uniformity I refer to both equal tax treatment and to equal access to loan markets for investments of equal expected returns and equal risk but unequal measures of cash flow or financial income.

Additional Supplies of Loanable Funds

A major and frequently advocated financial prescription is to increase the supply of loanable funds to the private sector through a change in the mix of fiscal and monetary policy. The objective of such a policy is to lower deficits through a combination of higher taxes and lower expenditures, while monetary policy would accommodate the fiscal change by increasing, or at least keeping constant, the rate of money growth in the economy. The reduced deficit would decrease the public demand for private deposits, thus freeing the loanable funds to be borrowed by the business and household sectors.

While uniformity in the treatment of capital income is not a goal commonly associated with a policy of smaller deficits or less restrictive monetary policy, it is one important result. Lower interest rates are a likely result of such policies, and these rates reduce the after-tax differences in the cost of borrowing among taxpayers: competition among businesses becomes based more upon differences in the actual returns possible from investment. At the same time, greater access to

181

the financial markets is gained by firms and households that are cash-constrained; with lower interest rates, it is more likely that the current cash flow, including that from the investment, will be sufficient to pay off the cash interest due on the loans.

The short-term benefits of this proposal are certainly not inconsequential: an increase in demand by cash-flow-constrained and interest-sensitive sectors, a more competitive position in the loan markets for new businesses and newly formed households, and the channeling of more loanable funds back to the private sector where they more likely will be used for private investment. Nonetheless, by itself, an increase in private loanable funds and a money-induced decrease in the interest rate will likely bring about several deleterious effects. Normal tax arbitrage will be made more profitable, and the prices of preferred assets (such as housing and land) sold in less liquid markets will probably increase. Inefficient investment in unproductive assets will be further encouraged if the after-tax interest rate is made negative for many taxpayers. In effect, as long as the proposal does not address the long-term allocation question, macro policy will still be left in the dilemma discussed in chapter 8.

Credit Controls

Among the most commonly heard prescriptions for the economy are various devices, direct or indirect, to provide for the control or allocation of credit. The basic notion behind all these proposals is that loans currently are being misallocated, and the government must step in to ensure that a sufficient share of loans goes to a disadvantaged sector.

An example of an indirect incentive approach to credit allocation is provided by the combination of tight money, high real interest rates, and tax incentives for investment. It has been argued that this policy—close to opposite of the proposal in the previous section—would be a means of countering a tendency in the economy to allocate too much scarce savings to investment in residential housing and other durables. Although tight money would tend to reduce investment in general, business investment in equipment and structures would be fostered by providing even further investment incentives for these items alone.[1]

1. See Martin Feldstein, "Inflation, Capital Taxation, and Monetary Policy," in Robert E. Hall, ed., *Inflation: Causes and Effects* (University of Chicago Press, 1982), pp. 153–67.

The direct allocation proposals are simply stated: the government steps in and provides credit to sectors that it considers disadvantaged. New businesses, for instance, are disadvantaged in the loan market, and the government might allocate credit through a small businesses administration; state and local governments might provide mortgage bonds and industrial revenue bonds; an industrial policy or an enterprise zone policy might favor loans to depressed industries or areas; and so forth. Often the rate of interest on such loans would be subsidized as well.

In some cases these proposals for direct and indirect credit allocation can be viewed, at least in part, as being aimed at the lack of uniformity in treatment of different households and businesses in the loan markets. Certainly previous analysis indicates that new businesses and newly formed households are put at a competitive disadvantage because of cash-flow constraints that would not be prevalent in a noninflationary economy. Businesses with lesser amounts of taxable income, including declining businesses with current losses, pay a higher after-tax interest rate on returns on borrowed dollars. And businesses pay higher rates of income tax to many forms of capital than do households to homes and durables. Investment in vacation homes, for example, is preferred to investment in industrial structures. Some disparities thus can be reduced either by reallocating credit to disadvantaged sectors or by denying interest deductions or otherwise raising costs in advantaged sectors.

Government identification of disadvantaged participants in the economic marketplace is not as easy as it may sound. Because most expenditures financed by loans—including expenditures for plant and equipment, housing, automobiles, basic industry, modern research and development, and education—are worthwhile, government often attempts to reallocate to all sectors of the economy at the same time. Sometimes to keep budgetary costs down yet make the programs appear significant in size, the subsidy rate is set high, while the amount of available loans is limited. In those cases there is only a small likelihood of reallocation to any particular sector, much less to the neediest parts of that sector. Instead, these types of government grants and subsidies often end up more as windfalls for those with the most access to government officials or the most knowledge of how administrative choices are made within government.

Even when disadvantaged sectors can be identified, there is a further problem in allocating money correctly within those sectors. Tight monetary policy, combined with immediate investment incentives, works greatly to the disadvantage of new business. Nor are subsidized rates of borrowing a correct means of helping new households that do suffer from a cash flow constraint.

Perhaps the greatest difficulty is that government is very poor at eliminating a credit or subsidy when the relative need of the government-favored sector declines or disappears. Many programs bring along an excess baggage of lobbyists and administrators. Participants themselves often become greatly dependent upon the programs. In any case, seldom is access to government funds abandoned, even when relative needs in society have changed over time. In the case of most tax programs, credits and deductions are made permanent, and no budget review process is required from year to year.

Government attempts to reallocate credit are often unsuccessful. Credit established for one purpose can be used for a variety of purposes. Business loans can finance home building. Loans for industrial development can finance activities of a company outside of the local jurisdiction. Homes can be put up as collateral for consumer purchases. Limitations or expansions of credit, therefore, cannot limit all borrowing for nonpreferred purposes nor ensure that all sponsored borrowing eventually goes for preferred purposes. Inequity among households and businesses is a related consequence.

It must be recognized that many of these proposals are only indirect ways of tackling the interaction between inflation and the interest rate. Practically all interest payments are subsidized under current tax law, not just those that are argued to support unfavored activity such as consumption. Many goals of these proposals would be met by simply imposing a more uniform tax on all real income from capital and by requiring a lower rate of amortization of the real value of debt in periods in which inflation tends to push up that rate.

Financial Innovation

Some allocation problems can be and have been mitigated through various forms of financial innovation. When financial arrangements are made more impervious to inflation, one consequence is a more uniform treatment of various borrowers. Financial institutions have slowly revised rules determining eligibility for loans on the basis of the relation between interest payments due and the current cash flow of the borrower.

In the farm sector, for instance, renegotiation of loans has become a more common practice over the years. In addition, new forms of lending instruments have been adapted to an inflationary economy. As an example, graduated payment loans essentially relend the borrower some of the interest due in the early years of the loan and slow the rate at which the real principal on a loan is paid off or amortized in an inflationary environment.

Futures and forwards contracts, as well as options to buy and sell commodities and securities at given prices, have also provided mechanisms for a variety of investors to hedge against the cost of inflation. A farmer who borrows and incurs current expense to produce a future crop, for instance, can hedge in the futures markets against the risk of both changes in crop prices and changes in the rate of interest. These devices have only begun to be developed, but they offer a large potential for shifting risks to those who have the ability to bear the losses, while in turn encouraging investment by those who would otherwise be deterred because of the risk.

Many of these financial innovations help reduce disparities among borrowers with equal investment prospects, but different rates of current cash flow relative to deferred income come from those investments. To the extent that risk of changes in interest rates and inflation rates can be assumed by persons other than borrowers and lenders, including financial institutions, both the borrowers and lenders may be more willing to look at economic returns as the primary basis by which to determine whether loans are secure. In some cases the development of devices such as graduated payment loans simply institutionalize recognition that inflation distorts the measure of income. These innovations help provide more uniform treatment of capital income by reducing the number of investors who are constrained primarily on the basis of cash flow but not the economic merit of the investment.

Given the above arguments, there seems to be every reason to support innovation in financial markets. New ways of risk sharing and better ways of measuring income certainly have a number of advantages, not the least of which is an increased likelihood of more uniform treatment of income from capital. But major issues remain, especially in the markets for futures, forwards, and options contracts. The U.S. economy still has little experience with new forms of financial instruments that can be held in negative amounts, that is, in short positions or in obligations to pay future amounts based upon rates of return other than the interest rate. A major concern of government commissions regulating the securities and commodities markets is that buyers and sellers of these new instruments should be sufficiently covered so that they can absorb the risks associated with their positions. More pertinent to the previous analysis, the asymmetric tax treatment of receipts and expenses, or of gains and losses, creates opportunities for new forms of pure tax arbitrage and other game-playing in the tax system. The failure to tax income uniformly, in other words, will continue to create serious distortions in these financial markets and prevent them from performing their functions efficiently.

A Commodity-Based Money Supply

In a world of inflation, even proposals considered extreme by many receive added attention. The merit of these proposals may also increase with inflation if they reduce many of the inflation-induced disparities in the treatment of capital income. An example is the return to a commodity-based money supply. Although gold is commonly proposed as the commodity to back money, the government could also design a commodity base using a weighted combination of other commodities. One of the factors used in choosing those commodities and their relative weightings would be the extent to which the commodity bundle is expected to fluctuate in price relative to the price of all other goods and services.

Although the aim of this type of proposal is to control the inflation rate, one consequence of a lower inflation rate would be the solving of many allocation problems posed by the lack of uniform measurement of capital income. Most important for the purposes of this discussion, the stated interest rate would more closely represent a real rate of interest. Indeed, Robert Mundell argues, "Perhaps the most significant objection to the existing [monetary] system is that it provides no basis . . . for incorporating the right *'inflation premium' into interest rates."*[2]

With no inflation, there would be no inflation premium in the interest rate. As a result, the incentive to borrow and invest in unproductive assets would be reduced, and other gains from tax arbitrage would be lessened significantly. Asset markets would be made more stable through

2. Italics are mine. See Robert Mundell, "The Debt Crisis: Causes and Solutions," *Wall Street Journal*, January 31, 1983.

the elimination of much of the conflict between tax arbitrage and financial arbitrage. In effect, in terms of the uniform taxation of capital income, converting to a commodity-based money supply would serve many of the same purposes as partial or complete indexing for inflation of the measures of capital income subject to taxation. The nominal rate of interest also would tend to be lowered, thus alleviating cash-flow problems and similar problems caused by the interaction of inflation with the operation of the loan markets.

Most economists and financial experts oppose a gold standard for a variety of reasons. Perhaps most important, the gold market is considered unstable. Unless one could be assured that the government could control the price of the gold, the economy could be made to face severe economic fluctuations in which there were alternating bouts of inflation and deflation.

A broader commodity base would alleviate this problem, but there remain the difficult issues of storage and delivery. Maintaining commodity reserves can be costly to society and provide lower social returns than alternative investments and uses of resources. As an investment, commodity reserves in general provide low or negative rates of return. One can reduce or even eliminate the amount of reserves kept, but then the problem of delivery is aggravated. Without any possibility of delivery of the supplies backing up the money supply, no one could be in a position to drive down rates of increase in the prices of the underlying commodities—and, through them, the prices of other goods in the economy—by threatening to turn to the government as an alternative supplier. The government is thus forced to enter into and partially control certain commodity markets—primarily as a major buyer and seller—and there is little experience by which to measure how smoothly or efficiently such operations would proceed.[3]

Summary

Although various proposals—increasing the supply of loanable funds, reallocating credit within the economy, promoting financial innovation,

3. For further discussions of commodity-based money supplies see Robert J. Barro, "United States Inflation and the Choice of Monetary Standard," in Hall, *Inflation: Causes and Effects*, pp. 99–110; and Robert E. Hall, "Explorations in the Gold Standard and Related Policies for Stabilizing the Dollar," in Hall, *Inflation: Causes and Effects*, pp. 111–22.

and backing the money supply with a commodity base—often seem aimed at different goals, each does address in part the issue of the uniform treatment of income from capital. None of these proposals is irrational, although many are incomplete or indirect approaches. As in the case of major tax prescriptions, the merit of each proposal depends partly upon whether it is being compared with the current tax and loan system or with alternative approaches to dealing with the problems addressed in this book.

CHAPTER FOURTEEN

Conclusion: An Agenda for Reform

BROAD DIFFERENCES exist today in the way various persons and corporations are treated by the tax structure and loan markets. These differences occur in such factors as type of investment, type of savings vehicle, liquidity constraints, immediacy of expected consumption expenses, need to report positive financial income, knowledge of tax system, and current cash flow. Flows of interest and borrowing are crucial, and the incorrect measure of real interest payments and receipts create opportunities for tax arbitrage, encourage investment in unproductive assets, leave an unstable financial market, and discriminate among borrowers in the loanable funds market. Inflation, of course, plays a central role.

With this background, one can see why simple macro policy changes in aggregate money supply or fiscal deficits have been limited in their long-term effect on the efficiency of the economy; why saving and investment incentives often have not worked and have created new sources of inefficiency and inequity; how new businesses have been discouraged, small businesses and farms have become tax shelters with liquidity problems; how a variety of organizational and financial incentives have been created that favor merger, leasing, buying, and selling whole companies or subsidiaries of companies; why some of society's brightest and most inventive people have been directing their otherwise productive energies to playing tax and financial games; how much of the progressivity of the tax system has been eliminated with respect to capital income; and why some types of "supply-side" tax cuts have not been so costly.

Once integrated, the themes of taxes, loans, and inflation help provide a unified story of many of the disparate economic problems in a modern economy. Although there may be some disagreement over details, this integration has potential appeal to individuals with a wide range of viewpoints and interests, both economic and political. One does not have to favor either higher or lower tax rates on income from capital to

189

support the conclusion that nonuniform treatment of this income, especially in an inflationary environment, creates some enormous costs and distortions within the economy.[1]

Whatever the actual agreement as to the analysis of causes, there certainly will be less consensus on what cures are most appropriate. These last chapters in part three of the book, nonetheless, outline how many types of proposed cures are not as different as they might first appear. The proposals include broad-base taxes, consumption taxes, commodity-based money supplies, and credit reallocations. Some of these proposals directly focus on the uniformity issue, others deal with nonuniformity only to the extent it is created by inflation, while still others address only some of the disparities, perceived or otherwise, in the treatment of capital income.

In this final chapter, I present what I believe to be a minimum, yet major and workable, list of reforms necessary to improve the allocation of capital, make the economy less prone to stagnation in periods of inflation, restore greater equity to the tax system, reduce the amount of resources devoted to unnecessary reorganizations, and eliminate some of the unfair, as well as debilitating, discrimination between potential new wealth holders and holders of existing wealth. All reforms I suggest can be justified in terms of the analysis presented in previous parts of the book. Some choices among alternatives, such as decisions to maintain some progressivity in the tax system and to minimize government interference in the credit markets, are based upon the additional premise that it is possible to address the economic problems without abandoning the principles under which the tax system and loan markets were meant to operate. My agenda for reform is contained in the following list of related proposals.

1. Every reasonable effort should be made to make the measures of taxable income and financial income as close as possible to economic income. This is a basic issue. Only with accurate accounting can questions be addressed such as how much should capital income be taxed, or how can society compensate for an inadequate supply of loans to disadvantaged sectors. Measures of economic income should not only be as accurate as possible; they should also be designed so that they do

---

1. The issue of how heavily capital income should be taxed has become the bellwether by which many persons decide the merits of almost all proposals that affect capital or capital income. This approach is reminiscent of an earlier attitude—that the merits of any policy proposal could be judged almost solely by its redistributional effect.

not change arbitrarily and randomly with the rate of inflation. The estimate of the real income from any asset or debt should be stated first on any financial statement, not hidden within. Similarly, a measure of economic income should be the classifier for income tax purposes, regardless of the taxes ultimately imposed.

A review of the tax and financial prescriptions in the last two chapters shows that several of them are really nothing more than movements in the direction of accounting for economic income accurately in determining, first, tax liability, and, second, eligibility for and conditions of loans. Because inflation so often worsens otherwise mild disparities in the treatment of returns from different assets, several prescriptions either provide directly for indexing or indirectly establish rules to effectively hold tax rates or loan conditions independent of or less dependent upon the rate of inflation.

The details of an accurate accounting system are essentially laid out in the discussions of a broad-base tax, indexing for inflation of the measure of taxable income, and financial innovations that would tend to measure real, rather than nominal, interest rates in determining eligibility for and conditions of loans. Deviations from such accounting should be allowed only on administrative grounds. Even if a subsidy is to be allowed for certain types of investment or saving, the process should not require that the subsidy be provided through the mismeasurement of income.

It needs to be emphasized that opposition to this move often results primarily from fear of consequences, not from considerations of the technicalities of accounting. Pure economic accounting is impossible; better economic accounting is quite feasible at reasonable costs to private businesses and households. The political fear is often that better accounting would eventually lead to the elimination of distinctions in the tax system among sources of capital income—as, indeed, it might. As we know by now, this is a negative sum game. All of us maintain various tax preferences, but the cost is an increase in the number of distortions in the economy. Our total income goes down, and in aggregate we become net losers in the process.

One aspect of uniform accounting for economic income—or economic consumption, for that matter—is that more complete accounting of wealth and income in different accounts is required. Because various sources of income are excluded or deferred from taxation under current law, there is a tendency not to require accounting for that income. As a result, many taxpayers actually have little idea of what their total income is. More important, it becomes difficult, if not impossible, to restrict manipulation of the tax system. Taxpayers thus can take advantage of saving incentives simply by changing assets from one account to another; they can borrow and purchase assets producing tax-exempt income, and so forth.

One interesting aspect of an expenditure tax is that it too solves the uniformity problem through more elaborate accounting of assets producing flows of income currently excluded from income taxation. In this case, the accounting is of wealth and wealth transfers rather than of income itself. Thus all flows of saving must be measured to provide uniform treatment of all saving, and all loan transactions must be measured to ensure uniform reciprocal treatment of both borrowing (dissaving) and saving.

In effect, regardless of the type of tax system under which one operates, more uniform treatment of capital income requires that the wealth, transactions, or income in all asset or debt accounts be treated similarly. Once certain assets, accounts, loans, or flows are excluded from accounting or treated differently from similar transactions, the tax system will begin to break down.

2. A broader-base and flatter-rate income tax should be adopted. Tax reform must be recognized as a fundamental component of macro policy, not just some tinkering to improve the marginal efficiency of the economy. Macro policy cannot succeed, or can succeed only at great costs, in an economy with so many distinctions among the ways in which capital income is taxed. A monetary policy that tends to lower interest rates, for instance, currently has as one probable consequence the encouragement of additional tax arbitrage and investment in less productive and sometimes unproductive assets, while a policy that tends to raise interest rates discourages competition for new business and discriminates against newly formed households.

Although alternative tax reforms may also move in the direction of uniform treatment of capital income, a broader-base, flatter-rate income tax in my view is a preferred option to a simple lowering of rates, to a flat-rate tax system, and to a consumption tax. Each of these latter types of changes has problems of redistribution, administration, or practicality that make them difficult to accept in either the short or long run.

Simply lowering tax rates is a half solution; if lower rates are desired, then base broadening is a natural corollary because it helps finance lower rates. If more uniform treatment of capital income is the goal, obviously one can achieve it by moving toward a zero rate of tax regardless of the definition of the tax base. Base broadening, however, moves toward that goal in a direct manner. Rate reduction and base broadening therefore go hand-in-hand.

A flat-rate tax, accompanied by a broader base, also has many features that make it appealing. Administratively it has a number of advantages relative to a progressive income tax. The great difficulty is that progressivity is abandoned. If progressivity is restored through an exemption or zero rate applied to the first dollars of income, the rate schedule is no longer flat. Even in such a modified flat system, tax burdens will be shifted substantially from the upper-income groups to middle-income groups if there is only one nonzero tax rate. When one also takes into account that upper-income groups are not subject to social security tax on their last dollars of income, such a shift in income taxation seems especially unwarranted.

A consumption tax can be designed to maintain existing degrees of progressivity for most income classes. The tax also eliminates many of the income-accounting problems present in an income tax. In a world of inflation especially, a zero rate of tax is particularly appealing because it is inflation-proof. These advantages, however, are more than offset by the disadvantages.

It is highly unlikely that society will accept a tax system in which accumulators of income, whether they become rich through merit or luck, pay little or no tax. This problem can be solved only through the taxation of wealth transfers; thus income is eventually taxed either when consumed or transferred. In addition, a consumption tax requires thorough accounting of existing wealth (to ensure that it is not hidden) and of additions and subtractions from wealth (to measure net saving). The administrative problems of accounting for transactions and transfers of wealth in a consumption tax closely parallel the administrative problems of accounting for income from wealth in an income tax. Under either tax system businesses have to keep income accounts.

In addition, it is not necessarily more rational to tax persons most heavily when they make withdrawals from accounts for large expenditures on education or other purchases, or when they are unemployed or facing hard times. States and localities would need to adopt consumption taxes for any gain in simplicity to be achieved, and many difficulties would be created in a world in which most major U.S. trading partners maintained income taxes, while the United States converted to a consumption tax. And huge transition problems would exist for the trillions of dollars of existing wealth that must either be allowed to be consumed tax-free, or else taxed for many persons who may have already been taxed on the income from that wealth. Other transition problems, such as the renegotiation of most major tax treaties, would not be simple.

Even those who favor consumption and flat taxes generally will admit that a broader-based, lower-rate income tax would achieve many, although not all, of the objectives that they seek. They may place different weights than I on other issues such as progressivity, transition problems, and the administrative problems of different tax systems. Thus, although I do not claim to have said the last word on the choice among tax systems that move toward solving many of the problems detailed in this book, adoption of a broader-base, lower-rate income tax must be viewed as a practical and rational step by those who adopt additional goals such as eliminating progressivity or exempting all saving from taxation.

Adoption of such a tax requires dispelling certain illusions that go with the current income tax. First to be discarded must be the notion that there are only small costs and distortions to the current political compromise of setting high statutory tax rates while eliminating taxes through a mix of provisions that mismeasure income and add to the distinctions among types of investment and saving.

Adoption of a broad-base, lower-rate tax also requires a willingness to forgo the use of provisions that "veil" the amount of taxes paid by capital owners. Double taxation of dividend income is no more justified on accounting, equity, or efficiency grounds than are saving incentives that primarily benefit those who alter the forms in which their wealth is held. The only possible justification for the use of veils is that they somehow cause an increase in saving or investment in society. Since the evidence for a saving or investment effect is so inconclusive, especially in the long run, and the costs in terms of inefficiency and inequity so certain, this justification is an inadequate reason to forgo adoption of a tax system that treats income from capital more uniformly. Moreover, those in favor of particular exceptions to the rule of uniform taxation must recognize that each exception sets precedence for many other exceptions that they do not support.

3. *As part of the movement toward a broader-based tax, the issue of tax arbitrage must be addressed through indexing or through limitations*

on artificial losses. Society cannot continue to grant different tax treatment to interest income on each side of the ledger. Depreciation allowances cannot be left so accelerated that whole tax shelter industries are created. Nor can society continue to allow investment with large negative real returns to generate positive real, after-tax income to investors. So many other problems—discrimination against new business, saving incentives that offer tax reductions to persons with zero or negative saving, broad reallocations of ownership of small businesses, farms, and homes according to tax rates of potential owners, and unnecessarily complicated reorganizations and financial arrangements among businesses—would be greatly mitigated simply through control of tax arbitrage.

One way to address this problem is simply to move toward indexing of the returns from all assets. Such an indexing system could replace whole series of ad hoc proposals in the tax code. Indexing of depreciation allowances would increase the value of later allowances. The effective tax rate on investment in plant and equipment would not change every time the inflation rate changed. Indexing of interest income by itself would eliminate much of the normal tax arbitrage problem. Even where tax arbitrage remained, there would be less possibility of investment in assets with negative expected rates of return as long as equity investments did not have negative tax rates. In the absence of indexing, of course, the justification for a flatter-rate tax or a consumption tax is much stronger.

Although indexing solves most of the normal tax arbitrage problems, it still leaves that part of the pure tax arbitrage problem that is caused when real interest payments are deducted immediately while real interest receipts are excluded or deferred from taxation. There are two additional ways to reduce opportunities for pure tax arbitrage. First, in moving to a broader-base tax, opportunities to exclude interest receipts can be reduced or eliminated. Second, interest flows can be traced through to ultimate recipients. Interest deductions would then be denied to persons to the extent that they exclude interest receipts on the other side of the ledger. For instance, households would not be allowed to deduct mortgage or business interest expense while excluding interest receipts in individual retirement accounts (IRAs) and insurance accounts. To minimize the number of people affected, some exemption could be granted for a limited amount of interest expense per taxpayer.

If indexing of interest is considered impractical, other limitations could be used to restrict tax arbitrage. Interest deductions from all borrowing—whether used to finance housing, consumption, financial assets, or business and farm assets—could be limited, or at least deferred, until income from investment or saving was recognized by the same taxpayer. Taxpayers could also be limited in taking deductions when those deductions exceed the maximum loss they can incur from an investment. Returns from IRAs and the savings accounts attached to many life insurance policies could be reported to individuals and interest deductions denied to the extent that income was excluded or deferred from taxation. Fractional exclusion of interest payments (in effect, partial indexing) could be applied to businesses and corporations that have high debt-to-equity ratios or make substantial use of other tax preferences.

The best time to adopt these types of limits is in a period of low inflation rather than when people become dependent upon the tax deduction of the inflationary component of the interest payment. Both monetary policy would be strengthened and the tendency toward inefficient investment would be decreased. Finally, substantial reduction in the benefits of tax arbitrage would help to limit the rise in nominal interest rates that accompanies a tight monetary policy and, correspondingly, would help limit the rise in the payments on the federal debt.

4. Depreciation deductions and investment credits must be changed so that they are available for all assets and between new and established businesses. Even if the total present value of investment incentives is kept constant, they can be made more uniform over qualifying types of investment. This, however, is not enough. The design of these incentives must be changed to eliminate the large tax advantage given to existing businesses. The current method of favoring owners of old wealth over potential owners of new wealth is a fundamental deterrent to innovation. A simple solution to this problem would again be to adopt measures of depreciation that more closely approximate real depreciation, and then index these measures for inflation. Such allowances would then be available over the lives of assets and would be more likely to match income flows from the investment itself rather than to offset taxable income from other sources.

In addition, if investment credits are maintained, they should be made refundable and targeted in a tax or expenditure process where they are better analyzed and controlled. Even then, it must be recognized that investment credits currently are a large source of discrimination, first, among assets with different real depreciation rates, and, second, between the qualifying investment and the less easily measured and, therefore, nonqualifying types of economic investment. Scaling investment credits more according to the lives of assets would help eliminate the first type of discrimination. The second could be solved through replacement of investment credits with a broader form of reduction in the tax rate on capital income, such as corporate rate reduction or partial integration of personal and corporate taxes. If investment credits are to be used as countercyclical rather than long-term policy, no credence should be given to those who argue that the credits are always necessary because the economy is going into a recession, is already in a recession, or is just recovering from one. If credits are meant as long-term policy, they are a poor substitute for corporate rate reduction.[2]

5. The development of new financial instruments should be encouraged, but their development will be constrained as long as tax arbitrage is not controlled. Financial innovation allows the development of instruments that give greater market access to borrowers who may have sufficient economic income to pay the real interest cost of a loan but inadequate cash flow to pay the nominal interest cost. At high interest rates associated with inflation, of course, both the lender and the borrower face the risk of substantial losses if the inflation rate increases or decreases. Thus the development of new hedging instruments, including those that would allow the risk of large increases or decreases in inflation to be borne by persons other than the lender or the borrower, may be crucial to the development of a loan market that would measure eligibility for loans mainly on the basis of potential real economic returns from an investment.

If the risk of losses can be transferred to parts of the economy that can bear such losses directly, of course, there is the additional benefit that uncovered losses will be less likely to multiply or snowball as they are passed from one household or firm to the next. Economic declines then would be less severe.

Innovation in the financial markets must be constrained by government policy, however, in a world in which tax arbitrage is not controlled. If interest payments continue to be deducted by the borrower but are not included in taxable income of the lender, and if capital losses are recognized while capital gains are not, many new financial instruments

2. As in the case of other proposals, however, some transition rules would be required to avoid large windfall gains and losses from the change.

will become tax shelter vehicles, and their primary social purpose—to improve the efficiency and liquidity of capital markets—will be distorted.

6. *Monetary, fiscal, financial, antitrust, and other economic policies must be better coordinated.* The disagreement among policymakers and economists about the proper mix of fiscal and monetary policy has tended to deter needed attention from the financial and tax policies that must be pursued to make macro policy more efficient—no matter what the fiscal-monetary mix. The adoption of a tighter monetary policy, for instance, currently will reduce housing investment most for those for whom the investment would be more efficient, while it will reduce that investment least for those who already have the maximum tax incentives for inefficient investment. A tighter monetary policy will also restrict new businesses more than it will old businesses. By the same token, a looser monetary policy may encourage even greater amounts of tax arbitrage by taxpayers and may make investment in unproductive assets profitable.

In a similar manner, antitrust policy often proceeds independently of the tax laws that favor the merger of some firms and the breakup of others. The regulators of commodities futures are encouraged to develop rules governing futures trading with insufficient consideration of the revenue consequences, or even market price effects, of greater opportunities for tax straddles. Immediate investment incentives are provided in the tax law with little regard for the additional policing activity required for regulators who try to protect investors from operators selling fraudulent tax shelters.

The problem here is primarily an institutional one. Fiscal policy, tax policy, monetary policy, antitrust policy, and so forth are each produced by fairly independent sets of actors. Coordinated policies are often not developed, although one group of policymakers will almost certainly react eventually to the circumstances created by another group's actions. Among some economists, too, there is a tendency to look at issues narrowly, as in the case of those who tend to advocate the changing of only one parameter—for example, the money supply, the full-employment budget deficit, or the average marginal tax rate—to meet most economic crises or problems.

Although this proposal may seem somewhat abstract, better coordination at the governmental level requires nothing more or less than the development and strengthening of institutions where such coordination is expected and required.

7. *If society agrees on the need for increased saving, it must be willing*

to consider direct ways to achieve that objective. Increased national saving is probably a good insurance policy for the future, but society cannot place complete trust in a vehicle—the tax code—that is both inadequate and not yet proven to be reliable. Moreover, with negative taxes on much capital income and on many investments, there is not much more the code can do.

A much more direct approach to increasing national saving is to lower the federal deficit, and thereby increase the amount of private saving available for private investment. Another direct approach would require that adequate saving and funding be maintained for social policies already adopted, including employer or employee funding of pension and un-employment benefits for persons who would not otherwise save. The point of these suggestions is to emphasize that direct methods have at least a high probability of being more effective and an almost certain probability of being less distorting than the indirect methods that have been adopted in the past.

Index

201